SEVEN MEN AT DAYBREAK

"A blessed companion is a book"—JERROLD

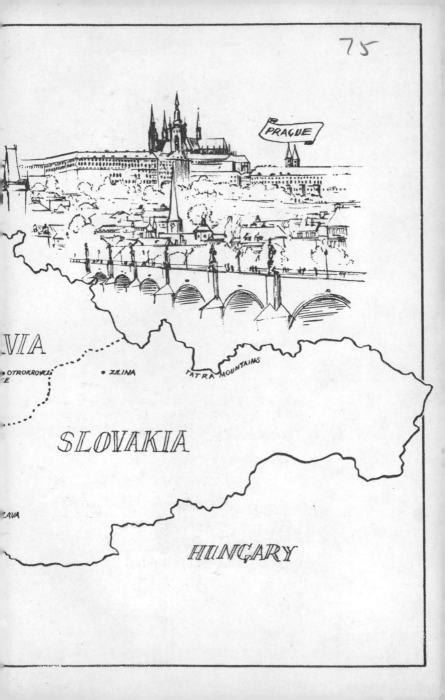

PRAGUE

VIA

• OTROKROVUE
E

• ZILINA

TATRA MOUNTAINS

SLOVAKIA

AVA

HUNGARY

SEVEN MEN
AT DAYBREAK

*

ALAN BURGESS

THE COMPANION BOOK CLUB
LONDON

*Made and printed in Great Britain
for The Companion Book Club (Odhams Press Ltd.)
by Odhams (Watford) Limited
Watford, Herts*
S.961.W.

. . . I don't say he's a great man . . . he's not the finest character that ever lived. But he's a human being, and a terrible thing is happening to him. So attention must be paid. He's not to be allowed to fall into his grave like an old dog. Attention, attention must be finally paid to such a person.

ARTHUR MILLER

CONTENTS

ILLUSTRATIONS

Note: the below-average quality of some of these photographs is due to several having been taken in difficult and dangerous circumstances immediately after the attempt on Heydrich

AUTHOR'S NOTE

I REMEMBER vividly how he opened the large hide-bound volume and flipped open its pages until he came to the section full of names which had been carefully ruled through with a line of red ink.

"A story here," said Mr. Wittmer, "to make your hair stand on end!"

The volume, it appeared, was one of the original records kept by the authorities of Mauthausen Concentration Camp, though I hasten to add that this story has nothing whatsoever to do with concentration camps.

The year was 1950. The place was Arolsen, a small town in northern Bavaria, where the International Tracing Service working within the orbit of the International Refugee Organization, had its headquarters. Mr. Wittmer was its Deputy Director.

At that time I was in the process of writing a B.B.C. feature programme about the Tracing Service which I later entitled with, I am afraid, a certain pretentiousness, "The Greatest Detective Story in History". However, from the moment Mr. Wittmer put me on the trail of Jan Kubis and Josef Gabchik, I have wanted to write their story.

To get to the heart of the matter meant visiting Czechoslovakia, and soon it became obvious that political events made it almost impossible to go there, and certainly quite impossible to do any research there.

It was not until the spring of 1958 that I was able to fulfil my ambition.

I am grateful to the Czech Ministry of Information for allowing my visit and putting no obstacles in the way of my research. On the other hand I formed the definite opinion that because Jan Kubis and Josef Gabchik and the others were trained in Britain, and the operation as a whole was conceived in Britain, the present Communist regime tends— if not to suppress—then at least to play down the story. I am therefore doubly grateful to all those people in Czechoslovakia, whose names I shall not enumerate, who helped me and gave me information.

I am also indebted to various published sources, particularly to the voluminous articles by Jan Drejs which appeared in 1947 in the now defunct magazine, *Kreten*; to the slim book, *The Truth About Heydrich* by Professor Ogoun, and also to the booklet published by the Czech Orthodox Church of St. Cyril and Method. I would also like to thank Mrs. Jeannette Simek and Mr. Geoffrey Tier for their excellent translations of this material. My gratitude is also due to Mr. Charles Laudau of the B.B.C. Monitoring Service at Caversham for allowing me to browse amongst their immense files; also to Mrs. Ellison of Ightfield, Cheshire, who knew both Jan Kubis and Josef Gabchik so well during their stay in Britain, and who told me so much about them.

One of the advantages of coming so late to this story is that one has the benefit of the records amassed by both friend and enemy. The years add a footnote of authority to a time which was bedevilled by censorship, confused by propaganda, and blurred by passion.

Because this is a story of such wide implication and background, I have, to avoid confusion, left out the names and exploits of many brave men and women working upon its fringes. I have also adopted the simplified form of Czech spelling used in this country during wartime.

On both counts I apologize in advance to any Czech who may chance to read this book.

ALAN BURGESS

Epsom
January, 1960

PROLOGUE

THAT night, at an altitude of two thousand feet, the huge Halifax aircraft roared out of the sky above the winter countryside of Czechoslovakia. The four airscrews churned through the drifts of low broken cloud, flailing them back against the wet black flanks of the machine, and in the cold fuselage Jan Kubis and Josef Gabchik stared down at their homeland through the open, coffin-shaped exit hatch cut in the floor.

Automatically they checked the release boxes and static lines of their parachute harnesses. Within minutes they were to plunge down through that darkness to the earth below, knowing that they were the first parachutists to come back to Czechoslovakia, and knowing also that their mission was as unique and hazardous as any that had yet been conceived.

The taller of the two, Jan Kubis, was twenty-seven years old and five feet ten inches in height. He had fair hair and grey, deep-set eyes which looked out at the world steadily from under pronounced brows. His mouth was firm, generous, the corners turned with laughter, and about his face was an air of authority. He possessed an athlete's shoulders and body; his hands were large and competent; when they shook your hand they grasped it firmly. But above all you remembered his eyes; they stared straight at you, not at your nose or chin, but directly into your iris with a direct and clear curiosity.

Jan Kubis was coming home. He was coming home in the middle of a war made more appalling by the diabolical diversions of man's inventive genius, yet for the young in heart made more exciting by the very diversity of adventure it offered. He was coming home delivered on to the doorstep as no warrior in history before him, equipped with weapons of such ferocity that in a different age their power would certainly have won him an empire.

But despite his utilitarian apparatus of violence, the mainspring of his purpose was still activated by an instinct primeval in origin. He was coming home impregnated by an emotion he had distilled and clarified in his mind over the years. The emotion of hatred: a hatred conceived and nourished by bitter experience.

During those war years, now well documented, and left as a well-stocked morgue of bones for historians to rattle, many young men, and indeed young women, stood or sat in the open hatchways of aircraft as they roared above territory occupied by the enemy, before plunging down into adventures as bizarre as any conceived by Homer in his *Odyssey*. But few underwent experiences as corrosive as those of Jan Kubis; and few indeed were as committed, as dedicated, or as resolved.

In England the people he met found him a normal and pleasant young man. Indeed, very few people knew he possessed one physical decoration which psychiatrists or even contemporary historians might find instructive. He was scarred in an extraordinary manner. Branded on his buttocks were seven small black swastikas. They had been burnt there some three years before with a red hot iron. What part they played in the formation of his character, and what measure of responsibility for the holocaust which was to follow could be attached to this stigmata, it is difficult to discern. But probably a great deal. He did not forget. In his nightmares he still felt the sizzle of flesh, and remembered his deep agony and shame. Because of that intense humiliation, he was standing now in this rocking pitching aircraft high above his own countryside. Because of the hatred stemming from that experience, he had been chosen for this special mission. Because he was imbued with a deep desire for vengeance he had been sent back to Czechoslovakia to kill a man. Not any man: not any cold-nosed German sentry, moodily patrolling an aerodrome or arms dump, but a man of spectacular importance: a man whom some people insisted was the most dangerous animal in the whole of Hitler's jungle.

As Jan Kubis stood there next to his great friend, Josef

Gabchik, looking down into two thousand feet of dark and freezing air which separated him from the earth, he could perhaps wonder where that man was. Beneath, on that December night of 1941 lay a rolling countryside, immemorially patterned by strip cultivation, a countryside thinly coated with snow and broken by black, close-packed clumps of pines.

Over the clustering villages where the dark ruts in the roads left by the high-wheeled cars glistened with ice, the Halifax droned, and the dogs, looking up, rumbled in their throats and showed white slits in their eyes.

In the farmhouses, men and women groping from sleep turned uneasily in their beds, a queasy sense of fear rising in their throats. There was always fear abroad these days; a thin, choking fear as all-pervading as the sifting snow; a fear that not even the daylight nor the winter sunshine could dispel. That aircraft low overhead was an intimidation, a threat, drying the saliva in the mouth, making the heart-beat quicken, and instinctively a man huddled closer to the small, warm security of his woman, trying to blot out the mechanical thunder in the sky.

Jan was afraid, too; gripped by a sick fear that had grown on the weary journey from the airfield in England. It is a feeling with which both airmen and parachutists are equally familiar. It is a fear that comes after midnight in the darkness over enemy territory. It is a fear that comes from the knowledge that suddenly passivity must accelerate into violent action; that this is the beginning of something to which you are irrevocably committed, and which might well destroy you.

Standing there waiting to jump, Jan knew all these fears. Not even the firm grip of Josef's hand on his shoulder next to the tight buckle of the parachute harness, could diminish them. Josef Gabchik was jumping with him; Josef was sharing the dangers and difficulties. It was a comradeship of much distinction; exposed by time to boredom and danger and the excitement of war; fretted by the stimulation of drink and women, and long late nights under foreign skies; affirmed by the rub and irritation and joy of close com-

17

munal living. Now it was to be confronted with its most demanding test.

In a few seconds the button lights would flick from red to green, and he would plunge out into the roaring torrent of air whipped along the fuselage by the four hammering airscrews. He tried to concentrate on the fact that this was simply a job to do; a mission to accomplish. As an antidote to his feelings he tried to summon up hate for the man they had come to find. As if his eyes might already seek him out, Jan stared down into the darkness.

Somewhere below in the night lay the man from whom the fear spread, the core of the malignancy. He would be sleeping no doubt, sleeping easily, sprawled next to the shapely blonde body of his wife, in the great manor house a few miles from Prague. Dreaming, possibly? But if his dreams encompassed anticipations or premonitions, it was almost certain they did not include an awareness that flying high in the sky were two young men who had come as assassins.

In the control cabin of the aircraft, the microphones built into the helmet of the Flight-Lieutenant of the Royal Canadian Air Force suddenly fizzed with static. The weary voice of the navigator came through.

"This is it, Skipper. Reach the dropping zone in five minutes."

It had been a long dangerous journey. Over Darmstadt, German fighters had isolated them against the night sky. There had been dicey moments before they shook them off, but the Flight-Lieutenant knew it was worse for those characters in the rear dressed in civilian clothes and stuffed in parachutes. He knew that this was the third time some of them had flown over Czechoslovakia in an effort to parachute down.

"Okay!" he said, and then lifted his voice to relay the information to the sergeant despatcher in the fuselage.

"D'you get that, Sarge? You've got your red. I'll give you a green in five minutes. You've got the first two standing by, I hope?"

In the strutted fuselage, astern, the eyes of the sergeant despatcher blinked briefly as he confirmed the message. The voice clicked off in his earpiece with a bleak finality. He unplugged his intercom and turned to Jan Kubis. He thrust his right hand towards him, thumb raised, and spread the fingers of the other hand wide.

Jan nodded, and felt Josef pat him encouragingly on the shoulder. He looked back into the fuselage at the others. They sat on the floor, their parachute straps loose. They were his friends; he had trained with them. Bartos, Valchik, and Potucek were jumping later. Their mission was quite different. To reopen contact with England was their chief aim, and in their containers was a radio transmitter and receiver with which they would seek to accomplish this task.

It was strange to think that this aircraft carried the first Czechs to parachute back into their own country since the war had started. Their reception when they landed had been a subject for considerable discussion amongst them during these past few months. And now this moment of such heated conjecture was close at hand.

Valchik grinned at Jan and raised his thumb encouragingly. Lieutenant Alfred Bartos raised his hands above his head in a boxer's handshake; Potucek, the radio operator, saluted gravely. If luck was on their side, they would all meet again somewhere in Czechoslovakia. If luck was against them, well at least they would all lie under their own soil.

Jan lifted his hand to return their gestures of good luck; he did not trust his facial muscles to react correctly. He turned back to look at the red light.

At that moment the face of the sergeant despatcher changed from a rosy pink to a phosphorescent mackerel shade, and Jan knew that the "green" was on. He heard the yelled "Go!", paused fractionally, willing himself to move, and then, stiffening and tightening his muscles as he had been taught, hurled himself outwards and downwards through the dark exit hatch. Airborne, the slip-stream snatched his feet upwards, and for a fraction of time he lay upon a blast of wind as solid as a plank. The tailfin of the aircraft slid away above his head like the flutes of a gigantic black whale. The rigging lines of his parachute streamed above and behind him, a thin, fluttering, silk arabesque. Then with a bank, air thrust its fist up into the canopy, punching it open so that it gaped, filled, breathed, and hung with infinite grace suspended against the night.

As he swung, Jan looked back and in the darkness saw dimly Josef's 'chute also break open against the sky. Even farther back the parachute bearing the bundle containing their arms and supplies suddenly appeared. The roaring engines of the Halifax dwindled to a soft bumble in the night. He shrugged down into his seat strap, reached for the rigging lines above his head, and peered down trying to make out the outlines of the earth. He could see the whiteness of the snow, feel the bite in the air.

These were the moments of pure magic and peace known to every parachutist: the moments separating the noisy, sick-making, windy plunge out of the aircraft from the painful reality of the crash upon the earth. He sensed rather than saw the earth coming up to meet him in a swift silent rush, and tensed, anticipating the shock. The snow was hard, frozen, and his feet jarred on the ground with metallic impact. He rolled over, twisting on his back, turning and banging the aluminium release box, jerking out his leg straps, struggling clear of the shoulder harness so that, freed from tension, the mushroom of silk collapsed into a soft heap on the ground.

He stood up, trembling slightly. The sickness he had felt in the aircraft had gone. He took a deep breath, holding it to listen, probing the air like an animal scenting danger. He could see very little. It was very quiet. Even the aircraft noise had died away. The snow was a thin and frozen crust on the ground. Satisfied that he was unobserved, he moved off to find Josef.

Had the Nazis been aware of the return of Jan Kubis to his homeland, it is doubtful if they would have evinced more than a mild interest in the event. In their brutal years of ascendancy to power, they had gained much experience of saboteurs and enemies of the Reich, and they were confident they could deal with all such minor irritations. The war was almost won; and it was being won by methods which they believed to be infallible. They possessed a fundamental belief that through animal processes of cruelty, bestiality, and utter ruthlessness, it was not difficult to inherit the earth, and they were willing to enlist all possible methods of intimidation to achieve this end. Ridicule, they knew, was a powerful weapon. They believed that seven swastikas branded on the behind of a young revolutionary were enough to discourage anyone's resolution. One could hardly boast of a war wound like that—eh?

They did not pause to reflect that throughout history, saints and sadists, revolutionaries, conquerors and assassins have often been driven forward to their destiny by a corrosive experience of similar intensity. They did not understand that to debase a man, to leave him without margin of human dignity, does not necessarily destroy him. It changes him, yes. Jan Kubis was changed. He was never a shy country boy again. He would never be a vague, hopeful patriot again. They had dedicated him to his hatred. He was a man in the grip of a wild rage of the spirit; he was possessed like a black witch of the Middle Ages.

The man who controlled Czechoslovakia for the Nazis, at the moment when the feet of Jan Kubis first touched the earth, was General of the S.S. Reinhard Heydrich, a human butcher of such sincerity and thoroughness that, at a memorable moment much later Hitler was to dub him "the man with the iron heart".

Now that the records are in our hands it is apparent that not only was Reinhard Heydrich one of the most powerful men in all Germany but also one of the most feared. He controlled the secret police within the Gestapo; the archives and apparatus of terror, known by its initials as R.S.H.A. Amongst its kindred activities this organization was responsible for the destruction of more than six million Jews.

The entire German police force was infiltrated by Heydrich's men, directly linked with his office in Berlin. In Berlin he possessed also a special "Alarm Group", a body of trained killers under his exclusive command, who murdered, kidnapped or tortured without hesitation or question. It is evident that he was secretly feared by both Hitler and Himmler. Walter Schellenburg, who later became chief of German Intelligence and for many years worked under Heydrich, declared that undeniably Heydrich was the hidden pivot around which the Nazi regime revolved, the true puppet master of the Third Reich.

In Prague upon September 27th, 1941, when Heydrich took over from the sick Baron von Neurath, as Acting Protector of Bohemia, he was at the height of his power. His task was to bring rebellious Czechoslovakia completely within the Nazi camp.

It was this man that the two Czechs, small in importance, one a farmer from Moravia, the other a locksmith from Slovakia, had come to kill.

CHAPTER ONE

THE major in the Special Training School for Czech saboteurs high on the north-west coast of Scotland knew most of his pupils very well. Some faces stuck in his memory more than others.

Gabchik and Kubis he could not forget because they were almost inseparable. During the entire training: the forced route marches, the long night treks in bitter weather, with only a compass to guide them across the mountains, the dynamiting of disused railway lines, the unarmed combat, the use of grenades and all makes of firearms, they had made it their business to train together. It was indeed this duality of purpose which singled them out and made them conspicuous.

Possibly because of the size of his hands and the strength of his wrists and forearms, Jan could throw the metal ball of a hand grenade a prodigious distance. "Farmer's hands," Josef called them; and indeed those sinewy fingers had been strengthened since childhood by using a spade and gripping the twisting handles of an ox-drawn plough.

The hand grenade was undoubtedly Jan's favourite weapon. Whereas other men like the compact exclusiveness of a Luger or a Smith and Wesson, or cherish a Mauser, a heavy Colt, or the sleek deadliness of a sub-machine gun—weapons designed to throw pellets of steel with phenomenal accuracy—Jan's affections rested conclusively with the dull sheen of the pineapple-cubed, Mills hand grenade. It satisfied a certain hunger in his soul. He would carry one in his pocket as other men carried a packet of sandwiches.

Already, because of his skill and courage with this weapon, he had won the Czechoslovakian War Cross. The occasion had been during the disastrous retreat through France in 1940, when the Germans had broken through on every side. It was Jan's first action against the enemy. His patrol was scouting through a wood, preparatory to falling back across a narrow bridge over a swift, deep stream. Their orders were to make a forward patrol; then retreat across the bridge, destroying it in the process, and rejoin the main forces. In the woods slightly above the bridge, Jan stayed on guard beside the detonating gear while the others moved cautiously across the concrete arch and fanned out amongst the trees.

Within half an hour of the patrol's departure, Jan was alerted suddenly by the grey-green movement of uniforms in the trees across the river. It was a Wehrmacht patrol obviously intent upon capturing an undamaged bridge. Jan could now do one of two things: he could blow the bridge and cut off his patrol, or he could try and hold off the Germans until they returned. He chose the latter course.

From his heavy bag he selected a grenade, weighing it in his fingers as one weighs a ball at a coconut shy. Wrenching out the pin with his teeth, he tossed it high into the air across the stream. The ball of metal dropped cleanly through the branches within ten feet of its intended target. He heard the cracking explosion, the noise of shrapnel hissing through the trees, the cries of alarm.

The bullets from the Germans followed swiftly: a quick angry chatter of lead, digging spurts of earth out of the hillside above his head, ricocheting off tree trunks and branches but causing him no damage. They had no idea where he was positioned. As far as they were concerned the grenade might have dropped from heaven.

Behind his screen of bushes he selected another grenade; he held the heavy ball in his hand; with one deft swift movement he extracted the pin, then, swinging back his arm, he heaved it high in the air, sending it soaring up like a lark against the blue sky to attain its maximum height, and drop swiftly downwards. It disintegrated in a great upward explosion of leaves and debris. Wild firing from the Germans followed, but it was more distant now. Jan sent three more grenades hurtling as far into the wood as he could, and the German patrol were now in ignominious retreat. Before they had time for a second cautious re-appraisal of the situation, Jan's patrol, alerted by the firing and explosions, had scampered safely back across the bridge. They panted up the hill and Jan waved them past. There was no point in wasting time. The Germans could probably call on artillery support to clear their path.

With a swift downward plunge of his hand he depressed the handle of the detonating box. The centre of the bridge bulged upwards, as a crimson-cored blast and a gust of black smoke hurled great lumps of masonry high into the air. The surface of the dark rushing stream was suddenly powdered white with a shower of plaster and small pieces of concrete. The bigger lumps churned sluggishly in the water as the current rolled them downstream.

As the cloud of dust settled, Jan saw that the middle arch was completely destroyed. Only a filigree pattern of pro-truding steel rods, pieces of concrete still adhering to them, hung dejectedly downwards.

As he hurried after the rest of the patrol, Jan thought of the men who must have laboured so long to build that graceful structure of concrete and steel. "Seemed such a waste," he said to Josef afterwards, and Josef knew he was referring to the bridge and not to the Germans who might have been killed in the action.

But it was a tiny isolated victory in a sea of confusion and defeat, and it was with a sense of despondency that they re-embarked for North Africa. After a short stay there, they went on to England and so eventually came to the Special Training School.

It was here they met the other Czechs who were to play such an important part in their lives within the next few months. Lieutenants Opalka and Pechal, both serious and determined young officers; Corporal Gerik, twenty years old and baby-faced; the gay, twenty-seven-year-old Valchik; Miks, with the figure and strength of a heavyweight boxer; and Karel Curda, thirty years old, strong, taciturn and reliable.

In the soft fogs and mists of the highlands they played at games of war and learnt its destructive skills, and in the evenings they talked of the future and what it held for them.

Jan and Josef made few friends in England, but in the village of Ightfield in Cheshire the Ellisons remember them very well indeed. Mrs. Ellison has often recalled, with some amusement, how she first met Jan. Her two daughters—they were fifteen and sixteen at the time—had returned from an afternoon in Whitchurch buzzing with excitement. They had been sitting in the homeward-bound bus waiting for it to start, when a good-looking young Czech soldier had tried to talk to them. Finding speech too difficult, he had at last passed a note through the window. It read, "Please meet me here tomorrow!"

It was a request to be turned down flat by Mrs. Ellison, who had heard all about the Free Poles, and the Free French, and the Free Norwegians, and the free rest-of-them. But during the following week when she herself had been in town with her daughters on the way to the pictures they met him again. They had almost collided in the street. He had stopped, saluted, and in his halting English tried to make polite conversation. On impulse, because he seemed a nice young man, and a lonely young man, she had invited him to accompany them to the cinema. After all, she had a son of her own in the R.A.F.; it would be very reassuring if she could think that some other mother was being kind to him in the same sort of way.

It was still early when they left the cinema, and she asked Jan if he would like to come home and have a cup of tea. She warned him that Ightfield was a tiny village four miles from Whitchurch, and that the last bus left early. Of course he might be able to get a lift back, she added.

He replied, in his stilted broken English, that he would be most happy to take tea with them. They had got off the bus at the corner, in the village, and she had seen his eyes pause upon the black and white cottage near the bus stop, and roam over the cow-pens opposite their own gate. On the long walk up the garden path, with the wired chicken run on the left, past the rows of potatoes and onions, the beets and the tall runner-bean sticks, to the delphiniums, and white stocks, and the roses under the windows, he had said very little. He sat there quietly drinking tea out of the flowered china cups, munching cake and smiling at the girls, who made enough noisy conversation for ten tea parties.

And Mrs. Ellison, motherly and intuitive, had been saddened by his silence. For in her wise and experienced heart, although she could not understand the cause for his despair, she could sense that it existed. And she was sad that she could do nothing to assuage or diminish it. She knew that there were soldiers dying in agony upon a hundred scattered battlefields all over the world; she knew that there were millions of lonely and dispirited soldiers and sailors and airmen of many nations everywhere; but somehow, because she knew this one, he had become a personal responsibility.

So strongly did he affect her that as he rose to go, she said, "Why don't you come and see us on your days off? Come and stay here if you get any leave. If you'd like to, that is."

She was rewarded, as she was always rewarded during those eighteen months she knew him, by his look of gratitude and his quick smile; he beamed with pleasure.

So to Jan Kubis the square, red brick cottage in the village of Ightfield became home, and Mrs. Ellison—for his own mother had died when he was very young—his foster mother. He joked and laughed with the girls; they were little more than children at the time, and there was scarcely a hint of romance between him and Lorna and Edna. But it was all great fun, and sometimes with their nonsense and their laughter they could make the war seem so far away it hardly mattered.

This was months before they did their special training; the Czech camp was at Cholmondeley, a few miles outside Whitchurch, so they saw much of him. Here were gathered some of the remnants of an army disbanded when Hitler marched into Prague; veterans, practically all of them, of actions in the French Foreign Legion, or the new Czech army formed in France in 1939.

Jan's delight at having, at last, got to know "the English" was touching. With each visit his knowledge of the language improved, and they learnt a little more about him. But he still often sat in the parlour by himself for long periods, looking out at the world with lonely eyes, and Mrs. Ellison would say, "What's the matter, Jan? Cheer up. It won't be as bad tomorrow." And he would smile back at her as if he knew that it was going to be much, much worse tomorrow.

It was because of his obvious loneliness that, one day, Mrs. Ellison asked him if he would like to bring a friend to stay with them to keep him company. By the delighted lift of his eyebrows, she knew at once that he had been longing for her to say this, and that only his natural good manners had prevented even a hint of such an idea escaping.

The very next week Josef appeared. Josef was fun; and his English was perfect. Josef rocked and roared with high spirits and laughter; he slapped Jan on the back and told the Ellisons that he was much too serious, but it was only to be expected as Jan came from Moravia whereas he, Josef, came from Slovakia, where everyone laughed and sang all day long amongst the green valleys and high mountains.

Josef had dark hair, white teeth, a thin brown face, a quick smile. He was as temperamental as a prima donna; a great table-banger and gesticulator. But of course, a Slovakian! Jan would patiently explain to Mrs. Ellison and her two pretty daughters the reason for Josef's idiosyncrasies.

Czechoslovakia, it appeared, was like a long sausage divided into three different regions; and the people of these regions were similar in temperament to those of England, Scotland and Wales. The Bohemians, with Prague as their capital city, were like the English; the Moravians, the central district where Jan came from, were like the Scots.

It was at this moment that Josef inevitably intervened to point out that the Moravians were mean, dour, cautious and bad-tempered.

Jan would ignore the interruption, seeking for serious comparisons, and liken the Slovakians to the Welsh and Irish; and interrupting blandly, Josef would extol how musical, how gay, how passionate, were his countrymen.

"Mad," Jan would insist, "mad as mountain bears! Moody, unpredictable, dangerous!"

"But handsome, very handsome," Josef would crow, always hugely enjoying his inevitable last word.

The Ellisons always laughed at this constantly reiterated and friendly rivalry. The world, it seemed, was full of young men at war, chaffing each other with their friendly enmities. Texan and New Englander; Welshman and Geordie; Scot and Irishman and Cockney; Digger and South African; and the "Frees", who did not laugh quite as much, because they had been so far closer to the real thing.

For over a year the two Czech boys spent all their leaves and all their free week-ends at the large, red-brick cottage, standing in the fields on the outskirts of the village of Ightfield. And often, peering at them wisely from behind her glasses, Mrs. Ellison would examine her "two boys" with motherly insight, and divine behind their laughter a bottled-up intensity, a bitter awareness that this was but a brief halt in a journey towards an unknown purgatory. Secretly she grieved for all that must lie before them.

She came to know them both well. The serious shy Jan, and the volatile Josef. If Josef missed a bus, or knocked a drink over, or broke a bootlace, it was sufficient to act as a match to the easily inflammable fuse of his temperament. Up he soared like a rocket, spurting rage, threats and abuse, to burst effectively, briefly and brightly at a high altitude; then with a wry appraisal of his own ridiculousness, he would laugh himself all the way down to ground level again.

Everything that Josef did was rather larger and noisier than life. Mrs. Ellison realized that Jan knew all about these physical gyrations and could sit back and thoroughly enjoy the performances.

Josef told them about Slovakia. In his rare moments of seriousness, he drew for them a picture of a country where the peaks of the High Tatras stretched to the sky, and mountain streams smashed down through the rocky gullies in a white rage of constriction. A territory, he explained, of dark pine forests and immense loneliness; the hamlets small and scattered, where lived people who had never seen the sea and would never see the sea, but where every child had heard stories of forest pixies dancing in the moonlight, and could recount fairy tales handed down from grandmother to child for twenty generations. Now, because of a deal made by its quisling Prime Minister with Hitler, after Munich, it was ostensibly a free and independent country, shorn of both Moravia and Bohemia, and able therefore to send regiments to fight at the side of the Nazis.

Mrs. Ellison also perceived that the friendship between the two men was more than mere comradeship; it was a need born of loneliness and, to a certain extent, despair. They intermeshed like cog and flywheel; they were completely unselfish, completely altruistic towards each other, and although their arguments and rivalries were constant, they were as complementary to each other as the rind to the fruit, the bullet to the barrel, the flesh to the bone.

When Jan brought Josef to the cottage at Ightfield for the first time, he at once took him up the stairs to show him their small square bedroom, with its pink walls, blue curtains and bed with matching counterpane. Outside were the green fields and trees and black and white cows drowsily munching. There was a wicker-work linen basket under the window, and at night they laid their loaded revolvers upon it, side by side.

When Mrs. Ellison brought them their early morning tea, the first thing she saw were the revolvers side by side. They took no chance of surprise, anywhere, any time— ever!

The revolvers and the photo album are amongst her unfading memories of Jan; these and his constantly reiterated dreams of "after the war". After the war, he declared, he would go back to Czechoslovakia carrying his assorted albums of photographs and astound all his friends at the diversity of his experiences. To Mrs. Ellison there was always something naive, and rather eager, about the way he insisted that any moment of friendship or happiness had to be captured by the blinking lens of his camera, then processed and printed, and carefully stuck in one of the small albums, and identified by his neat handwriting. There was something oddly touching about his pride in them; he had no other personal possessions.

He would show them one day, he declared, to his wife and children. "After the war" he would of course get married and bring his family back and stay with the Ellisons, and they would all come to Czechoslovakia and see the village where he lived, and he would show them Prague and his beautiful country.

When they rushed up to Ightfield for that last hectic week-end, before they went off "somewhere"—he could not tell Mrs. Ellison where it was—they left all their precious possessions with her. They would come back later for them, they said.

Yes, Mrs. Ellison learnt much about Jan Kubis during those months. Some things he could tell her plainly. Others were buried too deep in his soul ever to emerge clearly, or if they did emerge they were only inadequately expressed in words like courage, patriotism, loyalty; soiled little words that bobbed like debris on the great flood of rhetoric issuing almost every day from a world full of dictators and states-men.

He told her something about his family, his brother and his sister, and his father. His father was a small farmer in the tiny village of Dolnich Vilemovicich in Southern Moravia. It was a village so pastoral and hidden that unless you knew which white road to follow across the rolling green countryside, you would never find it. Trebic was the nearest town, a small place with a wide cobbled square, and a road that dipped to a narrow bridge over a shining stream, and beyond a white church with an onion-spire.

It was a countryside of utter enchantment: a countryside farmed medievally in long strips each no more than twenty yards wide: brown ploughed earth against a swathe of bright yellow mustard seed, green corn against the tassel-headed maize stalks. Threading through this countryside were roads edged by lime-banded fruit trees. Here you met white-faced, fawn-brown oxen pulling the creaking high-wheeled carts which carried the farm produce to market. And occasionally you passed a red-roofed, white-walled cottage, standing back off the road amongst its girdle of fruit trees.

Through all his boyhood Jan Kubis knew this countryside: the small dark pools lying in the arms of shady firs, where you could swim, cracking the smooth, sky-reflecting mirror of water with the impetus of your dive, and where, after-wards, sunning yourself on the grass, through half-closed

31

eyes you could see the hazy summer countryside, soaring and lifting endlessly until it merged with the hot blue sky. He could remember the avenues of fruit trees laden with spring blossom, white and scented in the moonlight. The village itself turned its back on the fields, looking inwards to the tiny white-wooden church with its bell mounted on top of the steeple. The house of the Kubis family stood up at the top of the village, and there Jan spent all his early years.

Even in those days of the 'thirties, when the rest of the world was in the grip of depression, the people in the inn, and the church, and around their kitchen fires, knew that a threat to their freedom—freedom not yet twenty years old —was gathering.

For a thousand years they had been under Austro-Hungarian domination, but they had never forgotten that once Bohemia and Prague and Moravia had been—not only free—but the most powerful and influential country in Central Europe.

A great war, and a regrouping of Powers, had returned that freedom to them in 1918. But now, again from across the border, newspaper and radio threats were roaring, and it seemed that they were never to be allowed to live in peace. Into the constitution of their democratic republic they had written the tenets of government, which other men in other free countries had affirmed by painful trial and error. Authority by parliament, elected by universal, equal, secret and compulsory suffrage, open to all citizens irrespective of sex. Equality before the law. Equal civil and political rights, irrespective of race, religion or language. Freedom of the press. Free assembly and association. Free expression of opinion by word, writing or print. Freedom of scientific research. Freedom of instruction, of conscience, of religious creed. Protection of minorities. Freedom for all.

Exactly what convinced Jan Kubis, the young farm boy, that this freedom was an integral and necessary part of his consciousness, it is difficult to know.

There is no reason why he should not have lived out his life in that quiet village, aware of the weather, and the countryside, and the things that grew from the earth, un-

"Somewhere in England", 1940:
Czech machine-gun crew in training

Jan (*left*) and Josef before they parachuted on their mission

S.S. General
Reinhard Heydrich

troubled by political clamour. What did freedom mean to him? Freedom did not stop the spring coming, or the birds singing, or the blossom powdering the trees in the first rush of April. Supposing the Germans did force their army across the border as they threatened? Why should a few Nazis in steel helmets and theatrical costumes bother him? The wheat would still grow and ripen on the golden stem, the horses would stand steaming in their stables; you would still be able to drink at the village inn, and hear the tiny bell on top of the church tolling you to mass on a Sunday morning. The snow would thicken on the eaves in the winter, the rain still fall. There would be cattle to be tended, and crops to be grown, and girls to be courted, despite all the Nazis in Christendom. Not a million Hitlers could stop that. His hands could still hold the plough. Why therefore should he—a simple countryman—feel this surge of sickness, as the radio and the newspapers and the endless gossip made all aware that Hitler was preparing to invade their country.

After all, what was freedom except the ability to go on doing what you wanted to do? And he could go on doing what he wanted to do; or at least, he thought he could?

But he knew, as they all knew, and what the whole world would know one day, that this was not a benevolent dictatorship that was threatening to sweep from the north. This was the old enemy, a tyrant bringing fear, distortion, hatred, corruption, slavery. For a thousand years the Germans had attempted—using every method from immigration to invasion—to impose their will upon the Czechs. For a thousand years they had been unsuccessful. To let them attack and not resist was to choke, to stifle for lack of clean air.

Jan Kubis knew, instinctively, that freedom was more than a word invented by man. Freedom was an infection against which there was no inoculation. Freedom was of your own conception; and you alone could defend its relative meaning.

When Jan left the farm and joined the Czech army he knew exactly what he was doing. It was an army, in 1937, of ten thousand officers and one hundred and fifty thousand men. It was a compact fully-mechanized army which was never to fight on its own soil. It was an army which, when the Nazis arrived in 1939, was immediately demobilized and told to go home. Some sections of it obeyed. Some companies of soldiers, sensing that the time was coming when the rest of Europe would inevitably have to fight the Nazi overlord or perish, travelled by night to other borders, and slipped across, seeking any friend who would aid and rearm them. Others formed underground resistance groups.

It was as a member of one of these groups that Jan was first captured by the Nazis, imprisoned and branded. It was simple, they thought, to crush this incipient revolt at source by such methods. They had done it successfully in their own country; there was no reason why such methods should not succeed in Czechoslovakia.

Jan Kubis was rescued by other members of his resistance group in the small hours of a dark morning. They overpowered the prison guards, forced their way into the prison and unlocked the cells. As they raced for safety into the darkness, Jan realized that his brother was amongst his rescuers. There was no time for more than a handshake and a quick word. It was imperative that he leave the country at once.

"Tell father," Jan said, "that I'll be back one day."

He travelled by night across a countryside that was now sad with autumn. The leaves had almost gone but the barns were full of warm hay where he could sleep. And in the farms were people who understood the bitterness of this hurrying young man on his journey to the Polish border, and they gave him food.

The border was not well guarded, and in Poland they were not surprised to see him come. They were expecting trouble themselves. The big men, the statesmen, could make all sorts of wordy prophecies and write their names on pieces of paper, but the people of Europe from the Baltic to the Mediterranean, from the Atlantic to the Black Sea, could smell war in the air, and were making—in their own hearts —that long and despairing acceptance of its coming. They showed him to a camp near Warsaw which was full of refugees: young men from half a dozen countries. The French Foreign Legion had a recruiting unit there. They were doing good business. It was in this camp that Jan first met Josef. He was a locksmith by trade, but had also worked in a chemical factory in Zilina, a town that lies in the foothills of the Tatra Mountains. Like Jan he was on the run. He had crossed the border just before the Gestapo got to him. Like Jan he had no money and few possessions. So, because their bond of friendship was apparent from the first moment they met, they teamed up. The only possible way for them to move onwards was to join the French Foreign Legion. At least there was a clause in the signing-on papers which promised that if war broke out, and a Czech Army was formed on French soil, Czech nationals would be allowed to transfer to that army.

It was the beginning of a long adventure that was to end in safety in England. An adventure which, however, was to have a second beginning.

When they were asked by the Czech Army in England if they were prepared to carry out a special assignment, the Czech military intelligence knew what they were doing. They chose well. They knew you do not fashion assassins by appealing only to their patriotic instinct. You do not manufacture killers by a short course in the apparatus and methods concerned with inflicting death. You pick out the man who will persevere, oblivious of danger and difficulties. You pick out the man who is so enraged that nothing will stand between him and his purpose. You pick out a man with seven swastikas branded on his buttocks.

CHAPTER TWO

WHEN Jan moved off across the Czechoslovakian snow in search of Josef, he knew exactly the danger they were in and the price the Germans would exact should they be caught. A quick death was a benevolence they could not expect. Continual, prolonged, agonizing torture was the certain means the Nazis would employ to extort every fragment of information from two such knowledgeable witnesses; and it was in anticipation of such a contingency—for they realized that shortly their lives might be of lesser importance than the secrets they hoarded—that they carried poison pills; small brown capsules swallowed in a second and bringing certain death within ten.

These, together with their revolvers, permitted a margin of mental peace, but there was no latitude of relaxation, no sanctuary anywhere, no moment asleep or awake when they were able to feel secure during all their time in Czechoslovakia. Aware of this situation Jan hurried across the snow-crusted grass in search of Josef, and it was with a quick surge of horror that he heard him muttering and cursing when he was still at least fifty feet away.

A moment later he understood the reason for Josef's anger. He had landed heavily against a frozen bank. His foot was broken or badly sprained. He hobbled around amidst the folds of his parachute, wild with pain and frustration.

The worst thing that could happen to a parachutist— injury upon landing—had occurred.

"Can you walk on it?" Jan asked quickly. "Can you manage to walk at all?"

Gingerly Josef tested it out, and Jan watched him anxiously. A painful, stumbling hobble was all he could manage; it was imperative they found shelter somewhere close and very quickly.

Jan looked up at the sky, at the hard clear stars embedded

in the black night between the ponderous and disinterested clouds, from which they had so recently descended. The clouds carried snow; there was the smell of snow in the air. If it snowed after they had found shelter, excellent: their tracks would be covered. If it snowed before they found refuge, hazards would increase and they might become dangerously lost. In the bundle dropped by the supply parachute they had food enough for several days as well as a large variety of weapons. But shelter was the primary consideration.

Before they left England the briefing officer had told them they would be dropped near Pilsen. They had been given three addresses of people it was believed would help them in that city, but there was no guarantee of this. For almost three years Czechoslovakia had been cut off. The important interests of the Allies had lain elsewhere. Jan and Josef were pioneers in a land which in all probability was unfriendly. Around Pilsen they had been told to expect hilly country, broken by deep swathes of pine forest where it would be easy to find shelter. But the country they stood in now, even in the darkness, had a feeling of being open and rolling, and there were certainly no trees in the vicinity.

It was Josef who said he had seen some dark objects over to the right as he came floating down. Sheds of some sort, he thought, where perhaps they might find shelter.

Jan put his arm around Josef's waist and together they hobbled across the frozen ground in that direction. It was very cold; breath gusted out of their mouths in quick jets like steam, and their breathing was laboured. They were intent upon their task, but both felt the thin coil of fear deep in their bellies; a fear which anticipated a sudden paralysing alarm which might spring from any quarter. This period—all their training and instruction had taught them—was the most dangerous time. They were comparatively defenceless now, like two hedgehogs crawling across a main road in broad daylight.

Within a few minutes, two low dark buildings loomed out of the darkness. Yes, they were huts. Jan left Josef and carefully scouted ahead. Both of the huts were unoccupied; one had a thin, triangular-shaped roof and was full of hay, the other was squat and square and apparently empty.

Jan went back to fetch Josef, and together they carefully examined the empty hut. Jan tried the door and found it locked, but above the door the flimsy boarding was rotten, and it was quite easy to pry the timber away from the corroded nail heads. They pulled back the boards to make an opening, and Jan gave Josef a leg up to wriggle through. He heard him groan as he dropped on to his injured foot inside the hut.

Except for boxes and oddments stacked against the walls, the hut was empty; the air inside was also several degrees warmer than outside.

Leaving Josef inside, Jan went back to collect the parachutes and to try and find the supply parachute which had carried the bundle containing their weapons and supplies. His eyes were used to the darkness now and he found it without difficulty. He made two journeys, one to bring back to the hut the two parachutes, and the other to bring in the supply bundle with its parachute still attached. This he pushed in through the hole above the door, and his own parachute after it. Josef's parachute he bundled up against the side of the hut and covered it with a thin covering of snow.

He knew very well that he was disobeying the primary law of the parachutist—reiterated over and over again during their training—"Bury your parachute as soon as you land!"

But Jan and Josef were not ordinary parachutists; from the very beginning they made their own rules, although very often these seemed to collide with elementary common sense, and some were close to elementary madness. What other conclusion can one reach when one realizes that upon landing in a country where every shadow might conceal a quick ending to their lives, they decided to preserve their parachutes as *"souvenirs"*? Quite how they were going to do this, they had not yet decided, but when the war was over, they were determined that each parachute should hang in a special place in their own homes, fitting memorials to that day when they returned to Czechoslovakia to revenge, with one blow, a part of the injury the Nazis had done their country. Such was the measure of their confidence in their task, and such was the extent of their inspired foolishness.

In the dark interior of the hut they opened tins of bully beef and biscuits, scraped the congealed meat out of the tins on to the soft warm silk of the parachute, and divided it with their knives. It was good to eat and be back on firm earth again. With the future so full of doubt, the present was precious: the small, safe cocoon of the present, vital with the humdrum necessity of eating and drinking, warm with the knowledge of being alive and fairly safe.

They ate in silence, each engaged with his own thoughts. They could reflect now upon the orders which had brought them to this place, upon that first meeting with the senior officers of the Czechoslovakian Intelligence in London, who had told them how they had been kept under special observation from the moment they started training. Without preamble, they were asked if they were willing to return to Czechoslovakia together, upon a mission of the highest importance? When they said "yes", without hesitation, and the senior officers obviously expected them to say "yes", the magnitude of this mission was revealed.

The Reichsprotector of Bohemia and Moravia, Baron von Neurath, had resigned from his post ostensibly because of illness. It was a convenient excuse. He was a failure. Czechoslovakia, far from being the model dependency Hitler expected of a founder member of his empire, was sullen and unco-operative. Production had fallen; students had the impudence to demonstrate in the streets; it appeared that the puppet government could do nothing with these irascible Czechs.

Upon the 27th September, 1941, S.S. General Reinhard Heydrich arrived in Prague in the post of Acting Reichsprotector of Bohemia and Moravia to remedy this state of affairs. He at once called a press conference and announced a state of emergency from that moment onwards. He also handed out a list of the names of eminent Czech public figures and soldiers who had been imprisoned for many months, and who would now be executed. This, he made quite clear, was only a beginning. Within the next few weeks other lists of executions would be prepared. Those who would not co-operate with the Greater German Reich were expendable; their ashes in small urns, neatly labelled with exact time and date of execution, would be forwarded to their next-of-kin without delay. German rule was to be thorough, efficient and merciless.

Within a matter of days, intelligently appraising the situation, Heydrich had also wooed the workers. Of what use were these Generals and intellectuals to the Czechs, he asked? He appealed on an effective materialistic level. For just a little extra work, extra fat coupons, meat coupons and bread coupons could be won. It was a belly bribery almost impossible to resist. And if a worker really cared to exert himself, there were holidays at the best Spa hotels—once the preserve of the aristocratic and the wealthy—for him and his family, higher wages, and food. Always the promise of more food. Within a month, production, especially war production, was rising.

Jan and Josef were shown the radio reports monitored by the B.B.C. Heydrich's success was self-evident:

"Heydrich, the friend of the workers. . . . Heydrich publishes an article on the traditions of Wenceslas. . . . Heydrich receives an address of loyalty. . . . Heydrich and his wife attend a Mozart evening in Prague."

It was insistent, insidious and constant propaganda, and it was having an effect upon the Czechs. No longer could the Allies expect resistance from them; each day they were passing more securely into the Nazi camp. And the Heydrich plan, eventually to be put into operation, was more ambitious than that.

As a gracious gesture from the Fuhrer, Heydrich would arrange for a measure of autonomy, more self-government, more apparent freedom to be conferred upon the Czechs for their co-operation with the Reich. The Czech puppet government would then return the favour—already its politicians were making speeches referring to "our two great nations hand in hand joining the struggle against Bolshevism and plutocracy"—and instead of remaining neutral, pass a bill legalizing conscription. What a propaganda victory it would be; what a military coup! Twenty fresh divisions on the side of the Nazis.

There was but one way to prevent this happening, declared the senior officers; one way of showing the world that Czechoslovakia was back in the fight on the side of the Allies. While the puppet government was fawning under the stroking Nazi hand, parachutists dropped secretly into the country, would bite off that hand. They would make such a gesture of defiance that the Germans would know they were dealing with an aggressive and not a defeated people.

That gesture was obvious. It was not simple, but it was obvious. They must assassinate Heydrich. If this was found to be impossible, they must try to kill Frank, the Nazi Secretary of State in Prague. But Heydrich was the bigger prize. If one of the leaders of the Nazi hierarchy could be killed, then the whole rotten edifice would shake and tremble. The Germans were dizzy with success; they believed their security precautions infallible; their power complex was so enormous that it was almost impossible for them to visualize anyone possessing the impertinence to attack one of their omniscient leaders.

Czech Intelligence in London had no such belief in Nazi immortality; they believed that two determined and dedicated men, trained and disciplined, could parachute into Czechoslovakia and kill Heydrich. They had chosen Jan Kubis and Josef Gabchik to carry out this task.

So now they were there, munching British bully beef in a gardener's hut somewhere in Czechoslovakia. They did not sleep much that night, and Josef, because of the pain in his foot, woke first. In the grey dawn light they discussed their next move. The thin light, seeping between the cracks in the rough timber walls, revealed the piles of boxes and wooden trays stacked everywhere; and the brooms and rakes and sacks. It would be quite simple to hide much of their equipment behind and under this paraphernalia. It was also important that they quickly find a safer hiding place. While Josef stumbled around and concealed their supplies, their guns, grenades and ammunition under the boxes, Jan decided to reconnoitre the surrounding countryside and see if he could find a better place.

He stripped off his parachute overalls, and scrambled out through the hole above the door. The earth was still hard and frozen, and the air clear and cold. He filled his lungs and set off.

Walking across the fields in the still, half-unwoken world on that winter morning, the cloud gone, and the sky a vague pale blue, the frost crisp on the tufty grass, the trees black and shiny with ice-encased twigs, an occasional lonely crow flapping across the sky, Jan felt a great exultation surging inside him. He was home again. As he plodded forwards, an undistinguished figure in a shabby overcoat and trilby hat, his eyes surveyed the broad sweep of the undulating fields, the row of houses, the church in the village behind him, the telegraph lines strung along a road a mile away. He could see no sign of a forest anywhere, yet they had been told that near Pilsen the country was heavily forested. It appeared that the aircraft must have dropped them off course.

He walked across the fields, across patches of frozen snow, and reached a narrow tarmac road. There was no one about and he walked along it for about a quarter of a mile. He was looking for a clump of trees, a small copse, any place which would give them a certain amount of cover, any place where they could hide until Josef's toe was a little better. Across to the right, as he walked, he glimpsed on rising ground the tops of a clump of trees, and decided to turn off and explore. The fields were hedgeless; it was quite easy to walk across the open ground. As he got closer, he saw that the trees fringed huge boulders, and with a sense of excitement realized that he had discovered a quarry. And by the look of it, a disused quarry.

In the centre of the quarry was a small pool, its edges glittering with ice, and to one side a small stone building which also looked abandoned. But what mainly attracted him was the quarry entrance. It was a dark tunnel opening into the interior of the hillside. Its entrance was grass-grown. Obviously no one used it or had visited it for a long time. The village was at least two miles away; there was no house closer than that. It seemed, at first sight, an ideal hiding place.

As he explored with his pocket torch, he saw it was even better than he had hoped. A labyrinth of stone passages turned and twisted inside the hill of granite. He found two other entrances, and did not stop to find more; the passages were very cold, but at least they would give them protection against the worst of the winter wind and weather.

He hurried back to tell Josef, and they decided to move at once while it was still very early. Jan helped Josef through the hole, and Josef limped along behind him as he led the way. Jan carried enough hard rations to last them for three days; they could replenish their stocks from the material they had hidden in the hut when they needed to; the primary need was to stay hidden and wait for Josef's toe to mend.

They spent a cold day and night in the corridors of the quarry, and next morning Jan made a cautious journey of exploration to the hut and walked a mile along the road. He met no one. Their parachute drop did not seem to have concerned anyone, but despite the discomfort of the quarry, they determined to hide there for at least another two or three days. And then, that afternoon they received their first shock.

They lunched on bully beef and biscuits and drank cold water from the pools gathered in the quarry floor; they had examined their maps for the hundredth time, and made vague guesses at which town they were near, and at last, for a little exercise, and to see if Josef's foot was any better, they walked out through the quarry entrance.

As they passed into the open air Josef said, "Look!" and they stopped dead. A burly, middle-aged man dressed in a heavy jacket and gaiters stood no more than ten yards away. He looked almost as if he were expecting them, but he stared at them without saying a word.

As Jan slid his hand inside his overcoat pocket and placed

43

his fingers around his revolver butt, the man's eyes flicked from one to the other, and he said quietly, "Good afternoon, gentlemen. What are you doing here?" There was no real animosity in his voice, no threat. The possibility that this question might be asked should they be discovered, had already occurred to them, and they had an answer ready.

"We are considering reopening the quarry," said Jan politely. "We see there is plenty of granite still worth working."

The man smiled. "It hasn't been worked for many years," he said dryly. "In fact, gentlemen, it might interest you to know that it was originally worked over six hundred years ago, when the stone for the Charles Bridge was quarried here.

There was a pause. They had not missed the friendly note in the man's voice, and they waited for him to continue. He was not hesitant.

"I am the gamekeeper here," he said. "It is my duty to go round the estate every day. I was passing the gardener's shed this morning . . ." he paused meaningly. "I saw your tracks in the snow. . . ."

Jan glanced quickly at Josef but the gamekeeper hurried on.

"Do not worry, gentlemen, you can trust me. I followed your tracks here."

"Did you find anything except our tracks in the snow?" asked Josef quietly.

The gamekeeper pause, "Yes," he said, "there was a parachute hidden under the snow outside the hut."

"You left it there?" asked Jan.

"Of course."

The eyes of Jan Kubis and Josef Gabchik met again; luck was on their side, it seemed. They had met their first Czechoslovakian, and he was friendly. He looked a decent, honest countryman, and sooner or later they had to start trusting people.

"We are parachutists from England," said Jan simply. "Will you help us? We need the help of good Czechs."

"You are?" said the gamekeeper delightedly, as if para-

44

chutists dropping in on his estate were as common as spring partridges. "Of course I'll help you. I live in Nehvizdy, the village nearby...."

"Nehvizdy," said Josef quickly. "Where's that?"

"Our nearest big town is Prague," said the gamekeeper. "About twenty kilometres away. It's about an hour's journey by train." He paused. "You look astonished gentlemen."

"We are," said Jan grimly. "We thought we were near Pilsen."

"Pilsen!" The gamekeeper chortled. Nothing seemed to disturb this merry, unconcerned soul. "Oh no, Pilsen is a long way from here, a long way the other side of Prague."

This was something they had not expected. It meant that all the contacts given them in England were useless. They would have to start from scratch.

"Now what can I do to help you, gentlemen?" continued the gamekeeper. "I must get back to my duties now."

"Find out," said Jan quickly, "if the country police suspect anything."

The gamekeeper nodded. "I will do that, and come back tonight and tell you."

They watched his sturdy figure retreating across the snow-powdered grass, and realized that it was within his power to end their enterprise even before it had begun.

The Germans would pay him well for such information. Nevertheless, they would have to take many chances similar to this.

That night the gamekeeper came back with a loaf and sausage. Although food was severely rationed it had occurred to him that they might be hungry; he also brought with him the news that, as far as he could ascertain, no one seemed to know anything about them.

They were very relieved to hear this, and it was not until the next afternoon that they discovered just how wrong he had been. It was getting dark when they saw a figure in the entrance to the passage, whistling enquiringly. They thought it was the gamekeeper returning.

"We're here," called Jan. "Come on through." Then he felt Josef clutch his arm. Against the lighter entrance of the

45

cave, the figure was vaguely outlined, and it was a different figure. It was certainly not the gamekeeper, but someone shorter and fatter.

Jan held his torch in his left hand, his revolver in his right. He let the man approach to within ten paces, then clicked on the torch.

They saw a short fat man with a rubbery face. He wore a dark overcoat and a battered felt hat, and he look frightened.

"Stay where you are!" said Jan sharply. "And put up your hands."

"Please don't be alarmed," said the man quickly. "I'm a friend, I want to help you." But he held his hands high.

"Who are you?" said Jan.

"My name is Bauman. I'm the miller here in Nehvizdy." He added as if in explanation, "I am a Sokol." To Jan and Josef it was an explanation. The Czech Resistance had its origin in the Sokol movement. On the surface it was merely a sports and gymnastic organization, but since the First World War, it had taken on a much deeper significance; it was deeply patriotic and concerned with preserving the traditions and culture of Czechoslovakia.

"Did the gamekeeper send you?" asked Josef.

"The gamekeeper? What gamekeeper?"

"How did *you* know we were here then?" said Jan suspiciously.

"It was not hard," said Bauman. "Practically everybody in Nehvizdy knows there are parachutists in the district."

"Everybody knows? But how do they know?" demanded Josef angrily.

"They saw the parachutes in the sky as you dropped," said Bauman. "Indeed, the aeroplane woke me up, though I didn't bother to get up. We have never had an aeroplane of such power so low before. Several villagers thought it must be crashing. Some looked through their windows and saw the parachutes floating down."

"But the gamekeeper said no one knew."

Bauman chuckled. He was growing more at ease every minute. "I think for the first day they were all too frightened to speak, but this morning in the tavern someone made a

46

remark, and then it all came out that many people knew that parachutes had been seen in the night."

Jan and Josef looked at each other in alarm. If this was true, they had to leave at once.

"But it is not as bad as it sounds," continued Bauman. "The villagers have only whispered amongst themselves. They are all my friends, good Czechs. The police do not know. I cautioned the villagers not to gossip. I said, if the Germans discover this it might mean many deaths."

"And they *will* keep quiet?" demanded Jan.

"They have no love for the Germans," said Bauman with simplicity and fervour.

"But how did *you* know we were here in this quarry?" persisted Josef.

"I didn't," said Bauman. "But this is open country and there are not many good hiding places. This is the most obvious, and it is the first place I looked."

"The first place the Nazis would look then, if they knew we were here," commented Josef grimly.

"That is why I came," put in Bauman. He paused, and then said very simply. "So far in this war we have been able to do nothing, except wait and hope. Now we can do something."

There was a short pause, then Bauman continued, "It is obviously dangerous for you to remain here long. I also expect you have work to do which you cannot accomplish from the interior of a quarry."

They assured him he was perfectly correct.

"You wish to go to Prague?"

"We are aiming for Pilsen in the first place, but Prague will be better if we can find a good hiding place," they said.

"I have a friend who belongs to the Sokol Movement in the Holesovice area of Prague," said Bauman. "The members still meet secretly—you understand, the Sokol is now unlawful. They would help you I think. If you are in agreement, I will get in touch with them."

They discussed the idea between themselves for a few minutes. In the circumstances it seemed the best thing they could possibly do. They could not stay in the quarry much longer. They placed themselves in Bauman's hands, and when the gamekeeper arrived later that evening, they told him they would shortly be leaving.

Two days later, with Bauman as their guide, they left the quarry at seven-thirty in the morning. They had shaved and washed in a tinful of water gathered from rain puddles. They had eaten their usual breakfast of bully beef and bread. They wore overcoats and trilby hats, and carried the brief-cases that practically all town-dwellers used. Josef limped badly, otherwise there was nothing to distinguish them from a million other Czechs going about their business in various parts of the country at that time in the morning.

Mr. Bauman nodded approval of their appearance, and they set off down the straight tarmac road which led to the railway a short distance from the village. At the station there were only a few passengers. One of them was a slight man in a dark overcoat who raised his trilby hat politely when Bauman introduced them, revealing a balding head. They thanked Bauman and climbed aboard the train with their new guide; they never saw the miller or the gamekeeper again, but both survived the war.

As the train rattled and bumped its way towards Prague, the small bald-headed man said very little. Jan and Josef quietly read newspapers.

As they came closer to the city their excitement grew. The quarry near Nehvizdy was like any other quarry in any part of Europe; but this was the great city which had figured in their imaginations since they were children, and which Jan, in his army days, had come to know intimately. They looked out at the grey suburbs, the tenement blocks, the clanking trams, the dingy factories, and the dust-encrusted heaps of snow piled everywhere, but their eyes saw only beauty, and close to the old heart of the city they lifted to the church steeples, to the great walls of Hradcany Castle, dominating the hillside, and the tall spire of St. Vitus, with the wonder and devotion of returning pilgrims.

The station was crowded and noisy with tannoy announce-ments, train whistles and engine clatter. At the barrier the collector took their tickets without a glance at them. There were a few Wehrmacht soldiers waiting for trains, but they also were quite uninterested in other passengers.

They walked out of the station filled with a great feeling of exhilaration. They were home. Preparations for the killing could begin.

CHAPTER THREE

Jan watched Auntie Marie moving around the living-room preparing the table for lunch, and as usual asking him all sorts of questions about England. Her eldest son had escaped there two years previously and had joined the R.A.F. Auntie Marie wished to know all about the R.A.F.; even news of the type of piston rings used in Wellington bombers would have possessed a certain interest for her.

Marie Moravec, who was to play so large a part in the future destinies of Jan and Josef, was in her early fifties. Her large, glowing brown eyes, flish-flashed with sudden glints of humour. She had black hair curled in a heavy bun at the back of her neck, even features and a white skin, indicating that in those early, windy 'twenties, when Czecho-slovakia was a republic newly intoxicated by its escape from the Austro-Hungarian Empire, and Prague laughed and shouted, gambled and experimented with this new condi-tion called freedom, she had possessed a youthful beauty to match its rapture.

She was volatile and gay; she loved parties and people, arguments and laughter; and if her laughter sometimes caused both her husband and her second son, Ata, to regard her with the slight uneasiness common to more repressed husbands and sons, Auntie Marie did not mind at all. These were dangerous days and she was implicated in them to the full. To the cause of her country she was passionately dedi-cated. She adored sheltering the two parachutists in her flat, and she was prepared to risk her life to help them.

Around her ample Amazonian figure the household revolved; within her empire of lounge, living-room and kitchen Auntie Marie—for such was how Jan and Josef always addressed her—was queen. Mr. Moravec was a tall, lean man with a craggy face and thinning hair. He worked as a railway inspector. Compared with his wife he was shy and retiring, and as so often is the case with men who possess such bouncing zestful wives as Mrs. Moravec, he preserved a certain anonymity. But Jan could always discern the note of deep pride and love in his voice when he mentioned his wife. It was as if he was eternally amazed that someone as undistinguished as himself could capture and marry and have children by someone so elusive and so feminine and so full of fire as Marie Moravec.

Ata was twenty-one years old, "tall, dark and handsome", as his mother so often teased him. He had inherited her quick brown eyes, and her vitality; he was astonishingly mature for one so young. He also adored the adventure of living with two "real" parachutists. They did not know, and would not have wished to know, that later *all* would depend on young Ata.

The first month that Jan and Josef spent in Prague had passed quickly and comparatively uneventfully. Before they reached the flat of Auntie Moravec they experienced many temporary hiding places. The little man with the bald head had first of all delivered them to a small house in the suburbs of the city and told them to wait until they were called for. They were well looked after by the family who lived there, and Josef was able to rest his injured foot.

It was because of this injury that Jan went alone to meet the members of the resistance when their guide called a week later. As usual, he tucked his heavy, khaki-coloured revolver into his breast pocket. They caught a tram out to a suburb of Prague which Jan did not know at all.

It was a cold blustery day, with the wind gusting along the drab streets, and patches of snow, frozen and grey-veined with traffic dust, piled at the pavement edges. As the tram jerked and rattled along, Jan thought fleetingly of the icy stone passages of the Nahvizdy quarry, and reflected that at least they were lucky to have found shelter in a warm centrally-heated flat.

The block of apartments to which his guide led him was indistinguishable from a dozen others in Prague. Tall, grey-stoned, steam-heated; the glass-panelled entrance doors opened into a wide inner lobby where letter boxes lined the whole of one wall. A wire-enclosed lift whined up through seven floors of rather dingy concrete.

"The flat is number 67," whispered the guide. "Sixth floor." He walked quickly out through the entrance doors, leaving Jan alone, except for a hard-faced young man leaning against the wall reading a newspaper with an apparent rapt disinterest in all about him.

Jan pressed the button, and the lift took him to the sixth floor. He walked along the corridor. At either end other young men were lolling against the wall reading newspapers. Their interest in the black printed columns was so sincere that no one could have misunderstood their purpose. Obviously they were guards. They could be Gestapo guards for all Jan knew. Obviously they had all taken their postures and dress from the American movies of the 'thirties. It was odd to consider what an influence those gum-chewing, mackintoshed, trilby-hatted gunmen and G-men and gangsters, manufactured by Hollywood, had on the world.

He knocked at Number 67. A voice called, "Come in", and he realized the door had been left open.

Inside was a small hallway. Another open door led through to an inner room. It was furnished without ostentation: a settee, armchairs, a table set with tea things, a few hard chairs, three rugs on the polished wooden floor, two coloured photographs of the High Tatra peaks on the walls.

Three men stood by the table. Jan halted inside the room and considered them. The shorter one in the centre was obviously the leader; he had authority despite his rather slovenly dress. He was short, powerful and inclining to chubbiness. He wore a dark-blue serge suit, which was baggy at the knees and stained on the lapels; and the fingers of his right hand which extracted the cigarette from his mouth as Jan walked in were yellowish with nicotine. His fattish face was pale, the dark moustache scrubby and unclipped. Yet in spite of all this, there was an air of quiet command about him as tangible as his own cigarette smoke.

He said simply: "I am Jindra," and held out his hand. When Jan had shaken it, he continued, "And this is Uncle Hajsky."

The third man's name Jan did not catch correctly, but there seemed no point in asking for it to be repeated, as he guessed they all probably changed their names from week to week.

Jindra indicated a seat next to the table and Jan sat down. There were small cakes on a plate with a lace paper d'oyley, and a silver teapot steamed peacefully.

Jan eyed it, and said: "You expected me to be on time."

Jindra paused in the act of pouring the tea, peering across at him like a rather motherly old bird. "You understand," he said quietly, "that if you are not what you say you are, and if you cannot prove what you say, you will not leave this house alive."

The tiny waterfall of amber tea splashing into the cup was the only sound in the room. When it was full Jindra handed it to Jan. Above the coloured china his eyes were as cold and grey as the pavements outside.

"We are all armed. As you probably saw, this apartment is guarded by other armed men. You realize of course that as members of an illegal organization we are not in a position to take the slightest chance. Even to *think* against the Nazis is punishable by death. People accused of *plotting* against them are not allowed such a luxury; they are kept alive and in pain in a variety of ways."

Jan looked from Jindra to the others. They were all watching him carefully. Jindra finished pouring the tea and handed around the cups. No one added sugar or milk or lemon, or even sipped the hot liquid.

Jan had expected a welcome not an investigation. He realized that his position was by no means impregnable. How could he prove his identity? As if reading his thoughts, Jindra continued, "What for example do we know about you? You landed by parachute near Nehvizdy from an unidentified plane. That is proven, but the plane could have been German. Or perhaps, if the plane was British, the agents could have been captured and German agents substituted in their places." He paused. "It has happened before."

His eyes never left Jan's face. "Ever since you arrived you

have been extremely careless. You have asked far too many questions. You have made many attempts during the last week to contact people working against the Germans." He paused again and then went on. "These are the normal tactics used by the German agents attempting to infiltrate into our ranks."

He stopped, added lemon to his tea and sipped it thoughtfully.

Since Jindra began to speak the tension in the room had increased perceptibly. Jan realized now how badly he had been caught off guard. That he had not expected to have to prove his identity to his own people, was no excuse; he should have been more alert. He also knew that the next move was up to him and he chose his words carefully.

"You must also understand that the people who sent us from England to contact the resistance here and complete our—our mission—were also very careful," he said quietly. "They could hardly give us documents to prove our identity. My card proves that I am Otto Strnad, a workman from Brno. I was issued with five thousand Reich notes of five, ten, twenty and fifty mark values, and ten Czech fifty crown notes. We also have arms and ammunition well hidden." He paused. In his own heart he was quite certain that this was no trap, that these really were men of the Czech resistance, and he wanted desperately to win them over. Upon impulse he made a slightly melodramatic gesture of which he was sure Josef would have approved heartily.

He slowly put his hand into his inside breast pocket, pulled out his revolver and laid it next to his cup of tea. He placed a hand upon it.

"I too must be careful," he said.

The silence lasted perhaps four seconds. The eyes of the man called Jindra were still as cold as frosted glass. "You say you have come from England?" he asked.

"Yes."

"Therefore you would know many of the Czechs serving in the forces there?"

"Of course."

"Perhaps you could name a few."

Without hesitation Jan named half a dozen.

Jindra fished into his breast pocket and produced a photograph of a young man in civilian clothes. He handed it to Jan.

"Do you recognize this man?" he said.

The face was vaguely familiar to Jan. "Yes," he said, "he's also an officer in the Czech Army in England."

Jindra nodded, but he did not smile or express approval in any other way.

"Your accent?" he said, "is——?"

"I'm from Moravia," said Jan.

"From what district exactly?"

"Near Trebic."

Jindra lifted his eyes. "I know that district very well," he said warningly.

"So do I," said Jan meeting his gaze levelly. "I was born there."

"Perhaps then," asked Jindra evenly, "you can tell me about the railway station at Vladislav quite near to Trebic? You know Vladislav, of course?"

"Quite well," said Jan, "it's on the main road between Trebic and Brno."

"You know therefore why the railway station is exceptionally interesting?"

"I do," said Jan. "The station master is a famous amateur rose-grower. The whole station is a mass of blooms all the summer."

"Good," said Jindra, and for the first time the mistrust left his voice.

"I should know," said Jan. " I was born at Dolnich Vilemovicich only nine kilometres away. My family still live there. If you wanted any more proof we could go out and see them."

The icy atmosphere was broken. The other two lifted their cups and sipped thoughtfully. There was a feeling of relief in the air.

"No more proof is necessary," said Jindra. "But you understand that we had to know about you. Incidentally do not get in touch with your family. The fewer people who know you are here, the better."

Jan nodded and drank his tea. He picked up his revolver and put it back in his pocket.

"You see," explained Jindra, "you are the first parachutists to arrive here since the war began. We are not used to the idea yet."

"It's difficult for us to get used to the idea of being back," said Jan.

Jindra lit another cigarette and returned to his questioning.

"We would like to know other things about you. Why for example have you been dropped here?"

"To set up resistance. To work for Czechoslovakia against Germany."

Jindra took his cigarette out of his mouth and stared squarely at him.

"We understood," he said sombrely, "that you were sent upon a certain special mission."

This was news to Jan. How would these people know about his special mission? It was a dead secret. Jan's voice was guarded. "I am sure that although we may have been indiscreet on occasions, we have never made such a fact known," he said deliberately.

"But it is true, is it not?" persisted Jindra.

Jan paused and looked at the three faces regarding him inquisitively. "I arrive at a strange apartment," he said. "You cross-question me and satisfy yourselves about my identity. But I know nothing about you. You cannot expect me to reveal everything."

Jindra moved his cup to one side of the table. There was a certain deliberation about his action. After a few seconds he said, "Could it be possible that you were sent to kill Heydrich?"

Jan stared at him in amazement. "Good God!" he exclaimed.

For the first time Jindra smiled. "We too have our contact with London," he said. "They are not good enough, or safe enough, but they are contacts."

"But how did you know?" said Jan.

"We thought of the idea and asked for help," said Jindra.

"Maybe London thought of it at the same time. It doesn't matter. The main thing is, can we do it?"

"That's our job," said Jan quietly.

Jindra nodded his head. "We will give you all the help we can," he said. "We are glad you are here."

He went on to tell Jan how the arrival of Heydrich had been the signal for a wave of arrests from which the resistance had still not recovered. Anyone with any pretence to being an "intellectual" had been arrested, imprisoned, and in most cases executed. There was no reason in law, or indeed in any civilized code of conduct for such atrocity. But if you were an "intellectual" and therefore likely to think against the Reich it was enough.

He did not tell Jan everything. He did not tell him how in the early days of the Heydrich terror, he had belonged to the Sokol revolutionary committee in the town of Brno, and that all the committee had been caught and shot except himself. He, a grammar school master, had decided it was time to disappear. He had moved to Prague to carry on the struggle because it was the capital: he had adopted the code name of Jindra and was in contact with the other resistance leaders throughout Czechoslovakia.

But he did explain to Jan the difficulty they had in making contact without short-wave transmitters and receivers. It was almost impossible to send reports abroad without radio apparatus; how could they commit acts of sabotage without explosives? How could they train people to do all these things? That was the main reason why they had appealed to London for help.

"But I understand that the other group which dropped from our aircraft, after us, had radio transmitters and receivers," said Jan. "Their main task was to open a line to London. You have no contact with them?"

"Nothing yet," said Jindra, "but no doubt they will need time to become established. If they are safe we shall hear soon." He changed the subject. "Your own equipment? What has happened to it?"

"It's hidden in a gardener's shed at Nehvizdy. It's as safe as it can be."

"What have you got?"

"Mainly small arms and ammunition—grenades, explosives, a couple of Sten guns. We thought it safer to leave it there for the time being."

"You must arrange to bring it to Prague and disperse it here in the city," said Jindra. "You know, I am sure, that the inherent weakness of any resistance organization lies in too many people knowing too much. Therefore in future you will deal mainly through 'Uncle Hajsky'. We shall move your lodgings as often as we can and try and change your names fairly frequently. Uncle Hajsky will work with you upon all aspects of your plan, and I expect you will need some time to survey the ground. I wish you good luck."

Jindra never forgot that first meeting with Jan; he looked at the young man and liked him, and never dreamed what was ahead for all of them. More than any others, these three —Auntie Marie, Jindra and Uncle Hajsky—were to shape the lives and destinies of Jan and Josef throughout the next few months.

Uncle Hajsky they came to know intimately, but they never knew that his real name was Jan Zelenek; that when the Germans arrived he had been a respected schoolteacher in a small town in Northern Bohemia, leader of his district Sokol organization, and as such, deeply implicated in attempting to preserve Czech culture and freedom. But they soon discovered that Uncle Hajsky was a patriot, believing implicitly in the fundamental dignity of man.

He had fled to Prague because the German collaborators in his district had his name on their lists; he taught now in an undistinguished primary school in an obscure suburb of Prague, a post which provided a convenient guise for the continuance of his personal resistance.

He was turned fifty: a tall, thin, dried runner-bean of a man with a brown humorous face and wrinkled, kindly eyes behind large horn-rimmed spectacles. Not a man of violence; a man of peaceful theories, and a love of freedom. He had a wife who knew little about his activities—it was safer for her that way—and a seventeen-year-old son who was a student.

He had observed, with the kind of numbness which afflicted many of liberal opinion during those bitter years of the 'thirties, the preparations for war. He had said, as all humane considerate people in all countries had said in those days, "this is not possible. People are more intelligent than this. Reason and decency must prevail!" But reason and decency had not prevailed. Allies had deserted, pledges were but scraps of paper blown skywards in a wind of hate and fear. He remembered how the Nazis had marched in: conquerors without battle honours, contemptuously collecting the spoils of intimidation. They had talked loudly of "lebensraum" and freedom and "national dignity", and they had begun their regime with such miserable and greedy little measures, that within a matter of days all the Czechs held them in contempt. They had decreed one German mark worth twenty Czech crowns, and the Wehrmacht had bought up all the butter and fats and bacon in the shops, filling lorries and trains with their plunder and shipping it back to the Reich. They had made it plain that there was only one future in store for Bohemia and Moravia—slavery under the Reich. For daring to protest, or for refusing to co-operate, or for offering resistance, torture and death were the quick penalties.

So Uncle Hajsky had swallowed the bitter gall of his liberal, pacifist theories and looked round for a way to resist, a way to quieten the confusion and despair in his heart. And he had found many other Czechs who were desperately looking for answers to the same questions. Many fled to fight again; many died as the repressive measures of the Nazis began to take effect. And others waited, and watched and planned.

From the very beginning Uncle Hajsky observed with a certain curiosity the two young parachutists to whom he had been attached. He divined that the inner conflicts which troubled him were, to these two young men, mere superfluities. Sometimes, he wondered, if perhaps they were right? The philosophers, in whom he had once believed, were mostly examining the state of the universe over dishes of watery potato soup in a hundred concentration camps and prisons all over Europe. Experience dictated that, if civilization were to survive, it could not afford the luxury of compromise. Utilitarian measures of murder were not only necessary; they were inevitable.

After a lifetime spent in teaching; of believing, with passion, that the whole kernel of life was to be found in the acquisition of knowledge, empirical and spiritual; and that in the grey, rubbery convolutions behind the egg-shell skull, reposed as much of heaven or hell as any man could adequately handle, it was hard to subscribe to this credo of the brute: kill or be killed. Could God also be an assassin?

But Jindra had singled him out to act as father-confessor, nursemaid, estate agent, liaison officer and contact man to these two young embryo assassins, and he was determined to carry out these tasks with a devotion to duty which was completely single-minded.

Quickly he discovered that the security precautions observed by both Jan and Josef were negligible. One of his contacts, in whose flat the boys had stayed for a few nights during that first month in Prague, confirmed his misgivings.

Their suits were English; their shirts and underwear were marked with English laundry marks. They still possessed English banknotes which they showed around rather proudly. But Uncle Hajsky realized also that, despite these shortcomings, there was a direct simplicity about everything they did. It was almost as if they knew they were men marked by history, and that this flow of events could not be altered by something as inconsequential as laundry ink. Nevertheless, he made it one of his jobs, as far as he could, to see that their indiscretions did not get out of hand.

It was necessary, first of all, for Uncle Hajsky to provide the two parachutists not only with food and lodgings but also with identification papers which would allow them to move about freely in Prague and the surrounding countryside. The forged identity cards they had brought from England were not enough. Their first need was employment books; only people holding these books had the right to exist in the Czech Protectorate, and they were obtainable only through the National Insurance Office. So Uncle Hajsky quickly found "friends" in the insurance offices; two books were issued, and all trace of this transaction expunged from the official records.

Now another difficulty arose. If they had employment books, should they not be employed? And where? Or better still could they not be unemployed and unfit for work? If they were on the sick list, they could wander where they pleased, looking for a job or possibly convalescing in the pure air of approaching Spring?

A doctor would be needed to certify them unfit for work. Again Uncle Hajsky organized help. He knew not one, but two, doctors who would perform this service. A Dr. Hruby volunteered to make out the initial declaration, and a Dr. Lycka each week added his findings regarding the continued ill-health of both Jan and Josef. Jan it appeared had inflammation of the gall bladder; Josef—and this of course was true—had a broken and inflamed big toe.

There entered also, about this time, one other person who was to play a major part in the life of Jan Kubis during those months in Prague. Even this event was indirectly due to Uncle Hajsky. For it was at the flat of Auntie Marie that Jan Kubis first met the girl known as Anna Malinova.

During this early period Uncle Hajsky was slowly sounding out people he could trust. Through his school work he was in touch with the Red Cross, and through them he met one of its most ardent members, Mrs. Moravec; he found her extremely anxious to help. Her flat, situated in a large block, was comparatively unobtrusive, and therefore an ideal central point from which Jan and Josef could operate; his own flat was no more than a hundred yards away in the same street.

Auntie Marie often gave parties; there was small security danger attached to a party, for in those early days it was not hard to distinguish between a "good" Czech and a quisling. Jan and Josef were often present.

Of course no one mentioned parachutists. No one mentioned resistance. What Jan and Josef were doing no one asked. They were just two rather nice young men on sick

61

leave; one could easily see that the smaller of the two had a bad foot. But somehow, amid the smoke and the chatter and the laughter, every one knew a little about them. Tacitly, they understood and were secretly encouraged that here at last, growing in the heart of the old city, was a root of resistance and defiance.

Anna Malinova felt it. She stood in the lounge, a glass in her hand, looking round, listening, not talking to anyone. It was Auntie Marie who intercepted Jan's glance and his quick look away.

"Anna?" she said. "Anna Malinova. Pretty little thing, isn't she? A widow, poor girl. The Germans killed her husband. Hardly knew what it was like to be married. There must be millions like her all over Europe. Would you like to meet her?"

"Well——" said Jan, but it was too late. Auntie Marie, the incurable romantic, had him by the arm leading him across to Anna's side. She introduced them and left them alone.

"You're from England," said Anna Malinova after a moment.

It was such a direct, uncomplicated question that Jan did not dream of trying to deceive her.

"Yes," he said, then a little disquietened for having admitted it so readily, added, "How did you know?"

Simply she told him that she had known the Moravecs for a long time, that they had been good friends to her, that they were pro-resistance; therefore, when two strange young men suddenly appeared, it was not hard to understand what was happening.

Her eyes were large, serious and blue, and they stared up at him from under dark lashes. She had a soft red mouth, a clear white skin. She was wearing a simple black dress which suited her, and her dark hair, curled under at the ends, touched her shoulders.

Jan looked at her with a certain awe and a certain fear. Josef might fiddle around with girls in Czechoslovakia, Josef was always eager to laugh, wave to, chat with, or pursue any of the pretty girls on the streets or in the shops

62

of Prague. But not Jan. Although, quite blindly, he seemed to be willing to take the most preposterous risks to preserve his parachute as a souvenir, he was not prepared to take any risks regarding women. They were dangerous. They exposed the weaknesses in a man; they had no place in the philosophy of a dedicated assassin; they might dilute his hatred. Yet, believing all these things he still looked at Anna Malinova with a man's interest.

It was not only that she was pretty and that he had been without feminine company for so long; she was a believer; he knew that, without words passing between them. With an odd, feminine deliberation she wanted to be implicated in this business of resistance. The one man she loved—the man she had married—had been killed by the Nazis. She too had need of revenge.

Jan realized that, in the old days before he joined the army, he would have thought of her as a sophisticated city girl, as someone in whose company he would have been apprehensive; and possibly she, in her turn, would have thought of him as a simple country lad. The war had altered all those preconceived notions. His years in North Africa, France and England had brushed the hay from his hair; he had seen the world, he had things to say, a future to make, and a man to kill. All this, as she looked at him, she vaguely understood, and she was attracted by his obvious determination. But although he also was attracted, he was not prepared to take a single step towards her. Mentally, the little repeating clock chimed, "Women are dangerous!" And she was a particularly attractive member of that dangerous species.

It was Auntie Marie who forced his hand that evening, by suggesting that it would be the gentlemanly thing to do to see Anna Malinova back to her lodgings on the other bank of the river in the old town under Hradcany. It would have been churlish for Jan to refuse.

Outside, a cold February wind was blowing down the streets. He turned up his coat collar and took her arm as they hurried to the tram stop. There were patches of ice shining like glass on the pavements, and the steel tram track glistened in the light of the high, hard moon.

As they sat side by side on the hard seat of the jolting tram, his shoulders touching hers, Jan was irritated by the situation. He was irritated to find himself taking a girl home on a tram; this was so obviously out of character with the rôle he had planned that before very long the absurdity of the situation overwhelmed him and he began to chuckle. He apologized to Anna for not being able to tell her what amused him, but added that maybe one day it might be possible.

The tram took them to the foot of Charles Bridge. They got off, and walked over the bridge, pausing for a few seconds to watch the dark, snow-fed waters of the Vltava pouring through the arches and streaming away, foam-flecked, into the darkness. There were no lights anywhere. Like every other city in Europe the black-out was strictly enforced, but the winter sky was full of stars and the moon shimmered in the black water. This was the very heart of the old city; at either end of this ancient bridge the merchants had built their houses and the men-at-arms had built their walls and castles, and trade and the defence of trade had continued side by side. Up on the hillside, dominating the city, stood the castle of Hradcany. The Nazis had not been slow in utilizing this symbol of power, and it was now the head-quarters of Heydrich and his court. Standing there in the darkness, feeling the warm shoulder of Anna Malinova against him, Jan Kubis realized that against the power and evil that these people represented, he was puny indeed.

Up through the maze of narrow streets which followed the slope of the hill up towards the castle they climbed, their feet ringing on the cobbles. The ancient houses were black and white in the shadows cast by the moon. Anna Malinova stopped in front of a tall, thin house with latticed windows and stucco peeling from the front. When she opened the door, the stairs which led upwards were wooden and rickety.

Jan said goodnight abruptly, and went off smartly down the hill towards the town. He had already decided that in all probability he would never see her again.

Next day Anna told Auntie Marie what had happened.

64

Heydrich (*extreme right*) welcoming Himmler to Hradcany Castle on the hillside above the River Vltava overlooking Prague

Jindra

"Auntie" Marie

Professor Ogoun

"Uncle" Hajsky

THEY RISKED TORTURE AND DEATH

Long before this she had got into the habit of confiding in Auntie Marie, for after the death of her husband there was no one else except the elder woman to whom she could turn. Auntie Marie had comforted her, and helped her, and now there was a deep bond between them.

This bond, however, did not prevent Auntie Marie from passing many of Anna's confidences about Jan to Jindra. Auntie Marie decided it would do Jindra no harm to know what was going on in the head of his young parachutist.

It was quite some time, however, before even Auntie Marie knew that Anna Malinova and Jan Kubis were in the process of falling deeply in love.

65

CHAPTER FOUR

TOWARDS the end of February, Jan and Josef received a message from Uncle Hajsky, asking them to meet him at noon next day in a tavern with which they were all acquainted, in the heart of the old town.

They pushed open the heavy door leading into the dim interior of a long room compressed by a low, vaulted ceiling. Faded murals, depicting Czech country scenes, lingered uncertainly upon the dingy plaster walls. To one side stood a huge stove faced with green tiles. As in all these places at this time in the morning, a faint smell of stale beer hung in the air. It was empty except for the barman busy behind his counter, topped by stainless steel and mounted with gleaming urns. There were two other figures at the end of the room.

They approached, recognizing Uncle Hajsky immediately, pausing to see whom he was with, and then, recognizing the young blond man, almost leaping upon him in order to shake his hand and clap him on the back. It was Valchik, their comrade-in-arms, with whom they had trained for so many months back in England, and one of the three parachutists who had jumped from the aircraft a few minutes after them.

When the barman had set amber tankards of Pilsen beer in front of each of them, Valchik gave them his news. All three of his team had landed safely, but because the container holding the radio set had jammed in the exit hatch, Valchik, the last to jump, had been separated from the other two. However, he had found the container, buried it with his parachute and overalls, and smoking an English cigarette, had walked jauntily through the growing dawn towards the nearest village. There he had discovered, like Jan and Josef, that they had been dropped far off course. He had overcome this difficulty by blithely hiring a taxi driver to drive him to the address of his nearest contact forty miles away. This transaction was effected by the expenditure of some of the currency he had brought from England, and the intimation to the readily convinced taxi driver that he was an operator in the black market.

Eventually he had joined the other two in Pardubice and they had begun to insert themselves unobtrusively into the life of the town. They aroused no suspicion, and slowly their web of reliable contacts spread.

Their first requirement was a safe place from which they could transmit and receive radio messages. This was readily found—with the aid of a friendly quarry owner—in the alcove of a machinery shed in a quarry on the outskirts of the town. Only the owner and his foreman knew what was going on; the quarrymen and transport drivers were quite ignorant of what their engine shed concealed. Workmen were always coming and going; lorries trundled busily backwards and forwards with their loads; and all this activity provided excellent cover. As soon as they were installed, the radio operator attempted to make contact with London. Upon the ninth of January London picked up their signal from the station they identified from that moment onwards as "Libuse".

Both Jan and Josef listened eagerly to Valchik's story. Both respected this young man whom they had known well at the training school. Before the war he had sold shoes in a Bata shoe shop, and much of that slick sales manner had stayed with him. Beneath his good-looking face and the smooth sweep of blond hair, underneath the grins, the easy laughter, the winks, the funny stories, the gestures, the recurrent affairs with girls, the contempt for "mugs", the obvious conceits; behind the candid blue eyes and the high forehead resided a second and different Valchik, puzzled and insecure; a Valchik who objectively disliked his own façade, his own mannerisms, his own glib philosophies. He was blood brother to hundreds of other young men who arrived upon the threshold of a war totally unequipped for its exigencies. Off they went to die without a faith or a philosophy, equipped only with a half-understood and indifferently accepted heritage, and a few gag lines produced by the music hall, the films, the radio, and the compelling cheap

67

materialism of their times. They did not "die gloriously" as of old; their comrades marked their passing with the terse understatements that "they had gone for a burton", "copped it", "bought it", or with elementary simplicity had just "had it".

Valchik was of this mould, but he quickly realized that the defeat and the ignominy of his own country had provided him with a sound reason for his own existence, and also with a direct challenge to his manhood. It was an historic, short-term and easily understandable challenge: to defeat the Nazis, to overthrow the tyrants who occupied Czechoslovakia. A cause worthy to die for, so thought Valchik, but there he was, lumbered with all the physical paraphernalia of a playboy, of a sophisticated shoe salesman, of the bright and breezy good-time Charlie, purveyor and exponent of the fashionable emptiness which in peacetime would have allowed him to rattle noisily through his chosen career, and all the time, under that glossy exterior, lurked the dedicated ascetic, the Knight Templar. Later, when the affair of Jan and Anna Malinova became obvious to everybody, it was Valchik, with a puritanism no one suspected, who harangued Jan and went so far as to write a letter to Jindra himself, protesting that such a situation was dangerous for all. But as Jindra both condoned and blessed the liaison, in the interests of organizational efficiency, Valchik's condemnation came to nothing.

When he heard from Jan and Josef that the objective of their mission was the actual assassination of Heydrich, he was very envious. It is more than probable that from that moment onwards he became determined to play some part in the final attack.

When Valchik and his two companions in the quarry near Pardubice sat in the engine shed patiently tapping out their call sign, they did not know then that London had already heard their signal and identified it correctly as "Libuse". The first Czechoslovakian resistance radio message had filtered through from the dark interior of Europe, and London frantically replied to their signals but realized that the parachutists were not getting their replies.

68

Night after night, at the agreed transmission time, this infuriating game of radio hide-and-seek continued. Each night, the radio operator of "Libuse" tapped out a message asking for recognition; each night, on three different wavelengths, London sought to reply, but without success, telling them that they were audible.

Czech Intelligence in London guessed what was happening. Valchik's radio operator was using his small receiver, a set which was built into his main transmitter. He possessed a second receiver, a modern set which was much more powerful, but how could they convey to him the fact that he *must* use it? It was not too difficult. This sort of emergency had been provided for. The Czechoslovakian Intelligence Service in London could request use of the B.B.C.'s powerful transmitters and insert a message into the regular broadcasts to Czechoslovakia. At forty-five minutes before midnight upon January 13th, 1941, they inserted this cryptic message into the Czech transmission from London: "We understand your painful silence up to now, but now we understand well, and hope that you understand us, too."

The message was heard by the Pardubice group. Shortly after midnight upon the 15th of January, the radio operator, using the second receiver, began to hear requests from England for communication. He answered at once with his identification signal. London replied that she could hear, and in the machine shed in the quarry a great shout of delight went up from Valchik and his two companions. The first contact between Britain and occupied Czechoslovakia had been made, and the first phonogram from London came silently through the dark night air.

"Inform us how and where you landed," it read. "Where and how are you situated? How are your personal and working conditions? Your reply will be invaluable. Reply in code. Use present code until further notice."

The next night there was another phonogram from London, congratulating the three of them upon the fact that they had been awarded the Czechoslovakian War Cross for bravery in the face of the enemy.

Now active resistance could really begin. Information

could be collected, collated and passed through to England along a secure channel. At last the Czech Intelligence Service in London could receive reliable reports of what was happening in their country. The Sokol organization in Pardubice had its contacts in Prague. Valchik was passed through to meet his old companions and to arrange for couriers to bring regular reports from the capital for transmission to London. Things were going well.

One disquieting revelation, however, came up in this conversation between Jan and Josef and Valchik. Jan told Valchik about their own adventures upon landing. He also told him how, shortly after they arrived in Prague, he had gone back to see if the arms and equipment they had hidden in the gardener's hut near Nehvizdy were still safe.

He had made the journey alone because Josef's foot was healing only slowly. A young woman had directed him to the gardener's cottage. He had knocked on the door and the old gardener had invited him in. Meeting the gardener and trusting him at first sight—an habitual reflex with Jan— he had confessed what they had hidden in his hut.

The gardener's amazement was ludicrous. The gamekeeper whom Jan and Josef had first met had told him nothing. He told Jan that when, shortly after the New Year, he had inspected his hut and found that it had been broken into, and that upon the floor were a couple of odd-looking tins, wrapped in peculiar labels, he had reported the fact to the local gendarmerie. No, he had not taken the tins along; he had thrown them away. Of what use were a couple of rusty and empty tins?

The sergeant from the gendarmerie when he arrived, days later, had been most impatient about the whole affair. Didn't the gardener know he had more important things to do than mess around looking at ramshackle huts? Did he think his rakes and baskets were all that valuable? Obviously the intruders had been poachers. He would make such a report to his commander. Coldly he had departed.

And now Jan had appeared with the fantastic story of parachutes, and weapons hidden beneath his seed boxes. And that fool sergeant had not suspected anything. The gardener roared his head off. It was like something you read about in the newspapers, wasn't it? Well, the best thing they could do was get that stuff out of the hut at once and hide it in his cellar, and then Jan could arrange to have it transported to Prague whenever he felt like it.

Jan echoed the gardener's laughter as he told the story, but there was no amusement in Valchik's voice as he told what had happened to him. As he had already explained, he had recovered the radio receivers and transmitters, but he had left his parachute and overalls still buried in a field awaiting another journey. Two weeks later, however, he had returned to the field, to find the hole excavated and empty. Cart tracks and a trail of manure were primary evidence of what could have happened. A farmer on a muck-spreading journey must have seen the patch of disturbed snow and investigated. If he was the same sort of simpleton as Jan's gardener, he would have undoubtedly reported his discovery to the local gendarmerie; they in their turn would report to the Gestapo, who would now know that parachutists from Britain had landed in that district.

They discussed this unfortunate turn of events for several minutes. There was, perhaps, a small chance that the farmer was a patriot who would realize what had occurred and destroy the evidence he had acquired; or if he was avaricious, he might even hand over the silk parachute to his wife or daughters, so that they could make underwear. But all this was pure supposition. From that moment onwards they must work, knowing that in all probability the Gestapo were aware of their presence and were attempting to infiltrate informers into their embryo organization.

Still, fortune had on the whole proved favourable. Valchik had already got himself a job as barman in the exclusive Veselka Hotel in the centre of Pardubice. It was a place patronized mainly by Gestapo, Wehrmacht and other German officials, and it should prove to be an ideal listening point to gather scraps of interesting military gossip.

Between them they also discussed the question of the couriers they would have to use to carry information between Prague and Pardubice. Valchik had already recruited one, a young and pretty married woman called Mrs. Krupka. Although he abhorred the idea of parachutists having love affairs, and he was absolutely fixed in his own celibacy, he favoured the use of women in their organization as couriers. Jan and Josef knew that Auntie Marie had volunteered to do all in her power to help them. They suggested she would welcome the chance of acting as a messenger.

Their hopes were high when Valchik eventually returned to Pardubice, and it was in these early days of the planning and plotting that Jan became an optimist again. He told Jindra as much. It was all right for Josef, eternally an optimist; nothing could alter *his* rainbow ego. But Jan, the realist, had landed in Czechoslovakia understanding plainly the suicidal nature of their mission. Amongst friends, amongst people willing to risk the same dangers as himself, against the serene and beautiful background of Prague, slowly he began to feel that perhaps after all there was a small, even a reasonable chance of success. With good planning, with good luck, perhaps they could accomplish their mission and still escape with their own lives. It might be a flimsy platform upon which to build a little outhouse of hope, but to exist without hope was impossible.

Some of this optimism was undoubtedly germinated by Uncle Hajsky's confident marshalling of the situation. He understood, at once, that an assassination attempt was a problem to be approached as clinically as a surgeon approaches a complex operation. In these academic beginnings he was expert. They all knew that Heydrich was no ordinary politician. In the business of extermination he had few equals in history; in the business of sadism, torture and human destruction, Torquemada, the Marquis de Sade and Genghis Khan were as amateurs compared with him. His security arrangements would undoubtedly be as infallible as experience in the murderous moods of Hitler's court could make them. To stay alive in that society needed above average skill; to advance to the position of chosen executioner, an outstanding talent was necessary. S.S. General Heydrich knew he was well hated, and correspondingly feared by most of his compatriots. He could not afford the smallest security

72

loophole. Enemies and treachery were to be expected at any, or every, moment of the day or night.

Nevertheless Heydrich was their chosen quarry and Uncle Hajsky knew they must examine, chart and annotate his movements, from daybreak to nightfall, probing for the smallest point of weakness.

With some difficulty and after much exhaustive and cautious research, Uncle Hajsky discovered a helper who could be invaluable to them. He introduced both Jan and Josef to him. His name was Frantisek Safarik. When the Nazis took over Hradcany Castle, its administration, repair and upkeep remained in the hands of the Czechs; Safarik, a furniture expert, was a member of that administration. The modern furniture in the castle, as well as the valuable antique pieces, were all in his care. To inspect them he could wander at will throughout the castle. He could also—if he so desired—acquaint himself with some of the habits and movements of the Reichsprotector.

Both Jan and Josef had many questions to ask him. Did Heydrich ever travel in the same car as Frank, the Secretary of State? Could they get near Heydrich in Hradcany Castle? What was his daily routine? Where did he live, what time did he leave, when did he arrive at Hradcany Castle, how did he travel?

Safarik was a small, neat little man with horn-rimmed spectacles and a grave pedantic manner, as became an expert in historical antiques. A more unlikely recruit to the art of assassination it was difficult to imagine.

He answered all their questions as well as he could. Frank did not travel in the same car as Heydrich, ever. He told them also that their chances were negligible of getting close to Heydrich in the castle of Hradcany. He was strongly guarded, and the slightest suspicious move would activate a swarm of alert S.S. men. Heydrich lived in a large and elegant château in a small village about fifteen miles from Prague, called Panenske Brezany. It lay in rolling, open country, and the village and château were under constant armed inspection. In the village or house, an assault against Heydrich was absolutely impossible.

73

These opening remarks of Safarik's brought no consolation to either Jan or Josef. They had often discussed possible methods of assassinating the Reichsprotector. They also knew that the desire to kill a man might be easy to acquire, but the attainment of that objective was much more difficult.

They knew that to kill a man, swiftly, quietly and decisively, requires no great skill. It requires a fundamental knowledge of the human body: the location of the heart, the jugular vein, the arteries, and if you are to kill surely and silently with bare hands, it needs familiarity with numerous pressure points and an understanding of various locks and holds. Indeed, this primary information was communicated to thousands of men during the war under the innocent euphemism of "unarmed combat".

Advanced courses in this type of human annihilation were usually given to special agents and parachutists: and both Jan and Josef had been adequately instructed in a number of refinements at their Special Training School.

Safarik's information, however, made it seem highly doubtful if either Jan or Josef were ever going to have the opportunity of using the skills they had acquired; their chances of slipping quietly into Heydrich's bedroom in the night and either slitting his throat or garroting him while he slept, seemed negligible. In fact, Safarik's evidence made it seem highly doubtful that they would ever succeed in getting close enough to him even to hurl a stone in his direction!

They were prepared for this disappointment and they possessed a variety of modern weapons to help them in their task. To execute someone with the maximum speed and efficiency was child's play—often a mere matter of a little pressure of the forefinger. In the hands of an expert a modern rifle will throw a steel pill with devastating accuracy for a quarter of a mile; in the hands of a schoolboy blessed with fair eyesight and given rudimentary instructions it can kill at two hundred yards.

A Sten gun will spray lead like water from a faucet; a Bren will pump bullet after bullet with phenomenal accuracy through the same hole at considerable distances; a Mills grenade will fragment with exterminating force at close quarters or in a confined space. With training, a Smith and Wesson or a Colt revolver is a useful weapon at close range; a portable anti-tank weapon will blow a hole in half an inch of steel, as easily as an infant pokes a finger through a paper bag.

They could choose from many of these weapons. Dismantled, carefully packed and coated with grease, they had sailed down with them out of the night sky at Nehvizdy, and after their initial period in the gardener's hut, these were now carefully stored in various private houses in Prague. But which weapon or weapons to choose? From Safarik's information it appeared that the only possible way they could attack Heydrich was out in the open, upon one of the innumerable journeys he was constantly making.

He travelled every day between his château in the village of Panenske Brezany to the heart of the Nazi-ruled Hradcany Castle in a fast open Mercedes. He left at about nine o'clock and arrived at the castle approximately forty-five minutes later. He was driven by his personal bodyguard, Oberscharfuhrer Klein, a man of immense physique and courage. His Mercedes was preceded and followed by other cars containing armed S.S. troops. But the convoy travelled at high speed, and if they made an attempt against Heydrich at any point on the road the chances were overwhelming that it would prove quite abortive; no one could be certain of killing a man in a car speeding along at over fifty miles an hour. And in any case a quick death at the hands of the guards in the other cars seemed inevitable for the attacker.

But Heydrich also made other journeys. These, said Safarik, might be worth investigation. He was constantly commuting between Prague and Berlin. Sometimes he travelled by plane, but more often by private train.

It was impossible to guard the entire train track to Berlin; a train had to stop and start, to slow down at various places. A weak point might be found there. At any rate, said Uncle Hajsky, it was worth looking into.

It was Safarik who later took Jan up to the square outside Hradcany so that he could identify both Heydrich and the Mercedes in which he drove.

Outside the first gates of Hradcany is a large open *place*, and behind the tall curving railings lies the first courtyard. Parked at one side stood the low, green Mercedes Safarik had described.

There were several sightseers in the square outside the gates, staring up at the black and red flag which flew from the flagpole close to where the Mercedes was parked. The sentries at the gate stood stiffly to attention, ignoring them.

Somewhere up above, a clock struck, and like mechanical soldiers, an armed guard strutted into the outer courtyard and lined up near the car. A moment or two later the clatter of arms and the stamp of jackboots announced the appearance of the Reichsprotector and his immense chauffeur and bodyguard, Klein.

Jan stared at the tall figure in the black and silver uniform of an S.S. General. From that distance it was difficult to make out his features, but he could see that the man was tall and powerfully built.

It was odd to realize that here was the man they had come to kill. He knew so little about him. But he knew that, as Acting Reichsprotector, he was callously and contemptuously murdering hundreds of Czechs, and for this alone Jan would feel no twinge of conscience or remorse should they succeed.

The engine of the green Mercedes exploded in a sudden fury of combustion, as the giant Klein pulled the starter and pumped the accelerator pedal. Heydrich took his place in the front seat next to the chauffeur; Jan noted that move carefully. Klein slipped into gear and accelerated noisily towards the gates. The Mercedes was followed by another open car containing S.S. troops armed with tommy guns. Their faces as they jolted past were grim and uncompromising. Jan watched them roar across the cobbled square and up the narrow road between the old houses which led to the wide tarmac of the main road.

CHAPTER FIVE

WHEN Jan Kubis and Josef Gabchik first arrived in Prague, Reinhard Heydrich was thirty-eight years old. He was six feet tall, an ex-Navy lieutenant, a fighter pilot who obtained leave of absence from his high-ranking posts to fly in combat during the first weeks of hostilities against the Soviets. A handsome man, even though on careful appraisal one would find something odd in the eyes or the mouth, and of undoubted courage. A man who would have been gladly accepted, with claps on the back and raised beer mugs, into almost any officers' mess in any military force in the world.

Accepted, at first cordially and then with slight astonishment; and as the true intent behind the cold eyes became clearer, with utter horror. For Reinhard Heydrich was, in the average concept of a man, not normal at all. Somewhere, a piece of the human jigsaw puzzle had been omitted; somewhere in the intricate convolutions of the brain, a duct had been left empty; somewhere in the human clay, the yeast of humanity had not risen. He was a man without pity, without kindness, without mercy; an egoist fired by ruthless ambition; a man who could enlist torture and blackmail, as normal everyday routines; a man who could order, observe and chart the degradation, misery and annihilation of literally millions of people, with untroubled belief in his own self-righteousness.

He was intelligent, perceptive, a first-class organizer and most willing to use all his skills to foster his perverted ends. When history signalled his cue to the wings, there he was, blond, teutonic and merciless, the man to match that bloody and festering moment in Hitler's reign.

Reinhard Heydrich's face was long and lean; his nose was thin and ran from between small, deep-set blue eyes. His mouth was thin, tight and hard above a bony chin. The hair was blond, plastered down above a domed intellectual forehead. It was a Nordic face structurally, technically and ethnologically. It combined, in correct degree, the handsome-ness, virility and strength extolled by his senior, Heinrich Himmler, who carried a *mystique* of race to a point where the shape of a nose could mean the difference between adula-tion and extermination. It was the face of an Aryan: a fact doubly fortunate for Heydrich because there is little doubt at all that he was one-quarter Jewish. The fundamental irony behind this fact is even more remarkable when one considers that he was undoubtedly the greatest persecutor of Jews in all history; the extermination machinery he set up being mainly responsible in the fullness of time for the deaths of some six million victims.

News of his Jewish ancestry was even rumoured publicly. Heydrich fought three libel actions against such "slanders" —these Western eccentricities were still possible in the early 'thirties before Hitler was securely in power—the first against a baker from Halle, where Heydrich spent his boy-hood, who declared that Heydrich's mother was half Jewish. When Heydrich produced his birth certificate, the baker's lawyer declared that it was a forgery. It appeared, in fact, that all the records relating to births in the Halle registry for the month of November, 1904, the month of Heydrich's birth, were missing.

Unkind people suggested that Heydrich in his omniscient rôle of head of S.D. might have brought this about. Interes-ted observers also noticed that a new tombstone appeared above his grandmother's grave in Leipzig, with the name Sarah omitted from its inscription.

The lawyer who defended the Halle baker joined the Military Intelligence Service at the beginning of the war, and it is known that he handed over the information at his disposal to Admiral Canaris. It is also believed that it pro-vided some of the reason why the Military Intelligence Ser-vice continued to function alongside the more nefarious S.D. in the years which followed. The use of blackmail was normal practice amongst those in high office in the days of Nazi power.

In the early days of the movement, Heydrich had been a young ex-naval officer. He joined the Party after being dismissed the service by the Officers' Court of Honour for a duel following a sordid love affair, but it also seems highly probable that Heydrich saw quicker advancement in the Nazi ranks, and his regret at leaving the German Navy never appears to have troubled him.

Quickly he found his level, specializing in gangster methods in and around the waterfront district of Hamburg. His disregard for the continuation of life amongst his adversaries isolated him immediately as a man ripe for rapid promotion. He was that rarity: the killer, possessing intelligence and lacking a conscience. He was, moreover, a killer who enjoyed his work and had administrative ability; and as extermination grew more necessary to the advancement of the Reich, he could delegate his authority, instruct his minions, dispense his offices, so that torture and murder became administrative processes as normal in their context as the activities of the Ministry of Health in dispensing drugs and pills. That was some small measure of the madness abroad in the Nazi State; a madness abetted and encouraged by all the scientific and mechanical inventions of the twentieth century.

When Himmler accepted him into his personal service and gave him as his first task the job of drafting a memorandum organizing a security service within the framework of the S.S. his fortune was made; his march upwards inevitable. Heydrich became the head of S.D., the master of the secret police within the secret police; a power which even Hitler feared. Amongst other things it spied on the powerful: gathering documents and information concerning scandals or indiscretions, which could be used to intimidate or blackmail every person of consequence in the country. In the use of this weapon, Heydrich had no equal, and no matter how many other important posts he might acquire, he never relinquished his hold upon the S.D.

By 1934, he was the power behind Himmler, feeding him ideas, and with his own murder squads fulfilling any plan which necessitated the abrupt physical extermination of an opponent. His qualifications as a human butcher were exceptional, and together with Himmler and Goering he played a major part in selecting the victims for the *putsch* of 1934.

His first major coup in international intrigue occurred in 1937. It was a coup of such fantastic importance and incredible impertinence that it is hardly believable. Its object was the destruction, at one stroke, of the entire Soviet High Command.

In 1937, a Russian refugee in Berlin communicated to one of Heydrich's agents the startling news that the Soviet High Command, under General Tukhachevsky, were collaborating with the German General Staff in a plan to destroy the Stalin regime. Heydrich, after checking his man and the rumour, and sensing that there was a grain of truth in it, passed this information through Himmler on to Hitler. He suggested that it opened a door for a number of devious schemes, any one of which might embarrass the Soviets considerably. Naturally enough, the Fuhrer was not at all pleased. It revealed that his own High Command were operating behind his back. It also placed him in a dilemma. Should he keep silent, and allow the *putsch* against Stalin to proceed? Or would it do greater harm to the Communist cause to reveal to Stalin, and indeed to the world, that his own generals were plotting against him?

Hitler, in conference with Himmler and Heydrich, decided to betray the Soviet Generals. He gave strict orders that the German High Command should not know of this decision. He did not want Tukhachevsky warned. The details were entrusted to Heydrich.

Heydrich, seeking further evidence, at once despatched his special burglar squads to break into the offices of both the German Army Intelligence Service and the secret archives of the German General Staff. Documents were discovered, photographed and replaced. They proved very little, except that collusion certainly was taking place between the General Staffs of Soviet Russia and Germany. But there was no evidence of an actual plot. This did not deter Reinhard Heydrich in the slightest degree. If there was smoke he would make it his own personal and devilish business to manufacture fire.

It was not difficult for him to fake the master blueprint of an imaginary *putsch* being prepared by the Soviet General Staff. A fantastic, dandelion spear-head of hooked seeds, lies, half truths, forgeries and false deductions was concocted. A quick sharp puff, and off went the little umbrella seeds of hate and suspicion, floating across borders and into embassies, springing up into fine seedlings of rumour, gossip and fear. In Prague the story reached Dr. Benes, who passed the information on to Stalin. Not long afterwards, Heydrich's secret agents were informed that the Soviet Embassy in Berlin was anxious to investigate certain rumours. Heydrich's men were also slightly startled to find that the Soviet authorities were willing, and indeed expected, to pay heavily to obtain this information. Heydrich made a quick decision. Three million roubles was the price he demanded; three million roubles for this evidence, which was really beyond price.

The money was quickly paid over. The German Foreign Intelligence Service were not violently surprised, however, when they discovered, months afterwards, that German agents in Russia using the high denomination rouble notes received for this transaction were quickly arrested. After losing several good men, what was left of the Russian bank notes was burned.

But the plot to destroy the Soviet High Command was completely successful. Tukhachevsky and his fellow generals were arrested, tried in camera and immediately shot; an internal purge of great ferocity started shortly afterwards which undermined the entire Soviet Military Staff. It was a coup of tremendous audacity, and up to that point the biggest political success of Heydrich's career.

It was with this fantastic success behind him, that, prior to Munich, he was appointed to be chief planner in the destruction of Czechoslovakia as an independent country. His terror squads in various guises infiltrated into the country at many points. He directed the campaign of propaganda reinforced by terror, brutality and murder which undermined the whole nation and indeed intimidated the whole of Europe. Heydrich's personal philosophy was brutally simple: be strong, vicious, merciless, and success must follow.

The conferences between Jan and Josef and Uncle Hajsky, and quite often Jindra, took place daily. While Uncle Hajsky was cautiously enlisting more helpers in his embryo resistance movement, Jan and Josef on two bicycles they had borrowed—Josef rode an old lady's bicycle belonging to Auntie Marie Moravec—tried to discover the daily routines of Heydrich.

They cycled out to the village of Panenske Brezany where he had his château. On the road leading from the château they hid in the hedges and watched his green Mercedes roar past; they noted at what time he arrived at Hradcany Castle and when he departed; they studied the train timetables and cautiously examined the railway tracks leading out of Prague in the direction of Berlin.

They decided, after these weeks of investigation, that the best opportunity of assassinating Heydrich, while still retaining some chance of surviving themselves, would occur during the time he was aboard his special train. Safarik usually knew when he was leaving for Berlin, and Jan and Josef carefully followed and plotted his route to and from the train on these occasions.

An attack while he was travelling by train had many advantages. If they could catch Heydrich at the window of a slowly-moving train, and direct a hail of Sten gunfire at him and his entourage, his death would be almost certain. Better still, the evidence of the action, the carriage full of dead and dying men, would be steadily drawn away from the scene of the assassination by a completely ignorant train driver. By the time the alarm was raised, the train stopped and the armed guards ready for their search, it would probably be at least a mile down the line. They would have had ample time to depart leisurely from the scene.

But where could they carry out this plan? The train line to Berlin followed roughly the bed of the River Vltava and its valley northwards. As the river neared the border the country became more and more mountainous. They might possibly wreck or derail his train in this area. At least they could investigate such a course of action; they might even rehearse such an occurrence with a different train. After all, troop trains were constantly ferrying the Wehrmacht and S.S. between Germany and Czechoslovakia. They both liked the idea of a rehearsal. If they were going to visit the country to the north, they might as well occupy their time usefully while they were doing it. They had modern explosives; a short refresher course in their use would certainly do them no harm.

Uncle Hajsky conferred with Jindra, who with some reluctance agreed to their suggestion. But he made one adamant proviso: the derailing must take place in some other part of the country, and not on the main line between Prague and Berlin. The reason was obvious. They would in all probability only get one chance to strike at Heydrich. Once it was known that he might be the object of an assassination attempt, security precautions would be doubled. If the Nazis realized that saboteurs were considering mining the railway over which the Reichsprotector travelled, they would take appropriate security precautions. At all costs, Heydrich, in the next few weeks, must be lulled into the feeling that all the Czechs, if they did not exactly love him, at least feared and respected his person, and that he was as safe in his car or in his train as he was in his own bed.

Both Uncle Hajsky and Jindra would have preferred Jan and Josef to remain inactive; they only gave permission for the attempt because they realized, only too well, that they must keep their two young parachutists occupied. They had to have action of some sort; plotting and planning was all very well; riding about upon bicycles and watching Heydrich from behind hedges and railings, from street corners and shop doorways was all very well, but it was a comparatively passive occupation. They had to complete some deed deliberate and direct; they had to hurt the Nazis!

It was during this affair of the railway that Anna Malinova first worked with them. Jindra was anxious that women should become an integral part of the resistance. Some jobs they did much better than men; and obviously some wives were bound to find out what their husbands were doing. Better to enlist their help than arouse their opposition. Anna Malinova had already done much good work as a messenger. She was absolutely trustworthy. Her papers were completely in order; she aroused no suspicion. She could act as a link between Jan and Josef in this task, and she could report back if things went wrong. She could accompany them; two men travelling together might arouse suspicion, but a young couple, and a single man, who apparently did not know each other, were a much less conspicuous combination.

Although Jan had seen Anna Malinova at the Moravecs' many times since that first evening, he had never escorted her home again. Admittedly he was attracted to her, but he had turned, so he thought, that side of his mind completely away from her. He had said as much to Auntie Marie, who had smiled in her motherly way and said: "You are only young once, Jan. Life goes on even though there is a war on."

She reported this conversation to Jindra who nodded agreement. He knew they were both young men itching to get on with the job; they were impatient with the attitudes of both Uncle Hajsky and Jindra himself; they did not understand and did not want to understand the organization of resistance. They simply wanted to kill Heydrich! If young women could curb their impatience for a while, so much the better.

Jan heard the news that Anna was to accompany them with absolute dismay. This was a serious job, he protested. A woman had no part in it. Josef had no such scruples; he thought it rather a good idea that Anna should go with them. Jan did not try and conceal his annoyance from Anna, and it was left to Josef, chuckling and affectionate, to try and salve her hurt feelings.

He sat next to her in the train which chugged them northwards towards the Sudetenland, and to take her mind off the sight of Jan's frozen face, he opened his briefcase, took

84

out the explosive and fuse they intended to use on the railway and explained how they worked.

It was a plastic explosive, invented by the British, and it was to prove the answer to every saboteur's dream. British planes were, in fact, dropping it to resistance groups all over Europe during those years. It was, oddly enough, this explosive which was used, much later, by Count von Stauffenberg of the German General Staff in the unsuccessful attempt upon Hitler's life in 1944.

It could be moulded into any shape, stuck to the side of a bridge or a railway line or a machine, and it possessed terrific explosive potentialities. Josef also showed Anna how the fuse worked. That also was of simple design; it was noiseless and could be set to operate instantly, or within ten minutes, half an hour, two hours. It was activated by a tiny glass ball filled with tremendously corrosive acid set in the neck. When the ball was broken the acid spilled on to a thin wire which, eaten through, released the firing pin, which struck a cap and set off the explosive.

The locality where they intended to put their plan into operation lay beyond the town of Liberec. Here was a marshalling yard and a junction for several lines; beyond the town the railway ran through the mountains and crossed the border heading for Breslau.

The plan was in every aspect simple. They knew from the friendly railwaymen in Prague that the troop trains passed through Liberec just before daybreak three times a week. A local train left for Prague at midnight. It should not be difficult therefore to walk a few miles outside the town, plant their delayed action explosives and be comfortably back in time to catch the midnight train. Anna would stay in Liberec and meet them at the barrier. By the time the troop train exploded its own death charge they would be well on the way back to Prague.

The plan went off without a hitch. In their mackintoshes, carrying briefcases, Jan and Josef looked no different from a thousand other Czechs as they marched along the country road in the fading light that evening. It was seven miles northwards to the village of Mniseh, and roughly half way towards it the railway crossed the road on its journey towards the border.

Their feet echoed loudly on the tarmac road as they approached the level crossing, but no voice challenged them and the barrier across the road was up. There appeared to be no German guards at all in this lonely corner of the country, and the local gendarmerie were plainly not expecting trouble. It was quite dark when they cut across country and descended to the railway line. Only a matter of minutes was needed to fix the explosive to the tracks. When the train wheels passed over it, the explosion would be almost instantaneous.

They headed back towards Liberec as jauntily as two schoolboys on a day out. They knew that personally they had risked very little, and that in terms of the overall impact on the war, their escapade was unimportant. But at least it was a job done. At least it was a blow against the Reich and right upon their front doorstep, too! One small part of the explosive equipment they had brought from England would have been put to very good use. Even though it got them no closer to the point where an attempt to kill the Reichs-protector might be made, it gave their morale a fillip. For Jan it did something else too. It began his involvement with Anna Malinova.

They met her at the station barrier, and she who had waited so anxiously for what seemed so long, could not restrain herself; she rushed up and embraced them each in turn. To Jan's astonishment he found himself returning the hug. As for Josef he swung her round on the platform and kissed her on both cheeks. Then they showed their tickets at the barrier and walked along the platform. Jan opened a carriage door and helped Anna in, but Josef to his astonishment pushed him in after her and slammed the door shut. Through the open window he winked broadly at Jan and whispered that "security arrangements" made it essential that he should travel alone. Then off he went down the platform, whistling loudly, to find a seat at the front of the train.

The carriage containing Jan and Anna Malinova was empty. The guard's whistle shrilled, the wheels slowly turned, and picking up speed the train rattled through the night towards Prague. They were alone in a small, dimly-lit world, and they could either be silent or talk. If they talked they had to learn about one another, and from that conversation liking or apathy might spring.

Jan was in a mood for talking. The night's adventure had invigorated him. He told her of his past, of England and of his hopes for the future. He did not tell her about Heydrich; he did not tell her that with this man standing astride his life, there seemed no way ahead until his removal. He talked, for that reason, only of the past.

There is no doubt that from the very first Anna Malinova liked this fair-haired young man with the clear blue eyes. At that moment also she needed a person as single-sighted, as simple and as uncomplicated as Jan. She also talked. She talked quite honestly and simply as one does at such an hour and in such a situation. She told him how she had been married before the war broke out, and how she had loved her young husband and their small flat. Her world had been full of housewifely trivialities, with the distant promise of a child perhaps, and money in the bank perhaps, and a car perhaps, and a holiday by the sea perhaps, somewhere far away. She wanted badly to go to the seaside for, like so many people in central Europe, she had never seen the sea.

Yes, Hitler had overwhelmed their country, but even that had hardly disturbed her. Maybe there was some good in the Germans? After all, the British and the French and the Americans had let them down, hadn't they, and the Germans couldn't be all bad? She had known quite a few Germans in her time and many of them seemed very affable people. Things would probably soon settle down again.

She was so much in love with her little life, so much in love with youth and the mere fact that the days were bright with sunshine, and the nights were warm in bed, that she did not notice as the days went by how the lines on her husband's face became stencilled a fraction more deeply, and how the shadows under his eyes slowly grew darker. She did not notice anything until it happened. He went off to the office one morning, kissing her as usual, waving from the front door. And he never came home again. At least not as the man she knew.

A friend had told her that he had been arrested, but that she must not worry; apparently quite a few of these young chaps had been mixed up in some resistance organization. He might even be put in prison for a while; it was very foolish of him to take such absurd risks in wartime, but she should not worry.

And then a few weeks later the postman had delivered a little brown paper package to her door, and she could tell by the greyness in his face that something was terribly wrong, for he had choked and hurried away without a word.

And when she had opened the parcel, she found a small urn full of ashes, with her husband's name stencilled on the side, together with the date and hour of his death. The fact that thousands upon thousands of people all over Europe had received in the past, and were to receive in the future similar, macabre mementoes of the executions of their near relations, did not, and could not, assuage her bewildered grief. She was stupefied.

In an agony of incomprehension she held the cold little pot in her hand and tried to equate its contents with the man who had lain so close to her and meant so much to her. It was just a small grey pot, inanimate and inhuman. She did not know what to do with it, whether to put it on the shelf or the table or just continue to hold it. She tried to reconcile her own tiny happiness with the magnitude of this punishment. She was paralysed with despair, and as she tried to tell Jan about it in the privacy of their dingy and dimly-lit carriage rattling and swaying through the cold and secret night, she wept again at the memory, and he held her hand, but could not find words to comfort her. Instead he told her about his own scars.

So the Nazis had another enemy, tempered and hardened in the fire of their cruelty, and Jan and Anna Malinova were, from that moment onwards, bonded by the depth of the revelations they each made, one to the other. When Josef met them on the platform in Prague he sensed that something had occurred between the two of them, and he said he would go off to Auntie Marie's alone, as Jan might wish to escort Anna towards her home.

There was no curfew in Prague in those days. It was a very secure corner of Hitler's empire and the Czechs were a people that Heydrich was quite certain he had tamed. So they walked through the night without hindrance and without fear. They walked in the old square and looked up into the darkness towards the turreted towers of the Tyn church, built five hundred years before they were born. They paused in front of the Old Town Hall, where long ago noblemen who led the rebellion against Ferdinand II were beheaded. There was not a sound in the wide dark square, and their feet clicked rhythmically on the broad flagstones. A policeman paused, shone his torch on them, and satisfied that they were merely lovers, and as so far there was no edict against such people in the Nazi empire, he wished them goodnight and passed on. They turned down the narrow streets leading to the old Jewish quarter where, almost a thousand years before, the old merchant, Ibrahim Ibn Jacob from Arabia, had warmly reported that Prague was a rich and beautiful capital built of fine stone and situated harmoniously on the banks of a swift dark river, a city goodly to observe and pleasant in which to live.

They came to the river and walked along its banks. They did not wish to separate, and their slow, pre-dawn walk through the old city they both loved so well brought a quietude and a peace to their minds.

They were still two ordinary little people, ravaged and inhibited and driven together by a hatred they had not sought and a despair they did not understand. But it lifted them to a level and gave them a force far beyond their own comprehension.

CHAPTER SIX

PRAGUE radio, in its morning news broadcast, reported that a train had been derailed in the north by a group of saboteurs. According to the announcer no damage had been done and casualties were light. Nevertheless the tone of the broadcast was grave. If the Czechs had committed this misdemeanour then they had better watch out! The magnanimity of the Acting Reichsprotector over the past few weeks had been due to the devotion to duty and the loyalty of the Czech people. This friendship, listeners were reminded, was a tenuous thing. Although the representatives of the Reich could be kind, they could also be stern, harsh and merciless. For anyone caught in the slightest act of sabotage, the penalty was instant death.

Jan, Josef and Anna were jubilant over their success. It proved to them one most important point: the railways were vulnerable. The Nazis could not, and indeed would not, attempt to protect hundreds of miles of steel rail, crisscrossing their newly acquired empire. If there was a weak point in the armadillo protection of the Acting Reichsprotector, surely it was this?

Quietly and effectively Uncle Hajsky had enlisted a number of railway workers to aid him in plotting Heydrich's movements. It is highly doubtful if any of them suspected for even one moment that they were collaborating in an assassination plot. Uncle Hajsky was more subtle than that; tacitly he merely let it be understood that he wished to chart the movements of the Acting Reichsprotector for future reference.

He learnt, for example, that the special train which carried Heydrich on his frequent journeys between Prague and Berlin always stopped at the railway station in the Royal Park on the outskirts of Prague. This was a branch line which connected with the main line running northwards from Prague; the train waited at this station for a signal which gave it clearance. The station, of course, would be well guarded, and S.S. men would most likely patrol the platform. But one important factor emerged from this discovery: from the station to the main line the track in its passage through the Royal Park ran through a thick screen of trees. In those trees a man could hide with a gun.

It was to this thickly-wooded fringe that Jan and Josef made a quick exploratory expedition. They paced out the distance from the station to a particularly sturdy and shady fir tree; it stood about three hundred yards from the platform. By the time the train reached this point, they reasoned, it would still be moving slowly enough to present a fair target. Of course, Heydrich might not be sitting in a place where he was easily recognizable; therefore, ideally, it would be better if they could acquire a weapon which would annihilate all the people in his compartment. Uncle Hajsky had obtained the ideal weapon: a bazooka-type anti-tank gun, which would throw a shell primed to explode on impact. If they could fire this directly through the right compartment window, there was every likelihood that all inside would be killed instantly.

The idea was so impressive that both Jan and Josef could not wait a minute to rehearse their plan and see if it would work. Heydrich was expected to use his special train upon a visit to Berlin the following week. They decided that when the train passed the fir tree, one of them would be sitting amongst its foliage awaiting him.

Primed by intelligence supplied by the railway employees, they cycled to the Royal Park on the following Thursday. Carefully they hid their machines in the thick screen of trees alongside the tracks; although this was to be only a rehearsal, there was absolutely no point in risking themselves unnecessarily, and a rehearsal meant that all weak points in the plan of attack must be exposed. A quick exit along the wooded paths, out into the streets, and so to the concealment of Prague's traffic, was of fundamental importance.

They arrived a full hour before Heydrich's train was due to halt at the Royal Park platform, and carefully they surveyed the railway lines to see that no guards were patrolling there. Everything was quiet.

They reached the foot of the tree. It was tall and gnarled and probably four hundred years old. Its branches were strong enough to stand the weight of the winter snows; its foliage was so thick that a man could hide in a fork of its trunk about half way up and be seen neither from the ground nor from the railway.

Because Josef's foot was still painful although it was healing now, Jan insisted that he should climb the tree while Josef acted as lookout on the ground. Josef gave him a leg up to the first branch, and from there he scrambled up to the fork. The bark was rough, the position not too secure, but he saw at once that it would be possible to fire a portable anti-tank gun from this position. He shouted the news down to Josef. When the train passed slowly across Jan's line of vision, the Acting Reichsprotector should be revealed as plainly as a goldfish in an opalescent tank.

Time passed slowly. It was a cold grey day in early March, and although Josef was able to keep warm on the ground by hobbling briskly around, Jan, immobile in the tree, got bluer and colder. He rubbed his legs to keep his circulation going and blew into his cupped hands, and then at last they both heard the train whistle as it signalled its approach and imminent halt at the Royal Park station.

It slid to a stop beside the platform with a cacophony of grating metallic acoustics. In a loud whisper peering down the track Josef reported that as far as he could see there were no S.S. troops on the platform, but that the train itself, consisting of three carriages, was full of soldiers. Jan could not see the station at all.

In the signal box, lower down the branch line, the signalman had obviously been warned that the Acting Reichsprotector was on his way, and that nothing must delay his progress; the train stood at the platform for no more than two minutes, before a sharp peep on its whistle proclaimed its departure. Jan, his coldness and stiffness suddenly gone, leaned forward eagerly.

To his dismay he saw at once that its rate of acceleration

was greater than they had anticipated. The engine was level and passing him almost before he realized it. His eyes became slits of intense concentration as he focused on the windows. Reflected light gleamed tantalizingly on the polished glass; and he glimpsed many men in Nazi uniforms in the carriages; no doubt they were the oleaginous companions of S.S. General Heydrich. But which one *was* Heydrich? Was *that* Heydrich or a minor official? Each carriage was crowded with men in uniform. Undoubtedly these trips to Berlin were occasions for a little junketry and celebration. Heydrich had quite a reputation in the brothels and night clubs of Berlin.

The last few windows of the last carriage passed in a blur of polished steel and reflecting glass. The rhythmic rattle of wheels died away. And Jan was again conscious of his coldness and stiffness. He scrambled slowly down the tree to where Josef was waiting. Josef had already guessed the truth; he, too, had noted the speed of the train and the almost hypnotic light reflections across the carriage windows.

They agreed that it was no good. There were too many windows, too much speed, too many reflections. Shooting a pheasant on the wing would be child's play compared with trying to pot Heydrich with an anti-tank gun in that train. If he sat with his back to the engine he would not be seen at all. They could pump a shell into one of the carriages and kill a few high-ranking Nazis, but Heydrich would probably not be amongst them.

Dejected and disappointed, they walked back to where they had concealed their cycles, mounted them and rode back into town to tell Uncle Hajsky that it was useless to persevere with any further plans for assassinating Heydrich while he was travelling by train.

Their dejection, however, did not last for long. There was too much work to be done in which they had to play a part. The whole movement of resistance was building up slowly and efficiently. There were several other resistance groups in Czechoslovakia, and Jindra was in liaison with most of them; he also possessed many influential official and political contacts. Uncle Hajsky and Jindra had realized at once that

93

the enlistment of railway employees was an essential priority, if the movement of resistance was to spread. The Czech railways—mainly beyond range of Allied bombing raids—were still functioning smoothly and punctually. Travel by car, because of petrol rationing, was almost impossible. But railwaymen moved all over the country with no difficulty at all.

So contacts were made in Pilsen and other large cities, and information began to pour in from Bohemia, Moravia and even Slovakia. News of airfields, of troop dispositions, of public morale, of points where sabotage was possible. The radio transmitter and receiver, "Libuse", was operating effectively in Pardubice, but radio transmitters were also being constructed in secret, because not only was the burden extremely heavy for Valchik and his team in Pardubice, but Jindra thought it safer to try and equip many more transmitting stations in various parts of the country. Then all could take turns in operating and so further confuse the listening enemy. London was constantly asking for fresh information regarding conditions inside Czechoslovakia, and for reliable "addresses" which new parachutists could contact upon landing.

This, Jindra decided, was the next priority. More parachutists were needed trained to operate radio transmitters, to instruct people in the acts of sabotage, to train groups of resistance men for guerilla warfare. London was co-operative; they assured him that within a matter of weeks, reinforcements would be dropping out of the night skies to aid his organization in their work.

Then came the first mistake. Further to conceal his tracks, Valchik accepted ill-timed advice and registered at the lodgings in which he was staying under a name different from the one upon his faked identity card. The police never checked such things, he was told. But on this occasion the police did check, and they reported the discrepancy to the Gestapo. Fortunately, there were workers for the resistance within the ranks of the police. Valchik was tipped off in time. He left the town that night, crossing the woods on foot and went out into the country to hide. His usefulness in

Pardubice was at an end; his portrait—it was really quite unlike him—appeared on posters in all Czechoslovakian towns. He was a wanted man and one hundred thousand crowns were offered for his capture. After a period in hiding, it was decided by Jindra that he should join their organization in Prague.

The fact that it did not seem possible to assassinate Heydrich by train did not prevent Jan and Josef continuing their researches. Their patient bicycle rides had uncovered the fact that he was also vulnerable by car; it seemed that about this time he was so overwhelmingly confident, or foolhardy, about his own safety, that occasionally he travelled without any guard or escort, and that only his chauffeur and body-guard, Klein, accompanied him in the Mercedes. Even when they did travel with an escort, it seemed that Heydrich became so intoxicated with speed that they drove so fast that they left the escort far behind.

There was one stretch of road not far from his country villa that ran straight as a sword blade, slightly downhill, between two avenues of chestnut trees. The trees had tall straight trunks, and their branches, by now budding with spring, interlocked above the black tarmac ribbon. Very often the green Mercedes reached a speed of over a hundred miles an hour down this stretch. Surely, pondered Jan and Josef, they could use this speed to encompass Heydrich's self-destruction?

For a long time this plan was uppermost in their minds; they even acquired a piece of toughened steel wire to stretch across the road between two trees so that it might either slice off the head of the driver and of his passenger, or at least wreck the vehicle. Jan and Josef would be waiting with their revolvers to finish off the job. But eventually they decided that this plan also possessed too many flaws. The speed at which the car was travelling might snap the steel wire like a thread of cotton. In any case if the car did crash and the occupants were killed outright it might look like an accident. That was the last thing they wished to happen. It had to be shown to all Czechoslovakia, to the entire German empire and to the world, that Heydrich had been killed by representatives of the Czech people. In fact, that the Nazis were vulnerable.

There were also other drawbacks to this plan. How could they escape after such an attempt? There were only two routes available: the first down the long straight road towards Prague, and if they considered such an eventuality, they had to take into account the fact that elderly bicycles did not provide the best and fastest means of escaping; the second across the fields, and if they took to the fields, they would be in grave danger the whole time. The country was open, and they would be easily spotted; capture would only be a matter of time once the alarm was raised and the Nazis cordoned off the area. Capture was something they were determined would not happen to them; they were not prepared under any circumstances to surrender to the Nazis. Reluctantly they abandoned the idea of using the wire.

And yet, oddly enough, it was whilst returning from the last of their cycling expeditions to the stretch of road between the chestnuts, that they finally discovered a spot where an assassination attempt seemed possible.

The tarmac road ran downwards, and the road became rougher as tram tracks made their appearance. The cobblestones made their wheels bump. They passed a brick works and entered the suburb of Holesovice. As they cycled down the hill Jan saw, on a street corner. a blue street sign with white lettering which said, "Rude Armady VII". They were freewheeling rapidly now. They had to brake hard to turn the sharp near-hairpin bend which led to the Troja Bridge across the Vltava, a mile lower down. And as they spun round it, the same idea occurred to both of them simultaneously.

They both braked. They both stopped. Quite often this peculiar coincidence of mental processes happened to them. They had no need to say very much. Both knew *this* was the place.

They rested their bikes against a front garden fence and walked back up the hill. It was a wide road flanked on both sides by pleasant suburban houses. A double line of steel tram rails ran down the centre of the street. On the bend itself another wide road branched off to the right.

They stood by a stop pretending to be waiting for a tram, and watching the cars sweep down the hill and turn the corner. They had to slow almost to a halt. Although it was not a blind bend it was much too sharp to negotiate at speed. The downhill tram lines swept in to within a yard of the kerb. The trams coming up the hill were only a few yards farther out. It seemed an ideal spot for their purpose and they discussed their discovery eagerly.

They could stand there as if they were waiting for a tram, and as Heydrich's Mercedes slowed down on the corner, they could scythe the occupants of the car with a blast of Sten gun fire.

There was happy anticipation in Josef's voice, as he discussed the idea, and Jan knew it would not be too difficult for him to drop a grenade in the back seat just for luck!

They also discussed the deficiencies of the plan. There would almost certainly be people about at the time the car passed. Trams might foul up the whole thing. But much was in their favour. The district was full of side turnings. Prague itself was only a couple of miles away, and there were many houses in the intervening suburbs where they could arrange to find shelter.

They rode back to see Uncle Hajsky, talking excitedly. At last they seemed to have hit upon a scheme which gave them much more than a fifty per cent chance of pulling off the job.

That very night Jan explained it to Anna Malinova. Their love affair and their intimacy had progressed to this extent. Now she knew all about their mission to kill Heydrich, but to Jan's slight atonishment did not greet the news with the enthusiasm he had expected. He did not understand her attitude, and she could not really explain it herself. Her hatred for the Germans was undiminished, but with Jan she had found a compensation for her deep loss. She wanted to retain that compensation; she wanted to re-awake and live again. For a long time she concealed these thoughts from him. He had forgotten his first belief that it was impossible to fall in love and plan an assassination at the same time.

For Jan it *was* the first time he had been in love. Why should he, the dedicated assassin, conceal a human need as normal as the coming of the spring? Why should he not find time for an hour of enchantment? If Romeo could not spare a kiss for Juliet, surely nothing was worth while?

Not that he could help himself. In the luminosity of that early spring in Prague love could not be ignored or halted. It flowed like the darkly shimmering Vltava; it dropped in tiny, crimson-stained flowers from the candles of the chestnuts along its banks. Love and the spring arrived and collided, and for Jan and Anna it endowed the whole city with such enchantment, that even the bootlaces and the bread and the silly dummy packages in the shop windows took on a new mystery and meaning; a champagne effervescence entered the watery beer they drank in the riverside cafés. Sometimes in the chiming of the endless clocks that rationed the sunlight, they heard a faint echo of passing time. And sometimes Anna Malinova sensed that this time was important.

She was a girl of much passion, and she saw in this tall, fair-haired young parachutist someone to fill the empty spaces of her heart. If she saw also, with the intuitive clarity of her sex, the shadows of a bleak and bloody future, then who could blame them for not wasting the present? Flesh is a tangible consolation before the grave; and young love is an ecstasy running in the veins with the fury of creation as its eternal source.

Nowhere could have been more lovely than Prague in that spring of 1942. Somewhere, away from the city, the idiot war was shooting the branches from the trees, but here, in this oasis surrounded by war, and occupied by men of war, the white suds of blossom foamed up to the walls of the Hradcany itself, and below, in the old stone roots of the city, it was possible for two lovers to walk, and laugh and whisper, and plan together their part in the continuity of nature.

The black-out, as so many discovered, was made for

lovers. For five long years the lamplight and gaslight and electric light were banned from Europe's streets. You could see the frozen crackle of stars caught in the crook of a statue's arm, or framed by a gabled roof. Sometimes, it is true, the sky would be lit with the red glow of a burning town and the drone of the bombers overhead punctuated by the brilliant starbursts of high altitude shells. But even these happenings, through some peculiar alchemy of the mind, only seemed to heighten the moment, and emphasize the essential transience of the hands which sought, and the lips which clung and whispered. There was some small solace even in one's own impermanence.

For Jan lifting his eyes from the bleak and barren business of preparing to kill a man, it was as if the sun had suddenly come out. Now each moment together had to be filled and refilled, as every lover on every leave, in every corner of the whole wide, hating world, knew. Love and be merry; tomorrow I must go back to the battle, and a bomb might drop, or a bullet come. And perhaps this—and only this—is all I shall have to take with me into the darkness.

Jan and Anna saw and understood this, through their senses, and no longer could deny what they understood.

CHAPTER SEVEN

Upon the night of the 26th March, 1942, a message of much importance to those concerned was tapped out from a radio station in England and beamed through the darkness of occupied Europe. It cut silently through the intangible radio waves which filled the air. Through the barrier of war signals, and plays, and features, and hints to housewives in French, Dutch, German and Italian, through the nightly propaganda pieces by radio morale builders, through *Lili Marlene* sung in half a dozen languages, through the cookery lessons and news reports, and fatstock prices, and English by radio; through all this penetrable mass of diction, and rhetoric, and drama, inspiring, informing and threatening, which spread upwards towards the periphery of indifferent stars, it sped, to be netted by the tiny indoor aerial of a radio receiver in the machine shed of a quarry near Pardubice. Into the earphones of the operator crouching there crackled this enigmatic twittering of morse which sent the man racing to reach his superior officer.

Upon the first train which left Pardubice for Prague early next morning sat Mrs. Krupka, the young housewife, a little paler than usual perhaps at being roused from bed so early, but prettier than ever, and looking so innocent as she strove to memorize the message she had been entrusted to deliver to Jindra.

And so the news went from London to Prague and down through Uncle Hajsky to Jan and Josef. The reinforcements which Jindra had requested had taken off that night from an airfield somewhere in England, and should be arriving soon.

To Jan and Josef the news was exciting and stimulating, and they discussed animatedly which of their comrades in England would be sent. They had helped to supply London with a succession of fresh addresses, and the new parachutists should find things considerably easier than they had done.

They also discussed the probable areas into which the new-comers would be parachuted; London for obvious security reasons could not pass on such information. In any case the journey was so long and hazardous, and landmarks so difficult to define, that they would be lucky if they were dropped within ten miles of their objectives.

The nights of the 26th and 27th were foggy in Prague and Jan and Josef looked up at the swirling mists with anxious faces; it meant, they knew, added peril for the aircraft and its occupants.

Their anxieties were short-lived. Upon the 27th March London advised "Libuse" that the aircraft had reached Czechoslovakia to find the ground blanketed in fog. There was no alternative but to return to England. They would make a second attempt as soon as conditions made it possible.

A week later London radioed a second despatch. The parachutists had been dropped successfully, although apparently a number of mishaps had made their journey unpleasantly eventful. The aircraft had been delayed twenty minutes at take-off. The nights were shorter now, and the flight distance from an airfield in England to the heart of Czechoslovakia and back to base, represented the limit of the aircraft's capabilities. In this case the pilot had also met head winds, reducing the margin of safety even farther. He had estimated after a few hours' flying that they had no chance at all of reaching their chosen dropping zone. He had radioed this fact back to base in England and requested further instructions. The Czechoslovakian intelligence officer there had requested the pilot to ask the six parachut-ists if they were willing to take the risk of dropping in a different place. From the plane came back the information that the parachutists were, indeed, quite willing. New addresses were then passed out from base and these were handed to the two Czech officers commanding the parachut-ists. Somewhere over Czechoslovakia they had all jumped out into the cold night air.

Obviously, London reported, they would need a day or two to re-orientate themselves. Prague should not worry and should not expect to hear from them for several hours, but eventually news of their whereabouts should filter through to reach some branch of the resistance.

The days passed, and no news of the parachutists reached either Pardubice or Prague. Now it was London's turn to express concern. The parachutists should have made contact before this. Could Prague institute inquiries as to what had happened? This was more difficult and dangerous to do than those in Britain realized. If all the couriers, the railwaymen, the odd helpers, were given the information that new parachutists were at large somewhere in Czechoslovakia then obviously the chances of the Germans hearing this news was increased.

Uncle Hajsky gloomily discussed such a course. And then just before a decision was taken, news arrived. A new parachutist was passed through from the north into Prague. The only people who could adequately vouch for his identity were Jan and Josef; they were hurriedly summoned to that same flat where Jan had had his own first uncompromising interview with Jindra.

And there hunched in the chair, sullen and unco-operative, they found Sergeant Arnost Miks. They both shook him by the hand and congratulated him, and he tried to smile and return their greetings, but the events of the past few days had tensed and frozen his actions.

He sat there hunched in the chair in the sitting room. As he hesitantly recalled the details of a story which was to have such far-reaching implications, his voice was curiously passive and flat. Arnost Miks was a big man, a heavyweight, massive and reliable. He had a thick boxer's face, dark brown eyes, a full humorous mouth which curled slowly when he smiled. Jan and Josef recalled how easily he was amused, and how when he laughed he threw back his head and his whole body shook with uninhibited glee. But now he did not laugh.

Four of them were grouped around him: Jan and Josef, Uncle Hajsky and Jindra. Jan remembered Arnost Miks most of all from their training period in Scotland; he would always remember Miks because of the easy contemptuous way he handled weapons; rather like a small boy playing with toys. He was never very angry about anything; not really very angry with the Germans; they were just people who had to be dealt with. God had made him a gentle man.

His party of three had jumped first. It was commanded by Lieutenant Pechal, a young man with a dark, sensuous face and heavily lidded eyes. He was an intensely romantic figure, good-looking and courageous; and his courage never wavered, even though sometimes his judgment might have been at fault. The third in their party was Gerik, a youngster of twenty, the radio operator. Their objective was to establish a centre of resistance in Moravia. They had been given instructions that they were not in any circumstances in those first days to take chances or draw attention to themselves. They had been told that Heydrich had wiped out all resistance in Moravia, and that their job was to re-establish it. They were above all to stay alive, exist, settle in and wait. When they were absolutely certain that they were undetected, then they could use the radio transmitter and receiver, contact London and start the second free radio station "Libuse II" operating in Moravia.

They all landed safely and joined up in the darkness. They located the parachute carrying their supplies and the radio equipment without difficulty. They hid the case containing the large transmitter deep amongst the straw in a deserted barn and printed in large letters on the plywood case: "I beg the good person who finds this not to report it to the authorities but to keep it for himself, or better to destroy it."

It was the sort of naively hopeful action which characterized that group of Lieutenant Pechal. They ate, and at dawn left the barn. Pechal carried a fat briefcase stuffed with Czechoslovakian bank notes; Gerik carried his portable radio receiver and transmitter; Sergeant Arnost Miks carried a briefcase containing emergency rations. Two miles along the road in the grey light they came to a village. The signpost read: "Gbely". With a shock of dismay they realized that they had been dropped miles off target. They were not in Moravia at all but in Slovakia, the new State created by

103

Hitler at the outbreak of war. Border posts and customs had been set up which now barred them from the rest of Czechoslovakia. Before the Pechal group could even think of beginning operations, it was necessary to cross this artificial border.

They discussed what they should do, and decided that the crossing was the first and most essential priority, so they hurried onwards. Quietly they walked through a sleepy village, rounded a turn in the road, and came to a dead halt. About three hundred yards ahead stood a group of Slovak gendarmes. Both groups spotted each other at the same moment.

"Run for it," snapped Pechal.

They crashed through the hedge. Fortunately only a narrow strip of grass separated them from a thick wood skirting low foothills. As they ran through the undergrowth, they heard the guards shouting behind them, but they had a good start. After ten minutes' effort all was quiet except for the sound of their own laboured breathing, and they knew they had eluded their pursuers.

They moved on, more slowly now, deciding to stick to the forest until nightfall. It was a disastrous beginning. They guessed that army and police posts would be alerted, and that a search of the area would almost certainly begin. If the searchers discovered any of their hidden equipment, the hunt would really be on. And guards on the new border would probably be increased.

They examined the map, and Gerik remembered he had an aunt who lived in a nearby town which was also quite near this artificial frontier. If she was unable to offer them shelter, then at least she might give them a hot meal. They reached the town the next morning and he went on alone to investigate. His crestfallen face when he rejoined them told them enough. His aunt had left the town months before and moved to Bratislava.

Their objective now had to be the town of Buchlovice across the border in Moravia; they had a contact there—one of the new addresses radioed to them aboard the plane—which they hoped would be reliable.

It was at this point that Pechal decided it would be better if they separated and joined up again in Buchlovice, at this address. Three men travelling together would obviously attract attention. Possibly the Slovak gendarmes had already broadcast the fact that three suspicious characters were in the vicinity. He told Miks and Gerik to go ahead and said he would give them several hours' start, making his own attempt later that evening.

Miks shook his head sorrowfully at the memory. Jindra had made coffee and he poured this out while Jan and Josef commiserated with Miks and went on asking him questions. Did Miks know, for example, that Jan and Josef and the others in Pardubice were already operating there? Miks replied that they knew that some parachutists—he had no idea of their identity—had dropped safely some months before, and were operating successfully in Prague. They had been told that the contacts they had been given would lead them eventually to this unit of the resistance, but first they had to establish themselves. Miks went on with his story.

He and Gerik crossed the border without any trouble, walked to the nearest village and caught a train to Buchlovice, where their "address" was that of a merchant called Stokman who lived on the outskirts of the town.

They found it easily: a small shop. An elderly woman with a crabbed, worried face, her hair screwed up in a bun, looked at them suspiciously, and at that moment it occurred to Miks that two nights in the open had not improved their appearance.

Gerik acted as spokesman. "We wish to see Mr. Stokman, please."

"He is not here!" Her voice was not friendly.

Gerik rested the case containing the radio set on the counter.

"We'd like to wait for him, then. Will he be long?"

Her eyes were hard and suspicious. "God knows," she said, "he's in a concentration camp." The conversation died as quick a death as a clipped telephone wire. And somehow, in an odd and indefinable way, from that moment onwards,

Miks realized that Gerik was scared. The old woman's voice was almost threatening: "Most people around here are aware of what happened to Mr. Stokman," she said.

Gerik looked at Miks without speaking, and Miks saw his Adam's apple bob as he swallowed. Miks tried to explain how they felt at this juncture to Jan and the other three men listening to him, and they nodded sympathetically. This was the only address they had got; if it failed them, they were completely on their own.

It was Jindra who intervened at this point. It was obvious, he remarked, that when the Czech officer waiting at the airport in England heard that the plane could not reach its chosen dropping zone, he would have to give them the only contacts he had, contacts not necessarily vetted by Jan and Josef or the Jindra organization. Miks wearily agreed. It was because of this lack of contacts that they had got into such trouble.

"Perhaps there is a relative of Mr. Stokman's in the town?" Gerik had continued.

Corporal Gerik was just twenty-one years old, with a fresh baby face. As a radio operator he was quick and competent. His passing out report referred to him as someone who was never perturbed, maintained cheerfulness in the face of adversity and would do well in an emergency. He had seen this report and repeated it rather proudly to Miks.

"This," Miks had thought, "is an emergency. And if baby-face can't appeal to the old girl, what chance have I with my mug?"

"Relative!" said the old woman angrily. "I am his mother. Is that not good enough for you?" She added stonily, "I have another son and daughter living here with me. What do you want with us?"

Gerik licked his dry lips. And then to Miks' consternation, without any preamble, he said in a deflated voice, "We're from England, we landed in the forest some nights ago by parachute——"

The expression of horror which leapt to the old lady's face was almost comical.

"Parachutists! Then you must go, now! Now! We had

106

enough trouble last year. Do you know my son is in a concentration camp because of people like you! You can't stay here——"

Miks stopped the old woman before she got into her stride. His deep voice was tired. He thought that Gerik had been indiscreet. He did not care very much for the woman either. He thought her an old hag.

"Mother," he said, "we are tired and hungry! We've been running for three long days. We've come here to help you. We've come here to help Czechoslovakia. We ask only one night's shelter!"

The old woman was panic-stricken. "And what d'you think will happen to us if we let you stay here—eh? What will happen to us——?"

"Let them stay, mother!"

The voice was clear and young and it came from the side doorway. It came from a young dark girl who stood there regarding them seriously. She was not pretty. But she was a friend, and if anyone needed a friend at that moment, said Miks, they did.

Miks had looked up at the faces grouped around him in the Moravecs' flat as he recalled that moment.

"It was the first friendly voice we had heard since we arrived in Czechoslovakia," he said bitterly. "She did her best for us but it took her a long time to convince the woman. Eventually, however, she won her round and the old girl showed us up to a small room. I'll never forget the sight of that bed! A real bed, with sheets, blankets, pillows. It was heaven! Sleep, we thought, sleep!"

But then Gerik decided they ought to try and radio London. For the first time they had an electric plug to work with. And it was the regular and arranged hour that London had agreed they would listen out for them. They managed to plug into the electric light. They heard London, heard them calling their number, their own call sign. It was a wonderful moment. They tried to answer. Gerik spun the dials and adjusted the volume. Then, phut! Suddenly a valve went. Gerik shoved his hand in to the set trying to force it down its socket; there was a bang and he received a severe shock. They knew then that for the time being the set was useless. Oh well, they thought, they could repair it later. Now they could sleep! And then there was a knock on the door and the old woman pushed her way in.

Would they please leave? Please! They *must* leave! She had thought about it; she had examined her conscience. Her daughter had pleaded with her to let them stay, but it was no use. She would go mad with terror if they stayed. For sheltering people like them the Germans had only one penalty, death! She didn't want to die! Please, she didn't want to die!

Miks stopped and looked up at Jan and Josef, Uncle Hajsky and Jindra with round hurt eyes. "She was scared out of her wits," he said. "Her face was grey with terror. There was saliva of terror running down the side of her mouth."

They knew it was no use pleading any more. The old woman began to weep as Gerik packed up the case. They clumped slowly down the stairs. Miks felt a sickness in his stomach that they should be the cause of so much terror; it was as if his face was filled with a foul disease.

At the bottom of the stairs the girl was waiting. It was plain she had been crying also.

"Try Mr. Holsen, two streets down to the left," she whispered. "He is a good patriot. I'm sorry, I'm sorry——"

As he passed her, Miks took her hand and squeezed it, and he saw the tears start again into her eyes.

So they were outside in the darkening street again, with nowhere to go, and no food to eat. As they tramped along, an early moon was high in the sky and they knew the night would be clear and cold. Very cold. They knocked at two wrong doors before they were directed to that of Mr. Holsen. As Gerik raised his hand and rapped on the door, it was driven home to Miks that somewhere, somehow, something had been missed out in their training. It was all very well to learn how to shoot on sight, blow up bridges, make long marches, endure tiredness and fear and kill swiftly and efficiently. That was fine; that was how you read about it in story books. But how did you convince your friends, your own countrymen, that you had come to help them? How did you knock on a door just before dark and say: "We are parachutists. Please give us food and a bed for the night. But we can't guarantee that tomorrow, because of your hospitality, the Germans won't stick you up against a wall and shoot you."

All this passed through Miks' brain as the door opened, and a scared little man in his shirt sleeves peered out. What did they want? Could they talk to him in private? No, they could not. What did they want to talk to him privately about? He was an honest man and anything they had to say they could say on the doorstep. They explained that a friend had intimated he was a good patriot. Of course he was a patriot. He'd help if he could; he'd help any man within reason. They then asked if they could stay with him for one night; they'd sleep anywhere, on the floor, anywhere. But who were they, he demanded. There were regulations about sheltering people who were not registered with the police.

They decided to tell him they were parachutists from England. They said they had dropped to help form a resistance movement with people who believed in the future, who were willing to work for Czechoslovakia.

"His face," said Miks, "slowly changed like milk curdling. He didn't want to believe us. By not believing us and refusing to help us he could keep his self-respect. If he believed us, and did nothing, then he was a coward. We stood on the doorstep and haggled with him. We haggled with him! The whole business made me feel sick. And in the end he compromised by saying he would hide our transmitter for us, but otherwise we would have to look out for ourselves.

"So we told him about Pechal and said we expected him to join us, and we would contact him each day to see if Pechal had arrived. We slept in the woods that night, and the next two nights after that, and Pechal still did not come, so we decided we must go and look for him ourselves.

"You see, we knew Pechal's parents lived in Vresovice. That was near where we should have dropped in the first place, and we guessed that if anything had gone wrong, he would make for that district. We had our original addresses to contact when we got there, so in any case it was the best place to make for."

They caught a train—it was a fairly long journey—and arrived in the small town of Vresovice, and went to the first of the addresses they had been given; that of Pechal's brother. He stared at them with haggard eyes. Yes, Pechal had arrived but his description had arrived before him. It was plastered up everywhere. He was wanted for murder! There was a price on his head. The local gendarmerie had been alerted; no one dare shelter him, he was hiding in the forest.

Sickened and bewildered by this news they allowed Pechal's brother to lead them into the forest that night, and they met their leader again. He was unshaven, dirty, wild-eyed. They munched the loaf and the sausage that Pechal's brother had left with them, and slept in a rough shelter made from pine branches. And Pechal told them his story.

CHAPTER EIGHT

To the four listening men gathered around Arnost Miks it was a story of unrelieved tragedy. But none of them, upon that evening in March, realized that already the pattern of events had been shaped, and now each of them was irrevocably implicated. Jindra listened taciturnly, never saying a word; Uncle Hajsky tutted impatiently, and Jan and Josef interrupted again and again.

It appeared that after Pechal had sent Miks and Gerik on ahead he tried to sleep for an hour or two, but all he could manage was an uneasy doze. His face was unshaven and dirty; his mackintosh was now stained with damp and earth mould, and his trilby hat shapeless. If the occasion had been different, as he set off, clutching the briefcase containing thousands of Czech banknotes, he might well have smiled at the picture he presented. His faked identity card showed him as Oldrich Pesar, commercial traveller, but at that moment he looked a very down-and-out commercial gentleman. He knew that if only he could reach Moravia, he would stand a chance: it was his birthplace, his mother, father and brothers still lived there. Once established, who could tell; he might even be able to pay them a visit?

So Pechal walked slowly and cautiously upon his way. He knew from his map in which direction the border lay, and his progress through the forest was uneventful. It was quite dark when he came across the rough forest track which led in the general direction of the border. The possibility that in such a lonely part of the countryside the track might be guarded, seemed negligible. Nevertheless his pupils dilated with the effort of trying to pierce the darkness ahead of him, and he kept his right hand in his mackintosh pocket against the reassuring bulge of his Colt Service revolver.

The blinding light of a torch directed straight between his eyes shocked him to a standstill. The harsh "Halt!", and the even more ominous snap of a rifle bolt forcing a cartridge into the breech, reiterated the unhappy truth; he had walked straight into a border patrol. Worse still, as he quickly realized, a German patrol! Obviously the gendarmes who had first spotted them and had given chase, had raised the alarm and—as Pechal had feared—extra patrols had been posted.

He sensed, rather than saw, the rifle barrel pointing at him. A bulky figure moved towards him. Yes, they were Germans all right. He could make out their uniforms quite clearly.

"Your papers?"

Pechal took his hand off his revolver. He did not know how many rifles covered him in the darkness, and he fumbled in his inside breast pocket for his identity card. His mind was reacting quickly now. They were obviously oafs: if they had had any sense, they would have made him stand with his hands held high, while one searched him. Then he would have been revealed completely. But now he could try to bluff his way through using this commercial traveller guise. At least he could stick to it as long as possible.

"I'm sorry, gentlemen," he stammered, "I've just left Petrov . . ." He knew this village was nearby from their earlier examination of the map, "and I thought if I tried a short cut, I could get through——" The guard's voice was disinterested but not really suspicious.

"Silence! What are you doing out at this time of night?"

"Well, I've just explained. I was taking a short cut from Petrov. . . ."

Pechal could see another figure holding a second torch closely examining his identity card. It seemed there were only two of them. If only he was not so dirty and unshaven! He hoped they would not scrutinize him too closely.

The second German thrust the identity card into the breast pocket of his tunic. "A commercial traveller—uh?" he said. "You will come back to Petrov with us, to the police station. We'll soon see if your story is true, and who knows you there. Come on! Move!"

As they walked, Pechal's mind worked quickly. There was still hope. It would take perhaps twenty minutes before they

THE SECOND BATCH OF PARACHUTISTS TO DROP INTO CZECHOSLOVAKIA

(*Above*, *left*) Corporal Gerik, the youngest parachutist of them all

(*Above*, *right*) Ex-customs officer Karel Curda

(*Right*) Sergeant Miks, a plain, simple man with the face and build of a heavyweight boxer

ANCIENT PRAGUE,
AN ENCHANTED CITY

(*Left*) "Stone façade, turret and tower, mirrored and changing in the reflecting waters"

(*Right*) "Upon the central arch of ancient Charles Bridge Christ crucified in stone hangs upon His Cross"

(*Below*) "The arches of seven bridges link the city across the Vltava"

The arrow shows where Jan and Josef waited for Heydrich's arrival

Jan's grenade blew a hole in the rear of the Mercedes

The Sten gun which Josef abandoned in the roadway

reached Petrov. He still possessed both his loaded revolver and his briefcase. Maybe the contents of the briefcase contained the answer. He injected as much despondency as he could into his voice.

"This is all very difficult for me, gentlemen. I realize that I've broken a few regulations but as a matter of fact it will be most embarrassing for me back at Petrov. A matter of the heart, you understand. Her husband is looking for me. . . ."

He might just as well have been talking in Chinese for all the attention the guards paid to his speech. They plodded along slightly behind, one on either side. He realized also with a glimpse of hope that their rifle barrels no longer pointed at him with quite so much dramatic implication. They were merely carrying out a normal duty; they had not the slightest idea of the importance of their capture.

He tried again. "I'm not poor, gentlemen. Would a thousand crowns be of any use to you?"

"Shut up," said the guard on his right. And that was the end of that. They marched on in silence. Pechal raged inwardly. He could not believe that it was devotion to duty which animated these two surly guards; it must be stupidity. But if they were stupid, surely he must have a chance to escape them.

They came to the end of the forest track and turned along a narrow, metalled road. Three hundred yards ahead lights appeared at the outskirts of the village.

"Two thousand crowns each, gentlemen. That's a lot of money."

This time the guards did not even bother to reply, and Pechal knew he had to make a break for it now, or he was lost for ever. Either his revolver or the contents of the briefcase would ensure him some brisk attention from the Gestapo when they found them. His briefcase was in his left hand, his right hand thrust negligently into his pocket gripping his gun. As he strode out, he suddenly swung the briefcase high in the air and crashed it down on to the rifle of the guard on his left. The force of the blow spun the briefcase from his hand, but he jumped to the left and was five strides into the wood before the guard had recovered. He heard their shouted, "Halt!" and a rifle shot crashed past him, ricocheting in a wailing scream through the branches.

Pechal spun round, his revolver in his hand. Now was the opportunity to put to the test all those weeks of practice in snap shooting. He fired at the torch which the guard, with the utter stupidity which Pechal had sensed, was waving in his direction. A glare of flame-coloured light enveloped him for an instant, as the bullet belched from the barrel; he felt the weapon jerk in his hand. The guard screamed and dropped. The torch, its beam still bright, rolled aimlessly on the ground, and the man went on screaming.

He fired at the remaining guard. He had practised this sort of game so often in Scotland, and only half believed the burr-voiced instructor who always said, "Practise, laddie, practise! One day your life might depend on it!" Two more rifle shots crashed through the bushes. He steadied himself and fired twice at the figure outlined against the sky. His shooting was good. The second guard also screamed and dropped his rifle. He began to stagger in the direction of the village shouting "Help! Help!" The other guard lying on the ground was silent now.

For two seconds Pechal stood frozen. Should he chase him, kill him? The briefcase. Where was it? Somewhere on the ground? But the ground was pitch dark. "Oh Christ," he thought, "which shadow is it in?"

The firing had attracted attention. Shouts were coming from the village now. Lights were flashing along the road. Against their brilliance he could see the sentry staggering along yelling, "Help! Help! Murder!"

He scrabbled despairingly in the ditch. No briefcase! Well, to the devil with it! He jumped out of the bushes and raced back along the road, running at full speed. He turned off right when he got to the forest track. Obviously it led to the border, and it was unlikely they would have more than one patrol guarding that particular segment. He jog-trotted for half an hour before he permitted himself a rest. He sat with his back against a tree, the sweat pouring down his face and thickening in the stubble of his beard.

The sweat ran in cold rivulets down his back. He could hardly breathe. Then, as he remembered his elementary and fatal mistake, an awful sickness filled his stomach. His identity card! It was still in the breast pocket of one of the guards.

It was too much for him. He doubled over and was physically sick. Poor Pechal! He was such a brave and patriotic young man. But from the very start nothing went right for him. Nothing.

He was soon to know that he was hunted; but the train of events which led to this situation was yet another extension of his fatal ill-fortune.

When the wounded guard's cries brought help from the nearby village, the police had found his companion guard dead in the road with his torch, like a single glowing eye, still shining upon him. In the ditch they found Pechal's briefcase packed with banknotes. It was then they started waking senior Gestapo officers.

They carried the badly wounded guard back to the village, but Pechal's shooting had been accurate and deadly. He lapsed into unconsciousness and died as the sun came up next morning. He spoke not a single word, but in the breast pocket of his uniform, they discovered an identity card belonging to one Oldrich Pesar of Otrokrovice, and pasted inside was a photograph and description of this man.

As soon as it was light, German officials were on the phone to Otrokrovice, scaring out of bed registrars and civic officials, and all who had access to the records. In all the files there was no trace of "Oldrich Pesar". He simply did not exist.

Then, with one of those coincidences so commonplace in life, but so amateurish in any sort of fiction which seeks to imitate life, into the police station walked a Czech Sergeant of the Gendarmerie just coming on duty. He had heard that they had had a spot of trouble last night. Anything serious? Two German guards shot dead? That meant serious trouble for the whole district. Any clue as to who did it? Yes, one clue. They showed him the identity card, and the sergeant's eyes rounded in excited recognition.

"Why this fellow? What's he got to do with it? I know him! We did our army service together. Oldrich Pechal. His family live in Moravia. . . ." And then he became aware of the hush suddenly enclosing him, aware of the sudden movement of the German officials towards him. He looked around at the hostile eyes. He was an ordinary country policeman who wished to do his duty and no more; he did not want to implicate any of his own countrymen. But the words had jumped out, and it was too late now. It was all up with Oldrich Pechal!

When Pechal finished telling Miks and Gerik his story they tried to sleep in their rough forest shelter, and it was in the cold, grey light of morning that Pechal told them what he had decided.

"It's no use trying to go on," he said. "For the moment we can't operate as a team; it's every man for himself. None of the contacts we've been given is any good; people have no courage. We've just got to try and survive, each of us separately."

It was Miks who said he knew one more contact in the north who he was sure would help them.

"No," said Pechal, "it's no good."

"But what are you going to do?" demanded Miks.

"I don't know," said Pechal. "I shall stay here for a bit. I must see what happens to my family."

Miks shook his head in distress. Life to him had long been an affair of blacks and whites. People were either good or bad. If they were bad you fought them and destroyed them, but all this was puzzling beyond belief. If only he could have summoned rhetoric to his aid, if only his feeling of shame could have become articulate, he would have said: "We came here to fight, to resist, not to rejoin our families. We still have duties." But he did not have the words to fashion this verbal resistance, so he said nothing.

They left Pechal in the forest, and Gerik and Miks went by train to Brno. Gerik had memorized the address of a lady given to him in England. She lived in Wenceslas Square, Prague. Surely, if she could not help them they would find some sort of shelter amongst the thousands of people there? Surely in Prague they could get in touch with the resistance? But Miks was going north to his contact which he knew was good because it was his own fiancée, and invited Gerik to go with him.

Gerik was set on Prague. If Miks found shelter in the north perhaps they could join up later in that city. He would stay at the Hotel Julia and leave word there for Miks as to where he could be found. They parted on those terms.

So Miks travelled to his village to the north of Prague, and his fiancée, as he had hoped, welcomed him rapturously. He stayed there for a few days while careful inquiries were made by friends on his behalf, and then he was passed down the resistance line to Prague, and so into the company of the four men who sat around him.

For a few seconds after Miks had finished his story no one spoke. There was little they could say. This was a disaster they had not expected.

Then Jindra said, "This other friend of yours—Gerik. We must do something about him."

Miks had heard nothing more of Gerik. No, he had not yet called at the Hotel Julia. Someone could make inquiries there but it was most unlikely that he would still be there.

Jan volunteered to make the call that very evening; and Josef offered to go with him. Jindra vetoed that idea; only one must go. With Pechal lost, and four of the other parachutists still unaccounted for, no extra risks must be taken. Jan could investigate with Anna; they could drink a beer at the bar, if they had a bar, and afterwards decide on the spot if it was discreet to make inquiries.

That evening, Jan met Anna at Auntie Marie's. Mrs. Moravec saw quite a lot of them these days; she was in sympathy with their situation, and they understood this and were grateful to her. Her advice to them was perhaps unoriginal, but it gave much consolation. "Don't wait and don't waste time," she counselled. "You are young but once, and then shortly. If you are in love, marry if you can, but don't wait. You will have plenty of time to wait under the earth. That you should have fallen in love during a war is bad luck, but that you should have fallen in love at all is a God-granted compensation."

That night they walked out under a clear sky to search for Gerik, but it is doubtful if their thoughts wholly concerned him. At either end of the ancient Charles Bridge the old towns of Prague have grown: on the left bank the old houses stretch up to the castle, and on the right they turn and twist until they reach the old town square.

There is much more to Prague than this; there are sprawling suburbs, criss-crossed by tram tracks, upon which squat and dingy monsters jangle and screech; there are huge apartment houses without beauty or elegance, staring out of black utilitarian windows across grey pavements. But practically all that is lovely, historic, romantic and necessary to the mind's eye lies at either end of the bridge.

Across the river from the castle, the narrow streets wind below windows barred with heavy iron grilles fashioned five hundred years ago. From every dark cornice, medieval saints, fashioned from stone, look down upon you, and with a motionless, uplifted, bird-limed finger offer a prayer for your passing.

Upon the parapet of the ancient bridge which steps with eight high arches across the swirling Vltava, other saints petrified in stone are set above each buttress. And upon the central arch, Christ crucified in stone hangs upon His Cross. It is a noble bridge built by the greatest emperor Bohemia ever knew; and if the tyrant, Hitler, had had but the simple intelligence to erect just such another monument, celebrating the devoted and endless dignity of man, perhaps today he would be remembered for other things besides his villainy.

Under the arches of the seven bridges that link the city across the Vltava, the river moves tranquilly, and shining, making its smooth half-moon journey through the heart of the city with a gentle ever-present murmur of water. It flows smooth-backed over its many shallow weirs, between tall embankments of water-worn stone, and there is a singular beauty in this natural juxtaposition of stone façade, turret and tower, mirrored and changing in the reflecting water. When the dusk comes and the spires grow suddenly upwards against the darkening sky in bewildering profusion, there is in this ancient city of Prague a continuing and durable magic. For lovers, to be in Prague in the spring is pure enchantment. To Jan and Anna, all their journeyings through the old city, whether in rain or wind, in sunshine or moonlight, were moments of serene happiness.

But it was with caution that they approached the Hotel Julia, which lay in a side street near Wenceslas Square. It was dingy, and no suspicious characters appeared to hang around its door. They walked past it a couple of times, and Jan made his decision. It had no bar that they could see; therefore without preliminaries he had to inquire at the reception desk. He told Anna she must wait for him outside the Bata Shoe Shop in Wenceslas Square while he went inside. If anything looked the slightest bit suspicious when he reached the desk—if he suspected for one moment that the Nazis had baited a trap—he would ask for a room, haggle about the price and leave. If things seemed normal he would inquire directly about Gerik. If he did not reappear at the Bata Shoe Shop in twenty minutes, she could assume the worst and report to Jindra without wasting a second.

She knew him too well to protest, and with but one anguished glance left him to walk towards Wenceslas Square and her appointed station. Jan watched her out of sight, then he walked boldly through the hotel doors and approached the desk. The clerk was elderly, thin and appeared disinterested in everything except the newspaper he was reading. He turned his eyes wearily up from its pages. Jan drew in a breath and made his usual snap decision.

"You have a friend of mine staying here?" he asked. He stared straight at the clerk, his nerves taut, waiting for any sign that the old man was seeking to trap him. The clerk sighed, put down his paper and came to the desk. He swung open the big ledger on one side of the counter.

"Name?" he demanded.

Jan gave him the false name inscribed on Gerik's identity card, and the forefinger, yellowed with nicotine, traced its way down the lined page.

"A young man," said Jan, "with fair hair."

The clerk's finger stopped at a signature. "He's gone," he said. "Stayed for two nights, and then he left."

Jan asked as many more questions as he dared. Had he left a forwarding address? Had he moved to another hotel? Had the clerk any idea where he might find him? All the man's answers were negative. He was bored with the questions and wanted only to return to his newspaper.

Jan thanked him and walked back along the streets and into Wenceslas Square to rejoin Anna. She gripped his arm tightly, and he told her what had happened. They walked thoughtfully down the length of the long square, discussing all manner of possibilities. Where could he have got to? What could have happened to him? But in all their wild guesses they did not get near the truth. That—much later —the official German records would reveal.

Gerik had gone from Brno to Prague by train. With his forged identity card he had passed all the check points without trouble. He walked through the noisy streets and saw that people were shabby, wearing drab overcoats or raincoats, and that there was little to buy in the shop windows. He found the flat in Wenceslas Square he was looking for. The lady whose address he had memorized no longer lived there and no one knew where she had gone. So that was one more failure.

He had one last hope, a small one. On his training course as a radio operator, a friend had urged him that if he ever ended up in Prague, he must be sure to go and see his fiancée and give her his love. Her father kept a shop near the centre of Prague; Gerik had memorized that address also.

He decided to try it. The shop proved quite easy to find; the girl's father stood behind the counter. Gerik did not have to ask many questions. The fiancée, it seemed, had not bothered to wait for her boy friend in Britain; she had married someone else.

At this news Gerik paused irresolutely. But now things were so desperate that he decided to confide in the father; he seemed a good-natured, talkative fellow. Gerik began to explain his plight but at the word "parachutist", all the father's friendliness disappeared. Hide Gerik? Impossible! Sheltering an unregistered person was punishable by death. You couldn't trust anybody these days. It would soon get known that he was hiding a stranger. It needed only one word to the Germans and his life and Gerik's also would be forfeit. "Madness!" he muttered. "Madness!"

"But what can I do?" pleaded Gerik. "There's nothing left. Either I shoot myself—or give myself up!"

"Listen," said the shopkeeper, "do what you like, but don't hang around here. I don't know you, do I? I've never seen you before, have I? But I'm not a bad fellow and I'll tell you what I'll do. Here's a ration coupon for a pound of bread, and here's another for half a pound of meat. Sorry I can't do more. But you understand, don't you? It would be madness to hide you."

Dejectedly Gerik went back to Wenceslas Square. He found the Hotel Julia in a side street and registered there. He went up to his room and lay on the bed. He closed his eyes and tried to sleep, but sleep would not come. When sleep did come at last, it was broken with terrifying nightmares, and when he woke the sheets were wet with perspiration. If only Miks would come! Maybe then everything would turn out all right. What would happen when his money gave out? What would happen if Miks did not come? Whom could he turn to? He had an identity card, that was all; no job, no insurance cards. A sudden raid by the Gestapo, and where would he be? He passed his hand over his unshaven face and decided to go out and find a barber. At least it would pass the time and give him some small contact with humanity.

There was no one else in the barber's shop, and the man chatted about the weather, about the food situation and about the Germans. After ascertaining that his customer was Czech, he became very rude about the Germans. Realizing that Gerik was new to Prague, he fed him with all the current jokes. By now Gerik was prepared to try anything. Maybe the barber would help him. And so, with incredible naivety, he told his story once more; that he was a parachutist who had just landed. Could the barber help him? Otherwise he was finished. The barber was shocked into silence. Help him! But Heavens, what Gerik asked was impossible! He was sorry for him but he had a wife and family to consider. A man with a wife and family could not take risks like that, could he? If others better placed than he could not help, what could he, a poor barber, do? Maybe if Gerik hung on, something would turn up. He took his money, thanked him, and Gerik walked out into the streets again. And now it seemed to him that there was only one course left.

He had time. He had money. He had a false identity card. He knew that somewhere in Prague the resistance existed. But he had the wrong sort of courage. The barber was the last person he turned to. He went back to the hotel and spent the night there. In the morning Miks had still not arrived. Gerik went downstairs into the lobby and paid his bill. He walked through Wenceslas Square, turned into National Street and made his way to Police Headquarters. He went inside. There was a policeman at a small desk and Gerik said, "Can you take me to the Chief?"

The policeman's eyes opened. "What do you want?"

"I have some information for him," said Gerik.

Something in Gerik's voice convinced the man he was not joking. He beckoned to another policeman lounging against the wall and they led him through into an office where a third and older man was sitting.

The position of the average Czech policeman at this time was difficult. When the Nazis took over Czechoslovakia in 1939 they also took over the police. To achieve promotion you had to please the Nazis. Many of the senior officers made certain they did this. Others had second and third thoughts. To resign meant you were protesting against the Nazi regime. Therefore few resigned. Many kept their noses clean, obeyed orders, kept on with their jobs. Others—the gallant ones—kept their jobs and did all they could for the forces of resistance.

"I am a parachutist," said Gerik simply. He was conscious now that the two policemen had taken up positions on either side of him. At a nod from their superior they pulled his arms roughly behind his back, handcuffed him, searched him and removed his revolver.

"A parachutist—eh?" The older policeman looked up with narrowed eyes. "The Gestapo will be interested in you." He picked up the phone and asked for a number.

Not far away stood the large bank called Petschek House. It had extensive vaults and strongrooms, and as soon as the Gestapo arrived in Prague they commandeered this building. It appeared that some of their macabre entertaining and questioning needed the security of sound-proof rooms and strong bars. They took Gerik to Petschek House. Few Czechs taken there after arrest ever talked about it, but Gerik was one of them.

At the Gestapo Headquarters he made a statement. "I became a parachutist simply to return to Czechoslovakia," he said. "I am a Slovak. I despise the resistance movement." He told them all he could. He told them where he had dropped and what had happened to him. He revealed all he knew about conditions in England and the names of all the men who had trained in Special Forces with him. He told them that there were six men in his plane—that three other parachutists had dropped after them; that Pechal was hiding in the forest near Vresovice; he gave them the home addresses of both Miks and Pechal. He also told them where they had hidden the transmitter the first night they had dropped. Never had the Gestapo possessed a more willing captive.

Fleischer, the Gestapo Chief who interrogated him, had no need to threaten torture. All he had to do was to suggest rewards and Gerik performed like a trained dog. With Gerik as guide and a squad of Gestapo men, Fleischer went to the barn where they had hidden the transmitter. A group of villagers gathered round wondering what was happening. The Gestapo left Gerik quite alone and the village people were able to talk to him.

He was full of self-importance, almost arrogant. He admitted he was a parachutist from England, but protested he had only become one in order to return to Czechoslovakia. He was going to take the transmitter back to Prague and use it to contact London. The Allies had lost the war. It was better to fight on the German side, anyhow.

He grew a little angry as the villagers cross-questioned him curiously. Naively he boasted of the money the Germans had given him, and of the fine life he was going to have. When the villagers were sceptical and suggested that as soon as the Gestapo had finished with him, he would be lucky to end up in a concentration camp, he became even angrier and blustered and swore. A gendarme who was there, ostensibly to keep the villagers at bay, whispered under his breath that if ever an opportunity to escape from the Gestapo appeared, he should avail himself of it rapidly for it was his only hope. Gerik laughed at this. He was much too valuable to the Germans, he bragged. They were going to see he had plenty of money and would be able to live exactly as he pleased.

It was not really strange that the Nazis should allow Gerik to talk openly to the villagers. He was the bait to attract bigger fish. They did not publish or broadcast the news of his treachery; they knew that by allowing the villagers to listen, the resistance would hear about it soon enough. And then who could tell what might happen? Perhaps other resistance men, other parachutists, hearing how well informers were treated, might also attempt to change sides.

They were correct in their elementary psychology. The resistance "grapevine" did pick up the news. The gendarme went back to his headquarters and talked, and there were many ears to appreciate his story. Within a few hours, the Jindra group knew that one of the men, whose arrival they had anticipated so eagerly, had turned traitor.

To Jan and Josef the news was unbelievable. Their immediate reaction was to demand that their plan to assassinate Heydrich should be carried out at once. Who knew how much the Nazis might already suspect? It was already early April. Heydrich must be killed now! It was Jindra who calmed them down. He assured them that Gerik knew nothing of importance; his knowledge was limited to his own experiences. He could betray Pechal and Miks and the names of the other three parachutists who had jumped after him, but he did not know what they were doing or where they were operating. He knew nothing of Jan or Josef and of their plan. He knew nothing of the Jindra group and its objectives. London could be warned that fake radio transmissions might be tried.

But where *were* the other three parachutists, protested Jan and Josef? What had happened to them?

In answering their question Jindra's face was as impassive as the trunk of a tree. They would turn up, he assured them; they would turn up in their own good time. And he was right, as so often he was right. But what he did not anticipate and what he could not predict, was the possibility that a second potential traitor might arrive with these newcomers.

CHAPTER NINE

JINDRA was right. News of the other trio of parachutists was not long in coming. Two days later, their leader, Lieutenant Adolph Opalka, arrived in Prague, and he brought with him plans for an exploit which vaguely disturbed both Jan and Josef.

When Opalka parachuted from the aircraft he joined up with his two companions in the darkness without much difficulty. They quickly ascertained where they were and discovered that luckily the homes of all three of them were within a radius of thirty miles. It would be better therefore, for the time being, decided Opalka, if they separated and sought shelter for a few days. When they were certain they were safe, they could make contact with their "address", a printer in the nearby town of Lazne Belohrad. This, although Opalka did not know it at the time, was a contact vetted by the Jindra group and perfectly safe.

Opalka reached the house of his aunt in Resice. He arrived late at night and at first she would not believe it was her nephew. He also met, for the first time in three years, his wife Miluska. It was a brief encounter which could last for three days only, for he had important news to give to Prague. So he went to find the printer in Lazne Belohrad and was passed on to the Jindra group.

They gathered again in the flat Jindra used for meetings of this kind and Opalka met Jan and Josef and Valchik, who had now come to join them in Prague, Jindra and Uncle Hajsky. He told them of the special requests he had brought from London.

One of the most important targets in Europe at that moment, as far as the R.A.F. were concerned, was the great Skoda arms factory at Pilsen, but it was a long, long journey through the night from England. For heavy bombers to reach it from their bases, and return safely, meant that they would have to pin-point their target with accuracy, spend but a short time above it, and turn quickly for home. What the R.A.F. bomber pilots would appreciate, above all, was some sort of identifying markers which would indicate the target. The task of the Czech resistance, said Opalka, was to place those markers.

"It will mean," he continued, "a party of us going to Pilsen to explore the countryside around the factory, and finding two beacons—a haystack or a barn full of hay—one on either side of the Skoda Works. When we have discovered these things we will radio the information to London, and they will tell us at which precise minute to light our beacons."

It was a challenging request, and it was Jan who made the first objection.

"What about *our* job?" he said. "Surely it should have absolute priority. It's all very well planning these other things, but we didn't come here to light bonfires for the R.A.F."

Jindra looked closely at him. The change in him was becoming more obvious every day. Both he and Josef had arrived self-confident, assertive, alert, watchful and suspicious. But the realization that they were among friends had slowly retarded their eagerness for action. They had become too relaxed and friendly. Jindra knew that, as far as Jan was concerned, Anna Malinova had had something to do with that process; and quite recently, Josef had also got himself, not only a girl friend, but a fiancée. After the Pechal incident it had been decided to move all the parachutists to different addresses. Jan and Josef had left Auntie Marie's, although they still made it their headquarters, and moved to the house of Mr. Fafka, an ex-soldier who worked for the Red Cross. Liboslava, his daughter, was nineteen, pretty and gay, and it took Josef approximately seven days to fall in love with her, and she with him.

But the Pechal disaster had provided a jolt for both Jan and Josef, which jerked them out of their state of indulgence; and Jan, particularly.

To Jindra, he seemed a young man who had added measurably to his stature since his arrival; there was now a maturity about everything he did. He was, reflected Jindra almost with sadness, growing up. And Jindra could also observe without much difficulty that he was entering a third phase; he was becoming irritable, edgy and nervous, not only because he knew they had a dangerous job to do, but because they seemed to be no closer to getting it done.

Jindra also knew that they were aware he was holding them back over a major issue; he had already told them that he thought their plan to attack Heydrich, in his car, in the open street was suicidal; he had requested an alternative plan. The least they could do, he said bluntly, was to continue their investigations. Surely there must be some other method which was both safe and more certain? Only reluctantly would he give his consent to their making the attempt in their own way.

Jindra knew he had no absolute authority to prevent Jan and Josef making the attempt how they chose. London had sent them, and London was still pressing for the job to be done. But both young men recognized Jindra's leadership; and also recognized that it was absurd to quarrel amongst themselves. Both protested that a swift attack on the bend at Kobylisky was the action most likely to succeed, and probably the best plan they would discover. If it was suicidal, then that was their hard luck; a chance they would have to take. They had come prepared for that. They considered that the most relevant and immensely important fact they had uncovered was that when Heydrich went by plane to Berlin, he almost invariably drove to the airport in his green Mercedes accompanied only by the chauffeur, and without any other escort. If they could catch Heydrich and Klein in their car, on that corner, they were certain they could kill both of them. Josef would sweep the windscreen of the car with a blast of Sten gun fire, and if necessary Jan would finish the job with a couple of grenades.

But Jindra did not agree. "Wait!" he said, knowing they were tired of waiting, knowing that they craved action at any price. Therefore, if for no other reason than that it kept the two boys occupied, he welcomed Lieutenant Opalka's arrival with the plan to reduce the Skoda Works to ruin.

He had already anticipated their resistance, and he went quietly about the job of demolishing their arguments.

"It's not a matter of priority," he explained patiently, "but of urgency. The nights are getting lighter now. Lighter and shorter. If the R.A.F. are to attempt the operation they will have to do it quickly, otherwise they will be caught by the dawn still over Germany and the Nazi fighters will have an easy killing." He could tell by Jan's face that he had scored a point. "I suggest therefore," he continued smoothly, "that we radio London through 'Libuse', letting them know that we will find and prepare our beacons before Friday, and that we will be prepared to light them on Saturday night. If the weather is favourable for flying, that is."

It did not need much argument like this to overcome the objections of Jan and Josef. Indeed, finally, it was Jan who said, "Then we haven't got much time, have we? We can start for Pilsen first thing tomorrow morning."

Jindra smiled inwardly. For the moment, Jan and Josef would be kept busy and would therefore be happy. But he was vitally aware that very soon he would not be able to restrain them any longer.

They discussed what they should do in Pilsen. Resistance was well organized amongst the railway workers there, and it would be fairly simple to find someone to put them up when they reached that town. They discussed who should go and decided upon Jan and Valchik, Josef and Opalka. Anna, also, who by now was a recognized member of the team.

They had also heard that day that one of the other members of Opalka's trio had already reported at the printers in Lazne Belohrad. This was Sergeant Major Karel Curda, a tough and taciturn n.c.o. in whom Opalka had great faith.

"I would like him to be included in the party if possible," said Opalka. "This was our special assignment when we left England. But can he reach us in time?"

It was Jan who suggested that he was certain Auntie Marie's son, Ata, would gladly make the journey to the printers at Lazne and bring the Sergeant Major back to

Prague. If necessary he could then take him on to Pilsen. Ata, Jan explained to Opalka, was a thoroughly reliable young man who had already acted as a courier upon several occasions. He seemed eager to become even more closely associated with their work.

Jindra thought it a good suggestion and the idea was approved. Before they left, they discussed the other news which Lieutenant Opalka brought. Opalka was tall, serious, almost thirty; he gave one the feeling of being reserved and withdrawn. He had a long lean face, a high forehead and blue eyes which looked out inquiringly into a complicated world. He spoke quietly and decisively, like a man whose purpose was clear and knew exactly where he was going, and what he intended to do when he got there. Both Jan and Josef knew him, but not well. His commission and the British officer system had kept them apart during their training period in England, but they had been on forced marches in his company, attended lectures, walked and talked on those high and misty moorlands of northern Scotland, and they knew he was someone upon whom reliance could be placed.

If Lieutenant Opalka possessed a weakness, it rested perhaps in his deep sensitivity: his overwhelming concern for his subordinates, for human values and relations, factors which are more often submerged and ignored in the exigencies of war. But these qualities were also his strengths. Determined above all things to acquit himself well in his rôle as a resistance worker, he had trained himself as zealously as a priest for his vocation. He was known as a man who walked often alone in the hills, a man who thought before he spoke, a man of inflexible determination and purpose.

Jindra was very content when he discerned the sort of man Opalka was. The addition of Valchik, to Jan and Josef, had meant that now he had three irrepressibly romantic, embryo assassins under his control. He did not doubt that one day, with or without his permission, he would wake up and find that the attempt to kill Heydrich had been made, and that the wrath he anticipated would be raging. But now, with Lieutenant Opalka nominally in charge, he felt he could rely upon him to have some sort of sobering influence upon them; now, Jindra decided, he could at least delegate a little of his authority.

The other news that Opalka brought was that London wished to parachute more teams into Czechoslovakia towards the end of April.

"But not with the same disastrous consequences as those of Pechal's party," he added seriously. "In future, we must be quite certain we know where, and when, they are going to land; and if we cannot meet them, they must have reliable addresses to contact as soon as they touch down. We must prepare adequate dropping zones, and unless aircraft can land the parachutists right on the appropriate D.Z. they must return with them to England. All this we must discuss with London before they drop another man."

The meeting broke up. They left the flat knowing exactly what each was supposed to do, and at what address in Pilsen they would meet.

Next morning Anna and Jan caught the first train alone. Lieutenant Opalka, Josef and Valchik were following at discreet intervals.

Anna sensed the unrest that the delay in the attempt upon Heydrich was causing Jan. She herself was secretly relieved at every delay, and she told Auntie Marie how she felt; but she also admitted that she understood Jan's feelings only too well.

"We could stay here in hiding until the end of the war and let others do the fighting for us," said Jan bitterly on several occasions. "You and I could slip away into the country somewhere, and I could get a job, and no one would be any the wiser!"

It was a temptation to which Anna might have surrendered only too readily, but Jan thrust it back into his subconscious. He was determined that "after the war" they should not be known as the brave parachutists who risked their lives to return to their homeland, but then took good care never to risk another thing. "The freedom of Czechoslovakia," he declared vehemently, and such trite phrases came easily and were perhaps necessary in wartime, "must be earned!"

But sometimes, when they were alone together, he sighed, "If only——"

How ironical it was, that he, strong in his purpose, shaping to deliver the blow which would kill the tyrant, had glanced aside and seen Anna. And fallen in love! His life, closed and dedicated to one narrow ambition, was now suddenly open and full of promise. The future, to a man with no future, was suddenly infinitely desirable.

To Auntie Marie, Anna revealed much of herself. Anna told her how she dreamed of waking up one morning and finding that the stupid war was over; she dreamed of having children to send to school; of seeing shop windows crammed with luxuries; of sleeping soundly each night, free from the inner dread that somewhere in the recurrent nightmare that hammering on the door would become real; she dreamed of opening a morning newspaper liberated from the tangible fear that there in the front columns, she would find the name or names of her friends, who but a few short hours previously had kept a final appointment with the executioner. All this she compressed inside herself, hiding it from Jan, because she knew that from her, above all from her, he needed reassurance and certitude. But sometimes when she could no longer control her feelings, she wept bitterly and hopelessly on Auntie Marie's shoulder.

And Auntie Marie, with her own son far away and in danger, and her own life possibly forfeit at a second's notice for the continuous help and encouragement she was giving to the group, still had enough motherliness and pity and deep humanity to hold her and comfort her, and tell her that the future was full of hope and that one day they would all laugh about these times of worry and trouble.

Above all it was Auntie Marie who realized that there was, in this love of Jan Kubis for Anna Malinova, some measure of desperate poetry, and perhaps some purposeful move in the enigmatic strategy of nature, and she told Jindra as much. It would seem that a man's love for a woman is the core of the matter, the recurrent cliché separating life from death, giving continuity to its grandeur and mystery and enchantment to its trivialities. She knew that there was a defiance in this sudden commitment which was not in accordance with the rest of Jan's character. He was a reserved, withdrawn young man, obsessed by his passion for revenge and dedicated to his task. But Auntie Marie knew that upon the lips and gently submissive breasts of Anna Malinova, he found a peace and an answer which was both an ecstasy and a completion.

He knew that a parachutist has no time for dalliance, no time for falling in love. It is woman with her immediate dreams who sends new thoughts and ideas racing through a man's head. Blue rifts open upon a horizon which should be grey and cold as a shroud. Jan knew himself that this had happened and Jindra sensed as much without being told by Auntie Marie. Jindra knew much more about Jan than Jan ever suspected. Jindra knew that there were moments with a woman close, and life as urgent as the spring, when it would seem such an arid and hopeless business, this daily tracking of a fellow human, intent only upon death.

Jindra knew that somehow Jan had to reaffirm his purpose and strengthen his will, drag himself out of the romantic, warm, secure and tender intimacies, endlessly original and endlessly surprising, that link a man and woman. Jindra knew that Valchik was right; that Jan should perhaps never have fallen in love. Love could make cowards of them all; love needed continuity, and for Jan that was certainly a situation he could neither envisage nor ensure.

Jindra knew all this and said nothing. He watched the tightness creeping into the set of Jan's mouth and said nothing. He observed his despair, excitements, passion and boredom, and still said nothing. He knew they were all symbols in a complicated equation, and that if one of the symbols—one of the minus or plus, alpha or beta signs were missing—the equation would not work out, and they would have failed. He also knew that it was possible, in the overall aspects of war strategy, that their particular equation might formulate something as unproductive as that of those indefatigable gentlemen in arithmetical problems, who endlessly walk from A to B, at so many miles an hour, or fill tanks with buckets of water at so many gallons a minute. But like those gentlemen, they were committed irrevocably to their task. And he knew Jan would not fail.

Anna Malinova also sensed this purpose in Jan; a purpose as uncomplicated, as deep and dedicated as that of any mystic or visionary. She felt also that this dedication might in the end destroy him. But that thought she kept concealed in some deep pocket of her subconscious, for she too in her way was equally dedicated. The Nazis had killed her husband. Without deference to her, they had taken her life and ripped it in half like an old bus ticket, and contemptuously thrown both pieces away. Although her grief was no longer bitter, she had not forgotten or forgiven, and because she found in Jan a compelling consolation for her deep sorrow this fact did not alter her hatred for the oppressors.

Many good things they had between them. They were never plagued by the thought that perhaps their dedication was all futility and moonshine, a chimera of nonsense. They were buttressed and strengthened by the thought that if they succeeded in killing Heydrich, the road was clear for another step towards victory. And with victory won they were certain common sense would prevail. Josef could wed his Liboslava; Adolf Opalka could return to his wife, and Jan and Anna could together start their journey into the future.

If they lived with danger, at least it heightened all their perceptions. There was stimulation in every dawn, and every dusk, and yesterday was a memory to be treasured. They discussed endlessly the house they would live in and the children they would bear. And if sometimes Anna would stop in the middle of a sentence with a small, cold mouse of despair gnawing at her heart, she revealed these thoughts only to Auntie Marie.

So they sat together in the train going to Pilsen, watching the countryside full of new leaves and spring blossoms moving past, watching the cows munching in the fields, watching the hills lift and fall about them, watching the sun rise up the blue sky.

They had no difficulty in finding the flat of a railway

worker who had already been informed that they needed accommodation. He told them that he had sent his wife away to her mother's for a few days; he himself expected to be away, travelling with his train for at least three nights. They would have the flat to themselves. He did not know what they were doing and did not wish to know. He handed Jan his keys and wished them good luck.

Josef, Valchik and Lieutenant Opalka were not long in arriving after them, Valchik carrying the suitcase which contained his portable radio transmitter and receiver. It was not the best of instruments, but it was powerful enough to transmit and receive a morse signal from London. There were several beds in the apartment, and they knew that at least they would have a comfortable night.

Josef laughed and joked with both Anna and Jan. And he had news for them.

"When we have finished with Heydrich," he said confidentially, "Liboslava and I are going to get married. Yes, at once!"

He laughed at Jan's raised eyebrows and pooh-poohed his suggestion that they might both be sent back to England, and that perhaps army regulations forbade a soldier to get married on active service.

Josef declared quite urbanely that he did not care. Liboslava and he would get married and consult the army authorities when and if they arrived in Prague.

For Josef, unlike Jan, was not prepared to wait until "after the war". Josef understood very well that there is only one time to laugh, and that is now, and that there is only one time to make love, and that is now. Josef knew in his bones that there was no time to waste. And how could Liboslava resist, confronted by this gay and passionate young man who urged her constantly to marry him?

Liboslava, gay and pretty as a lark, made up her mind very quickly. She said "Yes", and to the slight consternation of her parents they became engaged at once.

If Anna Malinova possessed any slight and private envy, she did not show it to Jan, either by look or word. Indeed it was a very gay and spirited little party that dined off bread and a peculiar assortment of tinned goods that night in the flat. Afterwards they gathered around Valchik's set to see if they could make contact with London. They could and did: it had never been easier. Valchik passed the message to London that they were in position in Pilsen, that the weather was mild and springlike and looked like continuing. Tomorrow, he informed London, they would search for inflammable barns, or haystacks, or buildings, which stood in the correct juxtaposition to the Skoda factory. Almost certainly, they would be ready to light these marker beacons on Saturday night, at any hour, if the R.A.F. were really coming.

The reply was also confident. The meteorological reports were good. If they continued good, the R.A.F. were certainly coming. On Friday night London would radio final instructions to them.

It was shortly after Valchik had signed off, that a knock came on the door and they found that Ata Moravec had arrived. He had had no difficulty in contacting Sergeant Major Karel Curda, and here he was, duly delivered. Ata was bright-eyed with excitement at his success. He found it all romantic and very thrilling. The thought that not only was he in the same room as real and experienced saboteurs but was also actually assisting them, was a kind of intoxication in his mind. His dark, curly hair was awry, his face was flushed and he was very happy. The man he had collected, and brought first to his mother's flat in Prague and then on to Pilsen, was of a completely different character. Although he shook hands all round and everyone welcomed him warmly, he did not smile.

Jan and Josef had known Karel Curda both before, and during, the training course in Scotland; and although they found him rather dogmatic and self-assured, they liked him well enough. He seemed a competent, reliable sort.

Curda was thirty years old, of medium height with a well-shaped head and brown eyes. Before he fled to Poland to continue the fight against the Nazis, he had worked as a customs officer. He rarely smiled because he rarely relaxed —and he was often afraid. The future would condemn him wholly, but in those early days he had put his courage to the test and so far it had not broken. Millions of men in those days endured and survived the war, fought if it was necessary, died if their luck was out, were content to obey orders, and never had to put their courage or their manhood decisively to the test.

The spirit and the manhood of Karel Curda were not in doubt. Facing other odds he might have emerged with honour and dignity. The odds he was to face were beyond his comprehension or his endurance. The wrong sluice gate was opened and his courage ran away. That was his tragedy.

They were all anxious to know what had happened to Curda after he parted from Opalka, and whether or not he had heard of the third member of their team. He told them that he had not, but he did tell them something of what had happened to him. He did not tell them that the girl he loved lived only a few miles from his mother's house, where he first found shelter. He did not tell them that risking more than he should, he had asked his sister to arrange a meeting with her. And there, meeting the girl he courted three years ago, before he fled the country, he had found that she had had a child. His child!

In tears because she was so happy to see him, she showed him a photograph of the son he had never seen. He stared at it solemnly and if there was some deep and fundamental cerebral change inside his head he did not reveal it, for his face did not alter. He, in his turn, gave her his own photograph, telling her to take it to the authorities after the war should anything happen to him. In this way, perhaps she and the baby would be cared for, and given a pension.

For an hour or two there was understanding and tenderness between them, and when she left, perhaps the first small seedling of resentment had rooted itself, that life could treat him so unjustly. He could not use his strength or intelligence to protect and cherish this girl and her son who depended upon him. Instead he must go out and live with fear and suspicion; the chance of a horrible death as close a neighbour as the beat of his own heart.

But in the flat with the others, Karel Curda did not talk like this. He told his story quietly and soberly and listened with interest when Opalka outlined plans for the next day. "We shall split into pairs and explore the countryside to the east and west of Pilsen and the Skoda factory on foot," said Opalka. "Within two miles on either side of the factory, we must find a barn filled with hay, or a haystack, something at least which will burn brightly, and quickly, and be easily seen from the air. With two blazing beacons on which to line up their bombing run, the R.A.F. should have no trouble at all in blasting the target."

And then it was Valchik's turn. He explained how they had to place a lighted candle amongst the straw, with a small, open bottle of petrol nearby. It was very simple really. The slow-burning candle gave one the opportunity to get well away; but as soon as the naked flame touched the straw, and the flame met the bottle of petrol—whoosh!

The prospect was exciting and no one slept very well that night. Next morning they set off in pairs, each to explore a different segment of the town. They travelled prosaically by tram to the outskirts. It was late when they came back that evening. Each couple had, without much difficulty, found various barns, haystacks and buildings which they were sure would burn. They compared their locations and marked their positions on the map. It was going to be very annoying for the owners, they decided, when they discovered that their fine barns were blazing pyres, but it was a sacrifice the farmers would have to match against the price of final victory. Maybe after the war some sort of compensation could be arranged.

After supper they gathered round Valchik's radio set, watching the glowing valves and mysterious coils, watching his forefinger bouncing on the Morse key, tapping the message out into the night, out across the black forest and hills, out from the heart of Europe to be caught upon the mysterious monitoring trapeze in England which netted a thousand messages from Occupied Europe every night. They watched the look of triumph on Valchik's face as the little tick-tacking answer spluttered back into his headphones, and his eager pencil raced over the block of paper. They watched until he switched off the set and slipped the earphones down to his neck.

"Tomorrow night," he said eagerly. "They'll be over the target at precisely one-fifteen a.m. We must have both barns blazing by one a.m."

Anna looked round at their excited faces, realizing that they were recapturing some of the exhilaration of those early days when they were training in Scotland, comrades aligned against a common enemy. But she knew also that this was the adventurous, the schoolboy war: tapping messages in the night, creeping out into the darkness and blowing things up with a satisfactory bang. This was war without the blood and pain, the inner betrayal, and the doubts which sat like small black crows on the clothes line of one's conscience.

Later that night they re-appraised their plan seeking for any weaknesses. They found none. For once Jan and Josef were going to split up. Josef would remain behind with Anna, so that they could examine the damage done by the bombing, and report back to Prague on Sunday. Jan and Valchik would act as one team, Opalka and Karel Curda as the other. When each team had ignited its beacon, they would make for the small town of Rokycany fifteen kilometres from Pilsen. They had checked that an early train from Pilsen stopped there on its way to Prague, and they could make the connection.

The hours next day dragged interminably; they simply did not know what to do with themselves.

Pilsen is a pleasant town lying in wooded rolling countryside, not far from the German border, but they had no mind for its pleasantries. It is famous as the home of a pale yellow lager to which it gives its name, but as far as the parachutists were concerned its interest rested only in the Skoda factory. From its assembly lines had poured the automatic weapons, the artillery, the tanks, which had once made Czechoslovakia's mechanized divisions the most potentially dangerous in pre-war Europe; weapons which were now doing that service for the Wehrmacht all over Europe.

It needed no highly skilled intelligence to deduce that a successful bombing raid upon the Skoda Works would seriously embarrass the Nazis. The area was not well defended by anti-aircraft guns. If only the R.A.F. could congregate enough bombers over the target, and if only the beacons shone brightly enough, they all knew there must be a reasonable chance that the following Sunday morning would find the factory a mass of tangled, burnt-out steel and masonry.

So they set out, late in the evening, each couple making for its appropriate destination.

Two hours later, in the darkness of the barn they had chosen, Valchik struck a match and examined the luminous dial of his watch, then put the flame to the stub of candle which Jan held in his hand. They knew that a few miles away, Opalka and Karel Curda would be doing exactly the same thing. Valchik watched while Jan placed it with reverent care amongst the straw close to the open bottle of petrol, his critical eye measuring the distance between them. The candle burned with a clear unwavering flame; it was shielded from draughts.

"That's fine," said Valchik. "Come on, no time to waste!"

Half an hour later from the vantage point of a small hill half a mile away they watched the flames shooting up from the barn. They fancied they heard the roar as the barn roof fell in and the torch of flame licked up against the dark night.

Away behind them they could see the glow of a similar fire in the sky where Opalka and Curda had accomplished their task and they congratulated themselves on their success.

When Jan and Valchik first heard the distant drone of high-flying aircraft, and then to join this basso profundo the contrapuntal crump-crump-crump of anti-aircraft batteries opening up, they could have sung aloud. They watched the pin-pricks of bright light as the shells burst high up in the darkness. The drone of the high-flying bombers was now a constant thunder overhead.

As they walked through the night towards the railway

station at Rokycany, they heard the boom of exploding bombs, and their minds formed technicolor pictures of machine-shop roofs blown skywards, and lathes and drills, unfinished tanks and guns and small arms, blackened and burned amongst the debris.

They caught the train without incident. In Prague Opalka thought it better for Karel Curda to stay only a short while and then, for the time being, return to his home in the country. But the following afternoon, Jan and Valchik and the Lieutenant met at Auntie Marie's awaiting Anna and Josef.

The radio had already broadcast the news that Sunday morning that a few Allied aircraft had penetrated the borders of Czechoslovakia and attempted to bomb Pilsen. It reported that all the bombs had fallen harmlessly in the fields on the outskirts of the town, and that no damage had been done.

None of them was prepared to believe a word of this; they waited impatiently for Josef and Anna to bring reports of spectacular damage. But as soon as they reached the flat and Jan saw their glum faces, he knew that the radio reports had not been lying propaganda. Josef informed them that the bombs had indeed been scattered in the fields far from the factory. Negligible damage had been done to the Skoda Works.

The raid had been a complete fiasco.

CHAPTER TEN

THROUGH the thin partition, separating his study from the dining-room, Professor Ogoun remembers how he often overheard the voices of the men raised in argument, and how he would feel the familiar thin dry fear begin to expand in his stomach as he listened.

Sometimes the absurdity of the entire business drove him to a point of utter frustration. He recalls how he imagined himself bursting in upon them, interrupting their conversation with a violent bang on the table, so that all the cheap little ashtrays and vases from Carlsbad and Pilsen and other tourist places, gathered by Mrs. Ogoun and the boys on a score of long-remembered holidays years ago, would quiver in sympathy upon their perches.

"What in the name of heaven do you think you're doing?" his imagination would shout. "How can you sit here, coolly and quietly in my respectable dining-room, and discuss whether you kill the man tomorrow or the day after? How can you discuss a political assassination—so perilous in its implications that I'm frightened even to think about it— as normally as you would discuss where you should go for your summer holidays?" Then—in this well-rehearsed imaginary scene—he would glare round at their astonished faces and continue, "Yes, I'm frightened! I wake in the night shaking with fright so that my wife thinks I've got ague and insists I prescribe something for myself. And what can I prescribe for sheer unadulterated fear—eh? Tell me a pill that will cure me. What you are attempting to do should be an impossibility, but because you are young and foolish and bold you might even succeed. And what will you have accomplished? Tell me that! Tell me that!"

With an effort Professor Ogoun would click his mind back to reality. He knew the strain was telling on him. He knew that his imaginary verbal gymnastics would peter out at this point; that he would be left standing there with his right hand stuck in the air like a cheap orator, and he would lower it uncomfortably to his side as if he was holding a wet dead fish. They would inevitably smile gently at him and say without the slightest rancour: "Now, Professor Ogoun, we respect your opinion. We admire your courage in sheltering such dangerous assassins as us, but really you must leave this business to people who know what they are doing."

He reflected how odd it was that one should slip so easily into these situations. Two months ago if someone had told him that he would be sheltering two young men, who tomorrow were going to attempt to assassinate Heydrich, he would have said they were mad.

A visit to the Red Cross had started off the whole absurd process. As senior professor in a Prague Modern High School for girls, he often had to go to the Red Cross offices. The book-keeper there was Peter Fafka. He liked the man very much; his wife also was a jolly, cheery soul. It was Mrs. Fafka who had told him that they had two parachutists hidden in their flat, two Czech soldiers noted for their bravery.

As they could not remain hidden for too long in one place, she inquired if the professor could possibly offer them accommodation for about fourteen days. He had not hesitated. He was a patriot. Of course they could stay. But, as he pointed out, they had no extra rations at home. With two teenage sons to feed it was difficult enough as it was. He could certainly take one parachutist and make do, but two would be difficult.

Mrs. Fafka had thanked him and told him not to worry about ration cards. The two boys refused to be separated; they were working on some special operation together. If he could provide accommodation, the ration books would be forthcoming.

"That is settled then," said Professor Ogoun. "They can stay and we will make them as welcome as possible." He knew as he spoke that the penalty for sheltering unregistered people was death; that the penalty for anyone working against the Reich was death. No matter how important or unimportant their contribution might be, the penalty was death for himself and all his family. But, as Professor Ogoun reflected in his philosophical way, the penalty for being a Czech was that you had to take these chances. That is, if you wished to retain your self-respect.

His youngest son was to sit for his matriculation in two weeks' time; his older son was a fine athlete busily engaged in breaking High School track records. As head of the household he was risking all their lives, but he considered it a moral obligation to do so.

His wife was gentle, calm and considerate; she did not demur when he told her what he had done; and she made a great fuss of Jan and Josef when they arrived. They were, it must be admitted, ideal guests; they rose early, at six o'clock, and did not return to the house until the evening. They helped with all the domestic duties they could. And his two sons were very thrilled to have them staying with them.

From the visits of Uncle Hajsky, a man after all in the same scholastic profession as himself, Professor Ogoun obtained a pretty fair idea of what was being planned.

In his household they made it something of a game. They drew up rules of work, agreed signals of identification and alarm and prepared answers if anything should go amiss. And in the evenings sometimes they played chess, and talked of what they would all do "after the war".

As Professor Ogoun sat in his reverie on that day, when as usual Jindra and Uncle Hajsky, Jan and Josef, Opalka and Valchik were arguing, he sighed heavily, and allowed his anger to syphon back into his body. He felt a little weary; he had been ill lately, confined to his bed with a gall-bladder complaint. In fact, nowadays, Uncle Hajsky always posed on his visits as a doctor specializing in such diseases. And he never failed to come and talk to him.

Professor Ogoun took off his glasses, polished the heavy lenses on his lawn handkerchief and replaced them on a thin, scholarly nose. He picked up his fountain pen. As he unscrewed the cap, he observed that the tiny mottled spots of brown pigmentation amongst the fine hairs on the back of his hand seemed to show up more in the strong light.

He sighed inwardly that age should so diminish a man.

He opened his pad and began to write quickly, without losing the meticulousness that always identified his handwriting. He was performing a task he considered imperative. Someone had to set on record an account of these days. He knew he could not alter the course events were taking. History had fixed the occasion firmly and immutably in its calendar of violence, and inevitably he, like everyone else, was implicated. He had examined the situation quite impartially, as one would examine a problem in chemistry. If one dipped blue litmus paper into an acid solution it turned red; if one heated mercury fulminate there was an explosion. The equation and result were known. He could see this human equation working out before his eyes. And he dreaded the result.

Therefore he had to set the story down while there was still time. He had chosen the place where he was going to bury his papers; a spot he had picked on the football pitch where his youngest son performed so creditably at right half back. He had a biscuit tin in which to hold his manuscript.

Even had the Professor known that the final fighting around Prague would so churn and burn the football pitch that his precious papers in their biscuit tin would be charred to ashes, he would not have halted in his work. Had he known also that for many months he would cower in a mental asylum in fear of his life, he would still not have halted his pen. Filling the pages in the fine small handwriting brought some peace to his soul. And someone had to leave behind an account of what they were going to do, and what they were talking about there in his dining-room. And he, if no one else, was going to do it because he believed fundamentally in the inevitability of their task, and the nobility of their purpose.

In the dining-room Jindra remembers that Jan could not understand, and did not like, the way Uncle Hajsky kept using the word "murder". He had never used it before in connection with Heydrich. Jindra knew how Jan felt; it was not murder; Josef and Jan did not think of it in that way at all. It was a necessary job; like treading on a slug, or swatting a plague-carrying fly.

Tomorrow, if all went well, the two of them would stand by that tram in Holesovice and with a shattering torrent of sub-machine gun fire, hosepipe their victim into his own, long-reserved and special corner of hell.

Murder? Certainly not! It was simple, carefully calculated justice. If ever a man deserved execution it was Acting Reichsprotector of Czechoslovakia Reinhard Heydrich.

Retribution? That was what Uncle Hajsky was harping upon. Of course it would bring retribution. This was war. You did not fight without casualties. Jan had confessed to Jindra that he sometimes wondered if Uncle Hajsky possessed the necessary "hate" which in both himself and Josef acted as a sort of internal yeast, fermenting every thought and deed. Maybe he was too academic. Uncle Hajsky had not experienced the bitterly corrosive education which both he and Josef had undergone. Ever since they arrived in Prague he had been an excellent "aide-de-camp", assisting in a variety of ways and apparently just as dedicated as they were to the task of annihilating Heydrich. But as the certainty of action grew closer his determination began to waver. He talked more of "postponement".

Jindra watched Jan turn his eyes away from Uncle Hajsky towards the blue sky filling the window. The spring in Prague was in full flood and the sunshine burst through the window in a great drift of gold. It bisected the dining-room carpet neatly in two, so that Uncle Hajsky, as he paced, was alternately in deep shadows or clear gold.

Lieutenant Opalka, Valchik, Josef and Jan had all put their points of view, but still Uncle Hajsky went on and on. Jindra knew that nothing was going to stop them now. They had waited long enough. The Sten gun and loaded magazine were already stowed neatly in Josef's bag. Jan's two hand grenades lay in the bottom of his briefcase, cool as cucumbers and much more deadly.

Jindra accepted this fact; Uncle Hajsky did not. So Jindra, understanding his dilemma, let him go on talking, although he knew the time for talking was past.

He never forgot that last meeting between them. The room, the furniture, the faces, the heated words, the arguments and counter-arguments remained fixed in his mind with the accuracy of a stenographer's report.

He recalled the events of the past month, all that had happened since the abortive raid on the Skoda factory. Another plane-load of parachutists had arrived from England; three teams, each consisting of three men, had parachuted down into a well-forested area fifty miles to the north of Prague. They had been picked up and all conveyed to safe hiding places in the city. It was only at the very last moment that tragedy had struck.

At two places in the forest they had buried transmitter gear. It was vital that this should be brought to Prague for use there. Valchik and young Ata Moravec volunteered to fetch one suitcase, Miks and one of the newly arrived parachutists, called Kouba, the other.

Jindra was glad of the opportunity of giving Miks a job to do, because he brooded constantly. It appeared that he felt he was partly responsible for Gerik's treachery and Pechal's irresolution. Where Pechal was at that moment no one knew; obviously he was living a nomad's existence in the forest somewhere.

It did not appear to be a difficult assignment and, without any premonition of danger, the two couples set off.

Valchik and Ata went by train. They got off at a lonely country station and started to walk. Their destination lay deep in the forest. They stumbled through rough country in the growing darkness, noting each landmark and hoping they were getting closer to their objective. And then suddenly the abrupt order, "Halt!" brought them to a standstill. A rifle pointed directly at them. They had walked into a guard.

It was a Czech gendarme. He approached them cautiously, warning them to keep their hands high. Both Valchik and Ata possessed revolvers, but Valchik knew at once that if either tried to draw them, one at least would die.

147

Complying with his demand, they each handed over their identity cards. He looked up into their faces, obviously making a decision far removed from his instructions.

"You fools," he said tersely. "Don't you know what's happened? Get out of here as quickly as you can. There's a path over there that isn't guarded. Now move! And quickly or you're for it."

As they hurried away into the darkness young Ata said anxiously, "What does he mean? D'you think they've discovered the radio equipment? Is that why the guards are mounted?"

"I think it's worse than that," said Valchik grimly. "It smells bad to me."

"Can't we warn Miks and Kouba?" asked Ata despairingly.

Valchik shook his head. "Too late for that. They'll have arrived before us. Let's hope to God they've had some luck. I'm beginning to think there's a jinx on poor Miks."

He was right. Miks had had no luck; no luck at all. An hour before, a few miles from the spot where Valchik and Ata were stopped, two gendarmes had suddenly moved out of the trees into the path Miks and Kouba were following.

"Halt," they shouted, rifles levelled. "Hands above your heads."

Neither Miks nor Kouba were prepared to do this. Kouba threw himself flat and rolled. Miks yanked out his pistol and fired once, twice, three times, and the rifles both spat back together. One gendarme was killed by the first shot, the other, badly wounded, slumped into a heap. But Miks was hit in the stomach. Kouba crawled towards him.

"Are you all right? Can you walk?" Miks' eyes were sick, glazed with pain and shock.

"No, I'm done for. I'm finished. You run for it."

In the distance they could hear shouting, voices drawing closer, as other patrols alerted by the sound of shots doubled towards them.

"You're not finished," said Kouba urgently. "Come on, let's get you up. I'll get my arms round you."

Miks stared at him as if he could not believe what he was

saying. "You go," he said painfully. "You've got a few minutes. I'll be all right."

"Not without you," said Kouba stubbornly. "Come on, we can hide."

"Go," said Miks. "You can still escape."

"Not without you."

"It's no use waiting for me," said Miks in agony. "I'm done for."

And to prove his contention, to leave his new comrade no alternative, to remove any sharp-edged grit of doubt that might lurk in some tiny pocket of Kouba's conscience in the future, he suddenly raised his revolver to his head, placed the muzzle against his temple and pulled the trigger.

Sickened and grief-stricken, Kouba jerked back, his face contorted. Unbelievingly he stared at the broken head, the massive body sagging in death.

The groans of the wounded guard lying nearby brought him back to the desperate reality of his own situation. He need stay no longer; Miks had removed all responsibility. He stumbled to his feet and raced back the way they had come. He ran until his heart pumped in his chest and he found tears mixed with his sweat.

When he reached Prague he told the others the story of the gallant Miks, whose luck had deserted him from the outset.

The newspapers carried other versions of the story. The German Press Agency said:

"On April 30th, 1942, at about 10 p.m. members of a Gendarmerie patrol from Kladno encountered two men of Czech nationality who were preparing to commit a felony with explosives. The criminals immediately began to fire at the Gendarmes. In the course of the shooting, Sergeant of Gendarmes Ometak was killed and Quartermaster Kominek gravely wounded. One of the perpetrators was shot. The Acting Reichsprotector has ordered the widow of Sergeant Ometak, who fell while doing his duty, to be looked after with magnanimity. The Acting Reichsprotector has expressed special recognition for the wounded quartermaster. Further, S.S. Obergruppenfuhrer Heydrich has had a suitable reward paid to the driver who contributed considerably to the discovery of the criminals, for in consequence of his presence of mind the prepared felony with explosives was successfully prevented."

It was all very simple. A farm driver had discovered the radio equipment and betrayed his discovery to the Gestapo. He had heard that the Nazis paid well for such information. He was right. They had set their trap and now Miks was dead.

They had also rewarded Gerik handsomely, although his whereabouts they did not publish. He was given an expensively furnished flat in Charles Square in the centre of Prague. He received from the police a new registration card; he was given a large weekly income, and he was allowed to come and go as he chose.

He had, of course, to be of service occasionally. On the night Miks died they came for him. Commissar Fleischer himself called at the apartment in his own car and personally drove him out to the scene.

They shone a torch down on Miks' bloody face and said, "Do you recognize him?"

And Gerik, trembling, said, "Yes, it is one of the two who dropped with me. His name is Arnost Miks."

The Gestapo Commissar himself took Gerik back to his flat and at the entrance wished him a courteous goodnight. Gerik climbed the stairs, unlocked his door and walked in upon his soft carpet. He undressed and got into his soft bed. And when he switched off his lights, he must have looked into the darkness with blank unseeing eyes, for he had much to think about.

Why Gerik should have broken and Miks endured, no one knows. What leads one man to persevere against all odds and another to break quickly like a dry stick, no one knows. During these past few decades, there have been invented a great number of methods of putting the human body and spirit to the test. But if any algebraic definitions of human suffering have been worked out, and if any graphs illustrating that despair moves upwards in a rising curve hang upon office walls, their distribution so far has been severely restricted.

It appears that the genes, and blood cells, and other physical apparatus containing the credo of human courage, have so far resisted all attempts to correlate them into a simple equation.

The death of Miks had a completely depressing effect upon the rest of the group. Another fact depressed them also. Heydrich was slowly and purposefully increasing his hold upon the country. Things were proceeding in exactly the manner which Czech intelligence in London had predicted. Soon he would have the country completely within the Nazi empire. This news affected Jan more than anyone else. After all, the task of Josef and himself was precisely to prevent this happening.

They had researched and explored diligently to try and find some other method of attacking the Acting Reichsprotector. But they were convinced that an attack upon his car at that corner in Holesovice still remained the best plan. And finally they decided they could wait no longer and would brook no more delays. When they next received word that Heydrich was leaving Prague, they were determined to put their plan into operation, no matter what Jindra said. Now they had received such news; next morning Heydrich was flying to Berlin.

Hour after hour, Jan argued with Jindra about their plan. All right, they agreed, they were just two young men on bicycles—one an old lady's machine—armed with a Sten gun, revolvers and hand grenades, against the head of the most ruthless terror organization the world had ever known. All right, it was suicidal! What did this matter if the attack was a success? And it would be a success, because they were going to press it home to the bitter end, come what may. Tomorrow Heydrich was flying to Berlin to meet the Fuhrer. Tomorrow, on that corner in Holesovice, Jan and Josef swore that their appointment should have priority.

Jindra brought his thoughts back to the present, to hear Lieutenant Opalka trying to convince Uncle Hajsky.

"We've been over it all before, gentlemen," said Opalka

wearily. "The proposed assassination of Reinhard Heydrich is not just an isolated act of revenge. Unless we kill him, the Czech people will be fighting on the side of the Nazis. Our divisions will be in action against the British and the Americans and the Russians. The Nazis will have achieved an unparalleled propaganda success. Other people, more important than ourselves, have decided that by this *one* act we can prevent that happening. We are merely the agents of the operation."

This was their credo. The Czech Government and army in London who had sent them here believed it. Jindra believed it. Heydrich himself was the architect of Nazi success. If he died, if he was assassinated, all would be changed. The Reich would have received such a blow in the face, such a staggering affront that collaboration would be impossible, and any reconciliation difficult.

"Today, there's been a further announcement," said Opalka slowly. "It was broadcast on the lunchtime news. Heydrich received members of the Protectorate Government this morning. That's why he's flying to Berlin. It's all been worked out. No doubt he'll explain to Hitler how successful he has been, and suggest that a few Czech divisions would be most useful on the eastern front."

"He will not arrive in Berlin," Jan cut in harshly. "He will be lying upon a marble slab in the mortuary."

It seemed to him, that to kill Heydrich on the eve of his departure for a conference which would further enslave Czechoslovakia, made justice both equitable and poetic. It was an opportunity without parallel.

They had warned a dozen members actively engaged in the resistance in the Holesovice area to stand by to help if need be. They had not told them what the plan was; merely to stand by. Valchik and one other resistance worker would be assisting in the actual attempt. Jan and Josef would pull the trigger.

So it was with much impatience that Jan listened to Uncle Hajsky going over and over the same argument, as if its very repetition would reveal some hidden merit.

"We've built up our organization slowly and painstakingly over the past few months," said Uncle Hajsky quietly. "If we succeed in killing Heydrich,"—he used *"we"* deliberately, and with pride—"we know we shall almost certainly bring down a terrible weight of retribution upon our heads."

"Well?" said Jan flatly.

"So?" added Josef truculently.

Lieutenant Opalka said nothing; neither did Jindra.

Uncle Hajsky stopped, sighed and shook his head in perplexity as if he could not properly explain what he meant. "I can't say I know exactly why I feel it's wrong to make the attempt tomorrow. I can't put my finger specifically on any fundamental flaw in the plan, except that we've built up our organization slowly and carefully and this might topple the whole thing over. We're not proved in action yet; and this is too big a test with which to try it out."

Jindra knew that according to his viewpoint Uncle Hajsky was right; but really he could not see the wood for the trees; the act of killing Heydrich was a culmination, not a *test* of organizational efficiency.

Jan got up. He could not sit still any longer.

"We've been here nearly six months, Uncle," he said passionately. "Six long months! What have we accomplished that has damaged the Nazi cause? Nothing." He ran on before Uncle Hajsky had time to reply. "All right, we've built up a new resistance organization all over the country. But what's the good of a resistance movement unless it's resisting. . . ."

"I agree," said Josef, who could keep out no longer. "That is what we are here for; to fight!"

He stood up, but Jan with a friendly shove pushed him back in his chair.

"You know as well as we do that we were sent from England to *get* Heydrich," continued Jan. "Karl Frank or Heydrich, they said. Whichever you can get, and whichever is the bigger prize." He paused for a moment to let his remark sink in. "Heydrich is the bigger prize and the bigger butcher. Outside Hitler there's no one more important in the entire Nazi pigsty. If we can kill him, we shall knock the first nail into the Nazi coffin. And it'll make such an almighty bang that it will be heard all over the world."

Uncle Hajsky blinked slightly at Jan's vehemence. He sighed as if he'd known all along that he could never win this battle. He turned to look at Opalka, and then at Jindra. He could tell by their faces that he had lost the argument.

Now Jindra spoke. He said sombrely, "I think we all agree with you, Uncle Hajsky, that we need more time; we need time to get arms and radio sets; our resistance workers need training; we need more parachutists from England. We need lots of things, and lots of time, but the war won't give us time. If Jan and Josef succeed in killing Heydrich we may bring down a wave of retribution upon our heads which will destroy us all." He paused. "But it is a hazard which in our occupation we must accept. Nothing is more important to our cause than to stop Heydrich integrating our country with the German Reich. We cannot let tomorrow's opportunity pass."

They all knew it was the last word on the subject and Uncle Hajsky blew out his breath in a long whistling sigh. "Then I suppose that's that," he said quietly. "I shall do my part." Jan jumped to his feet and slapped Josef on the back. Then he turned to Hajsky, still standing pale and irresolute in the centre of the room.

"Don't worry, Uncle, it'll be all right," he said. "Don't worry."

"Oh Christ!" said Hajsky, quietly, and he was not a man addicted to easy blasphemy, "I wish I didn't have to."

On the Charles Bridge Anna was waiting. She was leaning against the parapet on the centre arch. She turned towards him, smiling. He came close to her and thrust his hand under her arm, taking her hand and leaning over the parapet to look down at the water. She felt the warmth of his weight against her, and she knew they had decided.

Below, the river, broken into thick silk scarves of water by the triangular buttresses, rustled its way towards the sea. It was the evening of May 26th, 1942, and they could feel summer in the air. Along the river bank the chestnuts were heavy with blossom. They stood there in the growing dusk, and he talked slowly and painfully of why they must do what they had to do, repeating his arguments of that afternoon, almost as though he did not really believe them and needed some sort of reassurance which only she could give him. Their last four weeks together since the bombing raid at Pilsen had been weeks of quiet joy. Now she knew that their honeymoon of the senses, and of the flesh, was over.

She had heard him many times before talking in this manner, but on these other occasions the discussion had been purely academic. This was the real thing. Tomorrow morning, Josef and Jan would stand upon a street corner not as citizens, but as executioners. There would be no law to protect them. Their chances of survival were probably far less than those of their intended victim. Although she tried to conceal this knowledge from herself, sometimes a picture of them lying dead rose like a dreadful apparition before her eyes. The blood on the pavements could be theirs, not Heydrich's.

Jan was still talking, almost to himself, as if it was himself he had to convince; going over the same story of how, when they first arrived, the whole organization had been behind them. All were pledged to help. And then somehow, uncertainty, doubts, had crept in; something had gone wrong. Perhaps it was Gerik's betrayal or Miks' death that had caused this loss of confidence. He did not really know.

On the bridge, with the stars growing in the darkening sky overhead and the mysterious spires reaching upwards on either bank, they had a momentary sense of security.

Anna tried to explain this to Auntie Marie, and Auntie Marie in her turn understood. For here above all was the focal point of all Prague, and here all around them was their rightful inheritance. To regain it, to be worthy of this inheritance, it was necessary to plot and to kill, to risk their own lives and the lives of many other people. They could not turn back now. Perhaps Anna would never have her child; perhaps there would be no "after the war".

Tomorrow would bring them most of the answers.

CHAPTER ELEVEN

On that sunny morning of May 27th, a slight heat haze hung over the whole of Prague. It was a haze which would clear as the day progressed, and already up on the high ground, above the valley of the Vltava, the bright sun shone from a pale sapphire sky.

In the great house in the village of Panenske Brezany, Reinhard Heydrich was preparing for his journey to Berlin, and several miles away on a street corner in Holesovice Jan Kubis and Josef Gabchick were preparing to terminate that journey with abrupt and absolute finality.

On that morning, Heydrich's long fingers clipped the buttons embossed with the silver swastika through the cloth facings of his S.S. uniform, and he went down the stairs to bid his wife goodbye. Inga Heydrich was also tall, blonde and handsome. Heydrich had married her in 1932. A blonde wife of correct stock and social standing was an essential to a rising star in the S.S. in those years. Of the joy which came to both of them through this marriage, little can be assessed. According to Walter Schellenberg, the young lawyer who worked under Heydrich and knew him as well as any man, it was an uncertain liaison. Three children were born, and Heydrich, when not upon roistering expeditions around the town, was heard to talk of "the dear intimacy of the family circle". He played the violin well and enjoyed an evening of chamber music. There was a dichotomy about his character which any psychiatrist would find fascinating.

Panenske Brezany, the great house requisitioned as the home of the Reichsprotector, stood in a small village of the same name, in soft, rolling pastoral countryside about fourteen miles from Prague. It was a huge white building, its architecture owing much to the French château, and its large grounds, with clipped lawns and shady trees, were surrounded by a ten-foot wall capped with a tiny roof of red tiles. The village had been cleared of peasants, and only troops were stationed there. The country around was open and easy to patrol. Not that Heydrich had any fear for his life. His personal bravery was unquestioned; it amounted at times almost to foolhardiness.

When the elite S.S. Divisions were first formed it was Heydrich who suggested some of the standard tests for courage. One—reserved for embryo officers—demanded that the candidate withdraw the pin from a live grenade, and standing rigidly to attention, balance it upon his steel helmet until it exploded in the direction of the least resist-ance, upwards! At least, this was the theory to which those officer candidates hopefully subscribed.

Heydrich was quite confident that his strong-arm measures had intimidated the Czechs to a point where no resistance was possible. He knew that some parachutists were at large in the country, but compared with every other occupied territory, acts of sabotage and defiance were negligible. He had been a predatory animal for so long that he simply could not conceive that anyone would have the insolence to stalk his own person.

At the main door of the château, Oberscharfuhrer Klein was smoking a last cigarette and lounging by the green Mercedes. He was a huge man, six feet seven inches in height, with the shoulders of a dray horse and the broken-nosed face of an ex-boxer. He wore his best uniform and his medals flashed colourfully on his chest. It was an occasion for medals, for a guard of honour would present arms at the airport.

He saluted and swung open the door of the beautifully polished car. A small swastika flag was mounted on each mudguard. Heydrich sat in the front seat next to the driver behind the slightly raked windscreen. He waved to his wife as Klein drove the car down the drive. He returned the salute of the guard at the gate, and then with a blare of acceleration they turned into the lane and changed into top gear.

Before the Nazis arrived in Prague, all traffic drove on the left. A week of Nazi occupation ensured a new directive under which all traffic drove on the right. It had driven on the right ever since. Historically, one might wonder if this decision made any difference to the events which were to follow, in view of Heydrich's position in the car. Past the pond with its busy ducks, past the red brick cottages the car droned, the warm air flowing pleasantly against their faces, and then they hurtled along the narrow, dusty white road flanked with the full-blossomed apple and pear trees. On the right-hand side, a small lake gleamed; a yellow mustard field glowed like a burst of sunlight against the distant line of dark pines.

The car hummed through the small village of Predbon and then down on the main tarmac road where the signpost said, "Prague 16 kilometres". In the fields the peasant women in bulky skirts and headscarves bent over the weeding and hoeing; they ignored the fast green car which roared past them every morning. They passed through Libeznice, with its cobbled streets and tall spired church. A sharp left turn here brought them down the long, two-mile avenue straight through the tall chestnut trees, between which Jan and Josef had once considered stretching their steel cable. It was a pleasant drive. It gave Reichsprotector Heydrich time to consider his past triumphs and plan his future objective.

Two hours before Reinhard Heydrich left Panenske Brezany, Jan and Josef pushed their bikes up the long hill which led from the river, and their thoughts were not concerned at all with that lovely May morning.

Holesovice is a pleasant suburb: a conglomeration of small villas and shops, a quiet place of green trees and flowering shrubs, and milk bottles on front porches. On that morning, dogs, heads on their outstretched paws, blinked sleepy-eyed in the sunshine; cats washed their faces under blossom-laden trees in little gardens and surreptitiously eyed the singing birds in the branches. Housewives, now their husbands had gone to work, gossiped over back fences or tied their hair up in handkerchiefs to visit the local shops.

From the wide bridge at the bottom of the hill, twin tram-tracks wound upwards, gleaming in the sunshine. Occasionally the red trams—three squat coaches linked together—sucking power with thin black antennae from the web of overhead wires, lurched groaningly up or down the hill on their journeys out to the suburbs or back to the centre of Prague.

On the bend which curves upwards and round to the left, in a sharp near-hairpin, about a mile from the bridge, Josef went across to the phone box on the corner opposite and rang up Liboslava at Red Cross Headquarters.

He told her he loved her, and arranged to see her that evening. When she asked him where he was and what he was doing, he was evasive and said he was just doing some little job. Then he said goodbye and stepped out of the phone box into the sunshine.

On the corner, he rejoined Jan, who told him that both Valchik and the other resistance worker were in position: Valchik, three hundred yards up the street on a corner, and the first man a further three hundred yards higher up.

Ornamental iron railings, supported at intervals by brick pillars, separated the pavement where they stood from a small overgrown garden. Two trees in full foliage cast a deep shade over this corner. A little above it stood a tobacconist's kiosk. As he had already sold his weekly ration, business was negligible and the tobacconist sat reading the morning newspaper. Occasionally a few people would gather at the No. 14 stop to catch a tram. Trams stopped directly on the corner where the downhill tracks curved to within a yard of the pavement. If two arrived at the hairpin bend together, they completely blocked the road.

Jan and Josef had often discussed the problem of these trams. They were certainly a menace and might interfere with their plan, but there was nothing they could do about them. The vital operational point was that Heydrich's open car had to slow up here to negotiate the near-hairpin corner, and for perhaps five seconds it would provide an easy slowly-moving target.

It was a simple plan. The first man high up the street would see the Mercedes as it approached and flash the signal by mirror to Valchik, who would flash it on to Josef. They had rehearsed this mirror trick and it worked. Josef would have at least thirty seconds to walk slowly back around the corner and stand inconspicuously on the kerb as if waiting for the tram. Until Heydrich's car rounded the bend the occupants would not see him.

If luck was on Josef's side, the Nazis would then see him only briefly, as the business end of his Sten gun spouted bullets, and this should be the last picture of this earth they would carry with them on their journey to eternity. Ten yards lower down the hill, Jan waited, his empty briefcase in his left hand, his right hand in his coat pocket holding a grenade primed with a two second fuse. He was only a reserve; the actual annihilation was to be Josef's job.

With the shooting over, they expected to spring on their bicycles, Jan to race off down the hill, while Josef pedalled furiously along the broad avenue opposite, following another route down to the city. They needed a little luck, but in the confusion which would follow their action they hoped that luck would be on their side.

They knew that at nine a.m. Heydrich left Panenske Brezany. His car should round the bend where they stood between nine-twenty and nine-thirty.

They had half an hour to wait. Trams clanked and rattled up and down the hill. Passengers boarded them or disembarked. The sun shone from a cloudless sky. Bees hummed across the road in search of blossom. Jan and Josef changed positions often, strolling backwards and forwards. They consulted their watches. They tried to appear disinterested. They tried to look as if they were waiting for a tram or waiting to keep an appointment. And all the while the minutes crawled past with such agonizing slowness that one might have thought the clock finger was thrusting forward against the combined weight of a thousand hopes and fears. As indeed it was.

The Reichsprotector, spinning smoothly along in his gleaming open roadster, enjoyed the sparkling sunshine. What can one say of him? Two decades later, now that the period of propaganda hatred has passed, can one find any saving graces in this man, any flicker of humanity in the tall handsome figure? It is not easy. Like the other Nazi leaders he lived in an environment where orders of murder, torture and mass-extermination were the commonplace memoranda of in-trays. True, like Himmler, Heydrich's rôle was mainly administrative; the cries of the tortured, the drip-drip of blood, the smoke of the extermination camp crematoriums, were sufficiently far away not to trouble his conscience. But whereas Himmler was a weak-hearted theorist who sickened at the sight of actual physical brutality, Heydrich had no such scruples. His past was well-documented with examples of his personal efficiency as an executioner. He had served a long and willing apprenticeship to his trade.

Only two weeks before, he had addressed civilian officials at a conference in Berlin. The records report him as saying, "In great columns, with separation of sexes, those Jews fit for work are being despatched to the Eastern Territories, and in the process a considerable reduction of numbers will undoubtedly take place by natural means."

"Natural means" was the pleasant euphemism for an act terrifying in its brutality. Half-starved, terrified people were packed into carriages so that there was room only to stand side by side, and back to back. They were then shunted for days and nights, with no food or water or any attention, across vast distances of Europe.

Heydrich had continued: "If in the end an eventual remnant is left over, since this will undoubtedly consist of the most resistant elements, it will have to be handled accordingly, otherwise it would have to be regarded as the naturally selected nucleus of a renewal of the Jewish population."

Heydrich intended there should be no "renewal of the Jewish population". Yes, in the ten years he had come a long way. As he sped along in the Mercedes he might well reflect that his progress had been spectacular.

But it did not pay Reinhard Heydrich to reveal his hand. He was in no hurry. Always he had stood behind the leaders and waited. He was much younger than most of the other Nazi leaders; much younger and more feared. So far he had never failed. He had made mistakes but had always managed to bluff his way past them. As Deputy Reichs-protector in Czechoslovakia he had succeeded where his predecessor von Neurath had failed completely. Now, by bringing Czechoslovakia completely into the Nazi orbit, he was on the verge of a political coup which would mark a spectacular rise in his reputation.

The car turned on to the two-way road. The signpost indicated that it was ten kilometres to Prague. The city lay to the right in a faint haze of mist which rose from the river. Farther down the hill the trams began, their double tracks snaking along in the centre of the wide avenue. The street sign said "Rude Armady VII Kobylisky". The car purred smoothly over the tarmac down towards the point where the road turned in a tight near-hairpin bend, before running down to the Troja bridge across the Vltava.

The Fuhrer himself had sent personal congratulations to the Deputy Reichsprotector. But in point of fact, the Fuhrer himself was growing a little concerned at the limitless ambition of S.S. General Heydrich. Hitler himself would pass from the scene one day. Then who would take over the leading rôle? It was 1942. The Nazi fortunes were at their zenith. There were no boundaries to Heydrich's ambition if he waited long enough.

It was his ill fortune that others were waiting also. Two young men at the corner lower down.

They were worried. The clock in the Liben reformatory struck ten, and their faces were serious. Something must have gone wrong. He was late! Maybe he was not coming. Already when the tram stop was clear, Josef had unbuckled his briefcase, snapped the barrel of the Sten gun into the stock and slotted home the magazine. Now the automatic weapon was hidden under the mackintosh folded over his arm.

At ten twenty-seven, Jan idly watched a number three tram round the corner at the bottom of the hill and slowly start to climb. Two hundred yards below him it halted at a stop. At that moment he heard a sharp whistle behind him, and turned to find Josef hurrying to his position. From his face Jan knew at once that the Mercedes was approaching.

He glanced through the trees up towards where Valchik

stood, saw the bright reflected flash of sunlight in the mirror, and his throat went suddenly dry.

Below him, the tram started off up the hill again. With a feeling of alarm he realized it might well coincide with Heydrich's car at the corner, but it was too late to worry now. If passengers got off and were met by a spray of bullets it was their bad luck. This was no time for such muddling considerations. The green car was coming down the hill.

Above the clatter and clang of the approaching tram he heard the car's deep-throated engine, the quick crash of gears as the driver changed down to take the bend.

He saw Josef take two quick steps to the edge of the pavement, and throw down his mackintosh. He watched him bring the Sten gun up to his shoulder. He held his breath in anticipation. Two more seconds and a slashing hail of bullets would shatter the windscreen. Jan's right hand clenched excitedly on his grenade. Automatically he dropped his briefcase and wrenched the grenade from his pocket.

Shining in the sun, the swastika flag on either mudguard stiff in the breeze, the low green car swept round the corner. Behind the set-back windscreen he saw the two German uniforms, the peaked caps. He recognized the long pale face of Heydrich as he sat next to the driver. "Now!" he said under his breath.

"Now!" he yelled as the car sailed up to Josef. His mind was full of quick incoherent agony. Why didn't he fire? God, why didn't he fire?"

"Josef!" he yelled. "Josef!"

And the car had passed. Like a boy with a piece of wood shaped like a gun, Josef stood there pointing it uselessly. He swung round, traversing with its passage, his face a mask of agony.

The two Germans were now level with Jan. They looked very surprised and very angry. Heydrich's hands were tugging at his revolver holster. Jan heard the brakes squeal, the tyres begin to bite. That instinctive reaction of the driver was a bad one. The car passed Jan. It was now almost level with the approaching tram. Instinctively Jan acted. Instinctively his mind said, a two-second delay, don't throw too hard, lob into the back of the car.

He ran three strides after the Mercedes wrenching out the grenade pin. He hurled it—half lob, half throw—after the car. He saw the grey steel ball fly towards the rear near-side wheel. Then suddenly it was a flame-cored circle of blinding light. There was a loud bang as if someone down in hell had smashed his fist against an empty cauldron. The flame disintegrated into a great belch of black smoke. Jan felt a fierce blast of air, a sharp pain in his face near his right eye. Something else punched him in the chest sending him staggering back a yard.

The windows down one side of the tram shattered into pieces. A row of astonished white faces stared out at him. Two green Nazi jackets, which must have been folded on the back seat, flew high into the air. They caught on the overhead tram wires, swinging there empty and grotesque. Then they drooped and fluttered quietly back to earth.

The car gave two or three broken-back jumps, its back near-side tyre sagging on the rim, a great hole torn in the bodywork near the rear seat.

For one long second of time everything was isolated, silhouetted, frozen: the white faces in the tram, the two Nazi coats in the air, the open-mouthed tram driver. Then the scene dissolved, bunched, moved and leapt into complete confusion. Jan hesitated for only a fraction. As Heydrich and Klein swung open the car doors, revolvers in their hands, he heard the first bullet whizz past him. He turned on his heel and dashed back for his bicycle. Ten yards farther away Josef stood, still frozen, the useless Sten gun in his hand. Now he, seeing Jan, also ran for it.

As Jan grabbed his bicycle, he saw a second downhill tram slide smoothly around the corner and halt at the stop. He glimpsed the driver's astonished face. All this he saw as he wrenched round his bike and ran with it towards the gap between the two trams. Suddenly there were people from the trams everywhere, wide-eyed, shouting, furious people moving in towards him. They looked as if they wanted to interfere. He shouted at them, cursing. "Out of my way,

164

you fools!" he yelled. He dragged his revolver from his pocket and flourished it at them. One man waving his stick had started to rush towards him. His mouth opened and closed like that of a goldfish. Jan swung his revolver towards him. In a contortion of almost comic fear the man toppled backwards. Jan put one foot on the pedal and swung up into the saddle. His feet thrust hard against the pedals as he turned down the hill.

He could hear revolver shots, but whether they were directed at him or not he could not tell, for now he was hidden by the tram. People scattered in front of him. There was a crowd milling all around it, scared by the explosion, scared by the staccato reports of the German revolvers, scared by events they had not witnessed and did not understand. Two policemen were amongst them. One of them took a step forward and rapidly changed his mind, as Jan pointed the revolver at him. Not so the other. Arms outstretched, he jumped directly into his path.

"Out of the way!" Jan yelled.

He could see the man's face tensed for the impact of the bicycle wheel.

Jan pressed the trigger. There was a bang, a cloud of smoke. The policeman fell sideways. Then Jan was past, anger mounting in a wave inside him. He had not dreamt that a Czech policeman would try to stop him. He hoped he'd killed the swine! He hurtled down the hill away from the tram. A glance back and he saw that Klein was pursuing him. Revolver in hand, medals dancing, his knees jerking up and down, he pounded in his wake. Thirty yards down a woman was standing by the gutter with a pail in her hand. He realized that she must have been scrubbing her front door step and come out on to the street when she heard the explosion. Suddenly Jan's right eye was full of something warm and sticky which splashed down on to his handlebars. He saw it was blood. Behind him he could hear voices baying like a crowd at a bull fight.

Half blinded and five yards from the housewife, he saw her toss her bucket directly into his path. It clanged against his front wheel and for a second he thought he was off. He heard her scream after him, and his anger became more bitter than ever. These were his own people who were trying to stop him! A hundred yards farther down the street a second woman stood in his path obviously activated by the screams behind him. He could have killed the stupid bitch. As he swooped towards her, he dropped his shoulder, braced himself and knocked her flying into the gutter. He looked round as he free-wheeled down the hill and saw her stretched out flat on the ground. Far behind him was a small group of pursuers, and he could see they had almost given up.

The road was empty in front of him. He stuffed his revolver back into his pocket, pulled out his handkerchief and wiped his face. He folded the linen into a rough pad and held it against his eye which was now throbbing with pain. He was also conscious that he had no hat; the explosion must have blown it off his head.

His speed down the hill took him smoothly across the bridge. It was a wide road. The few pedestrians he passed ignored the bareheaded cyclist apparently blowing his nose. He crossed the bridge and swung right along the main road. It was almost deserted. A few hundred yards farther on was the house of a family in Liben called Novotna; it was the nearest place he could hope to find help.

Mr. Novotna and his wife were both good resistance workers, and Jan and Josef had visited them more than once. They had, in fact, been warned that either might need assistance some time during the day. Jan knew it was dangerous to arrive in his condition; he had not anticipated an emergency like this, but he had no other choice. He could not ride into Prague with blood all over his face and clothes. And he had to get rid of the blood-spattered bicycle quickly.

There were shops now, pedestrians in the distance. He slowed to a halt outside a Bata shoe store. Forcing himself to act with unconcern he propped his bicycle against the kerb. He pretended he was going into the shop, then moved down the side street. He knew the house. He pushed open the front gate and walked quickly up the path. He could feel the blood running down his face but kept his hand and the handkerchief away from it in case anyone should be looking out of their windows.

In an agony of impatience he pressed the bell. There was no movement inside. He could hear the bell and kept his finger on it, listening to its loud ringing. There was no answer. Everyone was out. Now he felt a wave of fear mount inside him. He would have to go back to the bicycle and go on to his next contact; the house of a railwayman two miles farther on. He had to find shelter quickly.

Sick at heart he turned away from the front door, and at that moment Mrs. Novotna opened the garden gate on her way in. He did not speak. He did not know what to say. She reacted quickly. She brushed past him, inserted her latch-key, thrust open the door and almost pushed him inside.

"What's happened to you? Oh, your poor face."

Jan walked into the room and sat down. The shock was beginning to make itself felt and he felt sick. Shock and loss of blood, pain, and the bitter disappointment at the realization of their failure depressed him completely. For failed they had. He had seen both Nazis leap athletically from the Mercedes. Their wounds—if any—must be slight. The car had protected them. All he had succeeded in doing was to get himself a faceful of shrapnel. And after all these risks and planning! After all their training, and scheming, and waiting, they had bungled the job hopelessly. He could have wept.

What had gone wrong? What the hell had gone wrong? Why hadn't Josef fired? Could he have frozen on the gun? Josef was not that sort of man, but what had gone wrong? And what was happening to Josef now?

"I'll boil the kettle," said Mrs. Novotna practically, "and bathe your wounds."

"We tried to get Heydrich," said Jan dully. "Josef was supposed to kill him with the Sten gun, but he didn't fire. Not a single shot. He just stood there and they sailed past as if he was pointing a water pistol at them. I threw a grenade but I was too late. We failed hopelessly."

Mrs. Novotna did not seem to be listening. "Take your coat off," she said. "And your shirt. Look, your chest's hurt.

You're covered in blood. We must burn all these clothes."

"He was so close to us we could have spat on him," went on Jan bitterly. "We had a Sten gun and two grenades, and a revolver each, and we didn't even mark him."

"Your hand too," said Mrs. Novotna. "It's pouring with blood. Heavens, what did you do to yourself?"

Jan lifted his left hand and looked at the deep wound. It was the first time he had realized his hand was hurt.

"Now, come, off with this shirt," said Mrs. Novotna. "And don't talk like that. At least you're alive to fight another day."

"There won't be another day," said Jan. "We'll never get another chance." He thought about all the people who had tried to intercept him during his escape. He told Mrs. Novotna, "They were Czechs. Would you believe it? Our own countrymen!"

"They didn't know what you were trying to do," she said quietly. But he was not comforted. He had risked his life believing he was helping his country, and this was how they had behaved.

She laid out clothes for him which belonged to her husband; they were both about the same size. She lit the boiler and stoked it preparatory to burning his bloodstained things.

"Oh God!" said Jan, suddenly remembering. "The bicycle!" Mrs. Novotna looked at him in surprise.

"I've left the bicycle at the kerb outside the Bata shop," he explained. "I'll have to get it—hide it."

"You can't go like that," she said "You must get out of those clothes."

It was at this moment that Jindriska, her fourteen-year-old daughter, returned from Mass. She was at first a little frightened by the young man with the damaged face who stared at her with such terrible eyes, but her mother reassured her. She had overheard about the bicycle.

"I'll go and fetch it, Mama," she said. "No one will notice me." She was a pretty little girl, slight and dark, with wide eyes that stared curiously out at the world.

Jan looked at her, remembering the man waving the stick,

the two policemen, the woman with the bucket, and the woman he had knocked down.

"No," he said thickly. "You're too young to get mixed up in this."

"All right, Jindriska," said her mother briskly. "Go and get it. It's standing outside the Bata shop."

"It's got blood on the handlebars," said Jan. "She shouldn't . . ."

"Wheel it away quietly and don't speak to anyone," continued Mrs. Novotna. "Come back by a roundabout route. Put it in the shed in the backyard."

"Yes, mama," said Jindriska, and closed the door quietly behind her.

Jan looked up at Mrs. Novotna with agony in his eyes, but all she said was, "Now go into the bathroom and take off all those clothes, and push them out through the door. I've got the boiler blazing and I'll burn them."

Jindriska walked quickly along the streets until she came to the main road. The bicycle—as Jan had told them—was standing by the kerb and no one was near it. As she got closer she could see the blood dappled on the handlebars and frame. She took it carefully by the grips and wheeled it away. She went first of all down the main road away from their turning, and several passers-by, seeing her with the blood-spattered machine asked, "Has there been an accident, little girl? Has anyone been hurt?"

Jindriska did not answer. With her face calm and impassive she turned off the main road down a side turning. She passed several other turnings which she knew from her games, and so came by a back way to the house. She put the bicycle in the shed against the wall, and covered it with sacks and went back into the kitchen. Her mother simply said, "Good girl. Now you'd better get on with your homework."

And Jan patted her head with his unwounded hand and said in a very gruff voice, "Thank you, Jindriska."

He knew now that their real ordeal was about to start. And he wondered what had become of Josef.

CHAPTER TWELVE

THAT moment when the green Mercedes slid swiftly, almost arrogantly, across his gun sights, and he realized that he most certainly could have done Heydrich and his chauffeur more harm by hurling his Sten through the windscreen, was for Josef the most bitter and agonizing of his entire life.

His index finger had almost cracked under the pressure he applied to the trigger. His face contorted with effort and frustration, vainly following the track of the car, but not a sound and not a single bullet left the barrel; it had jammed hopelessly. In a fury of disappointment and anger he threw it to the ground.

He heard Jan shout at him; he glimpsed his look of complete bewilderment and he stood hypnotized as Jan leapt after the car to throw the Mills grenade. It was the sound of the grenade exploding, and the sight of Heydrich and Klein swinging open their car doors, which jerked him back from stupefied immobility. Regrets and post mortems might come later; now escape must be his primary motive. A bullet whined past his head and with a quick glance over his shoulder he realized that it was Heydrich himself who had fired. With a quick appraisal of the odds, Heydrich and Klein had decided to do battle. Klein was pounding down the hill in the wake of Jan. Heydrich was after Josef.

Josef turned to run back to his bicycle. He took three steps towards it. Then with a quick shock of alarm he saw that people flooding from the tram which had come down the hill had cut him off from it. They advanced towards him, some plainly scared, some curious, some not knowing what had happened, and three or four of a more interfering type possibly prepared to engage him.

He jerked out his revolver and at the sight of it, the grim-faced ones, advancing on one who seemed so small and in-offensive, stopped dead in their tracks, their courage evaporating, reminding themselves suddenly that after all it was none of their business.

Josef glanced swiftly around him. He saw at once that like Jan his only escape route lay between the two halted trams. He would have to abandon his bicycle and make a dash for it on foot. Brandishing his revolver he raced through the growing crowd of astonished bystanders who seemed to have crept from a dozen corners. As he reached the opposite pavement another bullet ricocheted off the roadway and he jumped for the thin cover offered by a telegraph pole.

A glance from its shelter revealed that it was indeed Heydrich with whom he was duelling. The Reichsprotector had advanced from the car up the street and past the tram, and now he was taking pot shots across the road with his large revolver. A shot from Josef, however, sent him rapidly back to the shelter of the tram.

Even in that moment of dire personal peril, Josef had time to reflect sorrowfully that Jan's grenade seemed to have done him no harm.

He was quite wrong. From the very moment Jan's grenade had exploded, Heydrich was a dying man. Ten days it would take him to die, with the best doctors in the Reich fussing and fuming around his bedside, but die he would, as painfully and slowly as many of his own victims had died. The bursting grenade had exploded fine splinters of steel, horsehair and material from the seat covers upwards. They had penetrated deeply into the spleen and lumbar region of Heydrich's back. Blood poisoning would set in. No penance could save him now, and penicillin was beyond the range of even his most invidious intrigues.

Josef, trapped behind the telegraph pole, had little time to consider Heydrich's physical condition. The Nazi seemed extraordinarily hearty, as he pumped large and unhealthy bullets towards him. To rush up the hill, in the direction from which the Mercedes had come, making for the corner where Valchik had waited with his mirror, seemed to provide his best escape route. But to move from his shelter at that moment meant he would be an open, if not an easy, target for Heydrich's revolver. Although at thirty yards' range a revolver is an unconvincing weapon, a lucky bullet might bring him down. Therefore, all he could hope to do for the time being was to try to keep Heydrich under cover behind the tram.

So, with deadly absurdity, like two characters in a western film, the two of them fired single shots across the street at each other. The essential, and fascinating, difference between the film and reality rested in the fact that if one of the stray crumbs of lead flying through the air lodged in a vital spot, one of them would die and there would be no retakes in this particular sequence.

Josef also realized that the longer the game went on the worse his position would become; he was the one who stood to lose by delay; at any moment, reinforcements might arrive, and they could only be reinforcements for Heydrich.

The farcical nature of these proceedings was further heightened when, as Josef peered around the pole before firing another shot at Heydrich, he saw a young woman with a pram dashing down the hill, about to run behind the Reichsprotector. Josef waited until she had passed and then fired his shot; the bullet ricocheted screamingly towards a house behind Heydrich. A fraction of a second before Josef fired, the door of this house opened, and a man in shirt-sleeves, his face half covered in lather, came rushing down the steps crying, "Assassination! Assassination!"

The bullet evidently passed over his head and frightened the wits out of him. He skidded to a frantic halt, spun on his heel and bolted back to his door like a rabbit to its burrow. The slam of his front door was itself as loud as a pistol shot.

All around the trams people were lying in the roadway, covering their heads, peering incredulously from the broken windows, cowering uncertainly against the steel sides. And upon every face was a look of complete disbelief. These were quiet suburban trams in a quiet suburban street. The sun was still shining, the birds were still singing, the sky was still blue, but apparently the universe had gone quite mad. This might happen in battle, but surely not to good stolid Czech citizens in a suburb in Prague.

But it was happening and bullets were screeching and whining through the drowsy sunshine like furious hornets.

It did not seem more than two minutes to Josef when peering around the pole, he saw Heydrich's revolver pointing towards him, saw his hand jerk convulsively, and realized that no bullets were blasting from its barrel. Plainly his revolver was empty. At that precise moment, the enormous Klein, panting and red-faced after his useless pursuit of Jan, rejoined his chief. It was the opportunity Josef needed. Seizing that brief moment of diversion, he raced from the shelter of his telegraph pole and headed up the hill as fast as he could go.

Heydrich threw down his empty gun in disgust, and half bending hobbled across to the railings behind him. He leaned against them doubled up in pain. "Go after him, man," he shouted at Klein. "Go after him!" He gripped the railings tightly to prevent himself falling. His recent exertions had done him no good.

Klein hesitated, not willing to leave his master and yet anxious to avenge this terrible insult to German pride. Finally, spurred by Heydrich's angry gesture, he raced after Josef, who had now almost two telegraph posts' start on him. Glancing back, Josef saw him and jerked to a standstill behind another post. He had no desire to present his back to a revolver bullet. He watched the giant chauffeur steaming up the hill towards him, his medals clanking on his breast. His face was red from exertion. His polished jackboots crashed down on the pavement. He was obviously very angry, and he disdained the shelter of any pole.

Josef allowed him to close to within the distance of a telegraph pole and a half. He sighted carefully and squeezed the trigger. He saw the dust fly up a yard to the right of the polished boots, quickly adjusted his aim, and fired again.

The second bullet obviously passed close enough to Oberscharfuhrer Klein's head to insert into it serious doubts regarding his immortality, for he also slithered to a halt behind a telegraph pole. Panting there, he tried to withdraw his manly belly sufficiently to keep it out of target area. And the farcical but deadly duel reopened.

As Josef fired each single shot to keep Klein behind the pole, he reached into his coat pocket, extracted another round and reloaded. He knew that not only would he eventually run out of ammunition but also out of time. It was essential to keep moving.

He peered around the pole, fired two quick shots to keep Klein under cover and ran for it again. He had a twenty-five yard lead before the chauffeur realized he had gone.

The road curved round to the right and seeing that the bend gave him cover, Josef accelerated around it. In doing so, he almost ran into a man who had been loading logs of wood into his cart. The noise of the revolver shots had startled his horse, and now he was at its head quietening him. He took one quick look at Josef, saw the gun, released the horse, spun around so that his back was towards Josef, and threw his hands high in the air. Josef scooted past him.

A little farther up there was a side road running to the right, and instinctively Josef turned into it; the main road was too wide and straight for comfort. He could hear Klein in the distance berating the immobilized cart driver, and shouting, "After him! Stop the rogue!"

Josef's chest was heaving; he realized he was not in particularly good condition for this sort of cross-country flight; unless he stopped for a breather soon his legs would give out. But he also knew that Klein's bull-like voice might at any moment alert more pursuers.

As he raced along the side turning, he observed that each house was fronted by a small square garden. Forty yards along stood a butcher's shop. This front garden had been replaced by an open concrete area, and at the edge of it sat an old woman in a rocking chair. Her eyes widened with fright as he raced up. Her mouth opened but no words emerged.

A few yards behind her stood the butcher, a fat-jowled man, wearing a striped apron. He held his small daughter by the hand, and he too must have heard the shots for he was walking forward to investigate.

His eyes widened in astonishment as he saw Josef; and the small girl clung to her father's legs in fear.

"Don't tell them I'm here. Please help me," panted Josef.

He moved past the butcher, looking into his shop, wondering if there was a back entrance through which he might escape. His chest hurt; he had to rest for a few moments. He stumbled through the shop entrance and leant against the counter, his heart pumping furiously. Through eyes misted with perspiration he checked that all six chambers of his Colt were full.

Turning, he saw the butcher lead the small girl forward and hand her to the old woman. From the main road her chair must have been visible, for Josef heard Klein's voice yelling at her, demanding information. He saw her turn a terrified face to her son asking what she should do; he saw the butcher walk slowly into the centre of the road and turn towards the main road. It was then that Josef guessed he was going to betray him.

He saw the old woman's face turn back towards him, contorted with shame and fear. He knew then that the butcher was talking to Klein, presumably telling him what had occurred. Josef's eyes searched the interior of the shop. It had no back door. He was trapped between narrow walls and it was certainly no place to fight a defensive action.

The counter of thin wood offered no possible protection; a bullet from Klein's Luger would penetrate it like paper. He jumped quickly for the shelter of the door; at least it possessed a stout wooden frame. It was too late to run now; the duel must continue. He heard the angry voices getting closer, the clatter of running feet, and there was Klein, peering around the hedge of the next garden. He could have been no more than twenty feet away. By this time the old woman had left her chair, dragging the child with her. Josef heard the sound of their feet running out of danger.

Klein fired first, a snap instinctive shot. His bullet left a neat round hole in the butcher's shop window. Josef held his fire. Klein, over confident and certain of capturing his man, now made his major mistake. He took two steps forward. Josef, arm outstretched and eye glued to the foresight, fired deliberately. At twenty paces this was target practice. The bullet smacked into the German's thigh.

Klein yelled—in pain this time—grasped at the hedge for support and bending the twigs over with his weight, began to slide to the ground.

Josef judged his run to an inch. He leapt out from the doorway, scooted like a cat across the concrete pavement and fired another shot at Klein as he raced past him. This time the range was less than ten feet. He heard Klein scream a second time, and knew that this bullet had also lodged in flesh. Then he hared down the side street continuing in the direction he had first taken.

Klein, wounded and maddened with pain and frustration, bellowed in anger after him, but with one bullet in his thigh and one in his ankle, he would never run again. He tossed his revolver at the butcher and cart driver, who with bovine faces had advanced towards him. It clattered in the roadway. They looked at it with round, frightened eyes. Klein bellowed at them again, almost incoherent with rage, and reluctantly the butcher picked up the weapon, examining it warily, as if at any moment it might bite him.

Without enthusiasm, the two tradesmen, driven by the hysterical rage of the inert chauffeur, set off after Josef. They moved at little above walking pace. Their intentions were obscure.

They had no chance of catching Josef. As he reached the point where the side turning intersected the main road—it ran parallel to the one where they had attempted to kill Heydrich—a tram was just starting off from its stop. The conductor saw the running figure, and convinced he was simply anxious to catch his tram, obligingly left the side door open. Josef leapt aboard, his revolver now tucked safely in his pocket. There were few people on the tram and he slumped into an empty seat. Looking back he saw no sign of any pursuit. There was none; the courage of the butcher and cart driver had dwindled to nothing as soon as they were out of sight of the cursing Klein. Uneasily they played for time at the end of the side turning.

From the tram window Josef saw that the morning was still fine and sunny. There were no excited faces amongst the people they passed, no extraordinary activity anywhere.

Sitting on the hard seat with the sun hot on his face, he was overwhelmed with a sense of unreality about the past hour. Had he really stood at that corner and attempted to shoot Heydrich with that Sten gun? Had he really just emerged unscathed from a duel with both Heydrich and his bodyguard?

Yes, all this was true, but what had gone wrong? What in the name of heaven had gone wrong? From the very moment his index finger had squeezed that trigger and obtained no response, some inner cell in his mind had been searching for an adequate reason for the gun's failure. Now, sitting peacefully in the tram, he had time to ponder the enigma and he knew the reason. It was appallingly simple, and an appallingly stupid, reason. The safety catch had stuck. Under the cover of his mackintosh, he had thumbed it off several minutes before the Mercedes swept round the corner. Obviously in his excitement, he had not pushed it down far enough. With a utilitarian weapon like the Sten such a thing could happen very easily; in practice he had made the same mistake before. No weapon on earth would fire with the safety catch still on.

On that long jolting tram journey down into Wenceslas Square he was immensely depressed by his carelessness. And what had happened to Jan? At least, he could take some comfort from the fact that Jan had had a good start on his bicycle. They would not find him an easy man to catch.

He hung around in Wenceslas Square for some time, but all seemed normal and he caught a second tram out towards the Fafka household. He knew Liboslava would be home at lunch time and he wanted to tell her what happened. He did not have to. By the time he reached the house Prague radio was breaking into its programmes at regular intervals for a news flash. Josef heard it himself. The announcer's voice was loaded with quivering excitement:

"Listen to this official announcement. This morning on the 27th May at 10.30 a.m. an attempt on the life of the Deputy Reichsprotector Heydrich was made in Prague. A reward of ten million crowns is offered for the capture of the culprits. Whoever hides the criminals or gives them any help, or has any knowledge of their identity or description of their appearance and does not inform the authorities will be shot with his whole family. This is by order of the Oberlandrat in Prague. Other announcements will be made in due course."

Josef watched Liboslava's face as the announcer spoke, and saw the anxiety grow in her eyes. Before, it had all been a rather exciting game. Now it was a matter of deadly seriousness. He looked around at the other faces also: those of Mr. and Mrs. Fafka and their eldest daughter. Their eyes showed no fear, but they all knew this was only a beginning.

Jan had left Mrs. Novotna's house at lunch time, when the streets of Liben were crowded with workers going home for their midday meal. At the front door before she opened it, he took both her hands in his, leaned forward and kissed her cheek.

Jindriska was by her side looking up at him with grave quiet eyes. He put his arm around her thin shoulders and squeezed her tightly. She smiled up at him fleetingly. Mrs. Novotna opened the door and Jindriska went to the front gate to see that all was clear. Then with Mr. Novotna's hat pulled well down over his wounded eye, and keeping his head bent, Jan set off to walk two miles to the nearby house of a railway worker who he knew would help. This man had also been warned that he might be needed. He walked quickly and no one took the slightest notice of him.

He found the house and knocked at the door. It was opened by a short square man in the blue overalls of a railway worker. He had a cropped head bristling with grey stubble, a broken nose and small light blue eyes which now were hard and suspicious. Jan had met him only a few times before at a small meeting of the Sokols in this district, when volunteers had been called to help in any task which might arise.

By the look in his eyes Jan knew that he must have heard something of what had occurred. He stared at Jan's wounded face, then without a word opened the door wider and gestured for him to come in.

In the tiny lounge the railwayman examined his face and said he needed a doctor. He had heard the organization had one standing by for just such an emergency as this. Jan said there was no need to involve a doctor; he was all right. A short rest was all he needed. He was very grateful and if he could stay until dusk, he would leave and find shelter somewhere else.

The man, however, was insistent. If the organization had a doctor ready and willing to help in a case like this, why not use him? Determinedly, he put on his cap. Within an hour he returned with a young doctor wearing as a disguise a borrowed tram conductor's uniform. He carried in his leather pouch not fares he had collected, but disinfectant and bandages. He dressed Jan's chest and eye and hand injuries, and said they were not serious. He told him that if he waited until darkness, and kept his trilby hat well pulled down over his eye, he should escape detection, but he thought the eye needed more skilled attention than he could supply; it required the examination of a specialist. He knew the very person; a woman colleague of his. As soon as Jan was safely hidden somewhere, he would arrange for her to visit him.

After the doctor left, Jan sank back in his chair and closed his good eye. Like Josef, he was filled with a feeling of emptiness and despondency. Again and again he went over what had happened. How could they have failed with Heydrich right in their gun sights? They would never get a second chance now. He watched the railwayman put on his cap again to set off upon a second errand, but he could work up neither anxiety nor interest about its purpose. He just wanted to sit there, drained of emotion, and neither see nor think.

So the railwayman set off to meet the leader of his group and inform them that Jan was safe with him. He returned at dusk with instructions. Jan was to report at 1837 Bishop Street tomorrow afternoon at three o'clock.

"But what about tonight?" Jan asked dully. "Didn't they say anything about tonight?"

The man shook his head. Wearily Jan tried to orientate

his thoughts. Life had not ended even though they had failed. He was a hunted man, but the Nazis were not going to get him that easily. He considered his prospects. He could go back to the Ogouns, but they, poor people, had only known him for a few weeks; at a time like this it was hardly fair to load them with such a responsibility. The railwayman read his thoughts.

"You will stay here," he said in his gruff homely accents. His voice was friendly; he wanted to help. He had heard the radio announcements and he knew now what he had let himself in for when he offered to aid the resistance in any way he could. If the smallest rumour of what he had done ever reached the Nazis, he was doomed, and so were his wife and children. Yet he said quite simply—and this gesture of courage would never be rewarded, or recognized by anyone except perhaps by his own inner pride, "You will spend the night here."

Jan shook his head. He was grateful, but he explained that not only had the railwayman done enough, this district was too close to the scene of attempted assassination and the Germans might well cordon it off and make a search.

It was dark enough now for Jan to walk through the streets without looking conspicuous; there were still many people returning home from offices and factories. He could mingle with them and pass unnoticed. Grudgingly the railwayman agreed with him, and then had another idea. He possessed a spare set of overalls. They were baggy, dark blue in colour and worn by every driver and fireman who worked on the railway. Such clothing was commonplace in Prague. Worn with these overalls was a large-peaked cap; an ideal accessory to pull down over a bandaged eye.

Uncomfortable in Mr. Novotna's suit, Jan changed quickly and willingly, and his friend promised to deliver the borrowed suit back to its owner. He thanked the man, gripped his hand and stepped out into the dark street. He had now decided where he was going. To Auntie Marie's. With her he knew he could find shelter.

As he hurried through the streets he saw large notices pasted on many walls. Groups of people stood around them, shining torches to read what they announced. He did not stop. Newspapers were selling rapidly at the street corners but he did not dare pause to buy one. As he hurried along he overheard other scraps of information. "A curfew at ten o'clock! All people found out of doors after that will be shot!"

It was a Nazi reaction he might have anticipated, and it made it absolutely essential to find shelter before the streets began to fill with steel-helmeted troops. They would certainly cordon off many areas and search houses, but they could not search the whole of Prague. If only his face was unmarked he could take his chance anywhere. Now he was the most conspicuous man, and the most wanted, in the capital.

He pushed open the front door of the Moravecs' apartment house. Ignoring the lift, he walked up the stone stairs to the second floor. He pressed the bell using the special series of rings he always used. Auntie Marie opened the door. He lifted his head to look at her, and for three dramatic seconds she stared back, with pity flooding her face.

"Oh, you poor boy," she said. She took his arm and drew him inside the flat. He walked quickly through the wide hallway and into the lounge he knew so well. At last he felt secure.

Auntie Marie sat down beside him on the settee and he began to tell her what had happened. To him it was a confession of failure. To Auntie Marie, who had heard on the radio that both assailants had escaped after inflicting some sort of injury upon Heydrich, it was part of a crusade which would continue, and must continue, to the bitterest and most glorious conclusion.

There was no question of his leaving the flat, she declared. With his face in that condition it was much too dangerous. By tomorrow some of the swelling would have gone down, and then they could decide what to do.

Half an hour later they heard Ata Moravec's key in the latch. Auntie Marie got up to welcome him; Jan knew how much she adored her tall handsome son. They heard his footsteps crossing the hall and he came in. He saw Jan and stopped as though he could not believe what he saw. Under his dark mop of hair his face was sallow and his eyes seemed feverish. Before his mother could kiss him, he said accusingly, "You're here! Here!"

Gone was all the romanticism which had glossed his voice when previously he had spoken of resistance. Now his tone was harsh and angry.

"Ata!" said Auntie Marie reproachfully. "What do you mean?"

Ata tried to recover his poise, to start again, to appear normal, but he was young and he could not hide his feelings.

"The newspaper," he said thickly. "It's all about your bicycle." He looked at Jan. "My mother's bicycle which you borrowed."

Without a word Mrs. Moravec took the newspaper from him and spread it out on the table. There on the front page was a photograph of a lady's bicycle. Jan recognized it at once as Josef's, and realized with sickening abruptness that it was the machine they had borrowed from Auntie Marie.

Above it, the headline ran: "Attempted assassination of the Reichsprotector. Ten million crowns reward will be paid for information leading to the arrest of perpetrators." Translated into any currency it was a very large reward; in English money the reward was equal to about one hundred thousand pounds.

The newspaper went on to describe the incident. It said that the man who escaped upon a bicycle was "big-built with a full round face tanned by the sun, wide mouth with curved lips, dark hair combed back, and aged between thirty and thirty-five."

It was a description which did not even remotely fit Jan. But, more seriously, it numbered the items the attackers had left behind at that corner in Holesovice. Not only a bicycle —and both the trade mark, "Moto-Velo J. Kremar Teplice" and the number 40.363 were given—but two briefcases, a light beige raincoat with pale buttons—Josef had carried this across his arm to conceal the Sten gun—and one dirty camel-haired cap bearing the blue and yellow trade mark name, "White Swan".

With a second shock of apprehension Jan realized that he had taken the cap from the hall stand at the Ogouns' that morning almost without thinking. It belonged to one of their sons, and it might well be traceable!

The newspaper article concluded with a warning in heavy black type. Anyone discovered withholding information, anyone with information who did not proceed immediately to the police would be shot together with his entire family. But all information given—if so desired by the informer— would be treated as highly secret. It was also the duty of all householders, and owners of flats or hotels, to inform the police if any unregistered person was staying with them. All persons not registered, or failing to comply with the regulation, would also be shot.

Jan finished reading the paper, avoiding Ata's accusing eyes. Not only had they botched the operation but they had now incriminated dozens of other people.

Absurd though it seemed now, Josef and he had only analysed their plan in terms of success or defeat. Either they would wipe out Heydrich and his driver in one magnificent burst of fire, and then race for shelter, complete with weapons, bicycles and briefcases, or else they themselves would be killed. The outcome of this action, and indeed the responsibility for it, had seemed to be theirs alone. He realized too late that they had been blinded by the magnitude of their task and concerned only with its successful accomplishment. They had now implicated many people who had helped them, and as far as he was aware they had only slightly wounded Heydrich. After all these months of waiting and plotting, after all their training, after bolstering their determination and courage to a high peak, and risking all in one assault, they might just as well have stayed in England.

CHAPTER THIRTEEN

JOSEF escaped to the house of his fiancée; Jan found shelter with Auntie Marie; Valchik, after Heydrich's car passed him, pocketed his hand mirror and took the side turning—afterwards used by Josef—and caught a tram back to his lodgings. Until an ambulance arrived, Klein lay sprawled outside the butcher's shop. But what of Heydrich? What of the man they had tried to murder?

After throwing down his revolver, Heydrich had walked slowly back to his damaged car through the curious knots of spectators. He leant against the hood bending over like someone out of breath after a hard race. His face was a pale shade of green. The crowd from the tram clustered round him but they did not come too close. They were frightened of the Nazi uniform. Curiosity at last overcame their fear. Whispers began to seethe among them like a sharp breeze eddying through a wheat field.

"It's Heydrich, the Reichsprotector!"

"No, it can't be!"

"It is, I tell you. I've seen his photograph."

"He's wounded. Look at his face."

"He's hurt, he's got it in the back!"

"Someone ought to help him."

But no one did help him. They just stood there, looking. There was no other German in sight. Then a blonde woman who had got off the tram took charge. She was young, smartly dressed and quite pretty.

She scolded the crowd angrily. "Can't you see it's the Reichsprotector? Can't you see he's hurt? He needs help. Stop a car! We must get him to the hospital."

No one moved to help. The crowd drew back, whispering like a ruminative herd of cows, seemingly incapable of action. A lorry was approaching. The blonde woman ran towards it, and the driver slowed down.

She shouted at him to stop and help, but the driver, seeing that it was not the blonde who needed his assistance, and catching sight of the German uniform, pressed his accelerator.

"Sorry, I'm full up. Overloaded now," he shouted above the roar of his engine. He drove off down the hill, leaving the woman fuming and shouting after him.

Oddly enough, no one seemed to think of the telephone box which Josef had used a little earlier. But then, no one wished to be implicated. The wise ones hurried off on their journeys on foot, not waiting for the trams to restart. Only the stupidly inquisitive remained, and of course the faithful pro-Nazis.

The two policemen who had chased Jan almost as far as the bridge now panted up the hill again. The one at whom Jan had fired was quite unhurt; he had dived sideways in time. Now he took charge. An affair like this could mean promotion. At that moment a small baker's van came down the hill, and this older policeman raised his hand importantly. The van stopped and a bewildered and troubled little man poked his head out of his side window.

"You will take the Reichsprotector to Bulov Hospital at once," said the policeman sternly, the scent of promotion now keen in his nostrils.

"But I'm delivering——" began the baker, scared by the uniform but trying to stand on his rights.

"Don't argue," said the policeman warningly. "You will do as we say. This is urgent."

Heydrich's face was now as green as his uniform. There were two or three small incisions in the back of his jacket, but they looked of no consequence. He had one hand pressed against his kidney. The policeman assisted him into the seat next to the driver. Heydrich groaned, and with tight lips called for his briefcase from the car. The second policeman handed it to him. The driver got back in his cab and pulled the starter; but before he could engage a gear, Heydrich was shouting hysterically.

The little driver turned off the ignition key and scuttled outside seeking assistance.

"I can't understand," he bleated. "Doesn't the General understand, I can't speak German?" He was almost in tears.

Nothing but trouble would come from this. Why did this have to happen to a poor baker like him, minding his own business, staying out of politics, behaving himself, just doing his job as well as he could?

"Shut up," said the officious policeman and went round to talk to Heydrich. He came back to the baker and upbraided him as if the whole affair were his personal doing. Didn't he understand? The Reichsfuhrer could not bear the pain sitting up. He wanted to lie in the back.

"But it's floury, dirty old cases and crates. I didn't expect . . ." wailed the baker.

"Get a move on," groaned Heydrich. "Quickly!"

"At once, Herr General," said the policeman importantly. He waved the crowd back and assisted Heydrich round to the back of the van. It had no roof. They dropped the tailboard and Heydrich crawled in and lay back with his outstretched leg over one of the crates. They started off, the Acting Reichsprotector of Bohemia and Moravia, the hammer of the Czechs, the butcher of the Jews, the murderer, the torturer, the sadist, flinching at every bump in the road, the knuckles of his left hand which clung to the side of the van white with convulsive pressure.

At the hospital, startled attendants brought out a stretcher and carried him inside. From the porter's lodge the policeman rang up Hradcany Castle and asked to speak to some officer of rank. When he finally got through to a senior officer and told him the story, the earpiece of the phone almost exploded in the policeman's hand. An attempt on the Reichsprotector? Nonsense! Fantastic nonsense! No one would dare attempt such a thing! The Reichsprotector was at that moment driving to the airport.

The policeman, made slightly apprehensive by this rage, tried again. "I assure you, sir," he said, "he is at this moment lying in a bed at the Bulov Clinic. He has a wound in his back, I think. He is also holding what appears to be a very important briefcase."

At this news, the Nazi officer appeared to go quite mad. He insulted the policeman, he swore at him, he called him a fool. Politely and nervously, for he knew when he was talking to a very superior officer, the policeman waited for him to end, then repeated his story word for word. The important officer went berserk. Did he not realize that Reichsprotector Heydrich was head of the S.D.? Even the lowest member of the S.D. was sacrosanct. The idea that anyone could attempt to do injury to the *Head* of the S.D. was a very crucifixion of sanity. The polite policeman began all over again.

"I have to inform you, sir, that Reichsprotector Heydrich is at this moment lying in a bed in the Bulov Clinic in considerable pain . . ."

The officer rang off. Within half an hour the clinic was surrounded by picked squads of S.S. troops. Beds containing Czech patients were thrust impatiently into other wards. Cables went flashing backwards and forwards to Berlin. The Fuhrer himself was outraged. Himmler prepared to fly to Prague. The best German doctors and surgeons prepared to fly to Prague. Prague radio was monitored by other services everywhere, and throughout the world the story struck the headlines in a black banner.

The Nazi beehive buzzed as if it had been struck by a sledge hammer. Only the most terrible vengeance could now requite their madness.

At midnight the lorries started their engines, and the steel-helmeted German troops assembled from barracks and billets around and in Prague piled into them. They had been given their objectives; they knew their orders. All passes must be scrutinized, all houses in the chosen areas sealed off and searched. Any sign of resistance was to be met with instant execution; any suspicious person without papers was to be arrested at once and brought in for interrogation.

The engines roared and exhaust smoke billowed in thick clouds towards the stars. The hooded lorries rumbled through the streets, and the people of Prague hearing them turned uneasily in their beds.

Find the men who attacked Heydrich. The manhunt was on!

Jan Kubis, utterly exhausted, lay in a drugged sleep in the armchair at Auntie Marie's. Josef slept more easily at the Fafkas' house. And all over Prague, where the newly arrived parachutists were hiding, they slept uneasily and kept on their guard.

In the flat of a Mrs. Tereza, Lieutenant Opalka drowsed fully dressed in an armchair. Just before four o'clock in the morning he fell into a deep sleep. When both Jan and Josef had failed to turn up at the pre-arranged rendezvous to discuss future plans, he knew something must have gone wrong. The radio bulletins confirmed this. He was prepared now for the terror to start. It was Mrs. Tereza who first heard the bell ringing in the caretaker's flat downstairs. Peering through the window she saw below the glint of helmets, and heard the growl of voices.

She ran to wake Opalka, but he had heard also and was buttoning his jacket. She looked at him with terror-filled eyes. "It could be just a general search. I think they're soldiers, not Gestapo."

Opalka knew that the difference between Wehrmacht and Gestapo was purely academic. "The hiding-place— quick," he said.

It was a small flat: lounge, dining-room, kitchen and bedroom. They moved swiftly into the sitting-room at the rear. To an unobservant eye it seemed to offer no hiding-place at all. A round table and chairs; a settee with wooden arms upholstered in striped satin against one wall; two cushions propped up at the furthest end. There was a bookshelf fastened to the wall above it. To the right a small cupboard flush with the wall opened into a small space used as a place for brushes and dusting materials.

Together they heaved the settee away from the wall. Behind it was a cupboard similar to the other but slightly larger. Opalka crawled in and Mrs. Tereza closed the door behind him, pushing the settee back into position. The small door was completely obscured except for its top left-hand corner. By balancing the cushions precariously on top of the settee, she was just able to cover this up, but it was a flimsy concealment.

She heard a noise at the door and turned, her heart faltering. Her small daughter Alenka stood there. She was ten years old. She had been seven when the Gestapo came for her father; she had been awakened at the same hour and seen him hauled away. Now the remembered terror was in her eyes. It was a terror so naked and revealed that Mrs. Tereza wept inwardly that she should be so subjected again to this bleak and bitter experience.

She took her very gently in her arms, holding her tightly and securely for a second.

"Darling," she said, "don't be frightened. Sit in the chair where Uncle Adolph has been sleeping and don't say a word when the soldiers come in to search. If we say nothing they will soon go away."

The tramping feet sounded in the flat below. She looked round, trembling. Was there any sign of Opalka's presence? She hurried back into the sitting-room and whispered over the settee, "Don't worry, I'm sure it's only soldiers."

His voice was urgent. "I forgot my revolver. It's under the cushion. Is there time to get it?"

She flew back into the lounge, pulled Alenka off the chair and flipped over the cushion.

It was there. A Browning automatic, heavy, cold and dangerous. She snatched it up and raced back. She heaved away the settee, pulled open the door and thrust it into his hands.

"Good luck," he whispered, "good luck."

Almost simultaneously she heard the heavy banging on the door. She hurried across the lounge. As she passed the armchair for a second time, she saw his tie lying at the foot of the chair from which it had fallen. She grabbed it and stuffed it fiercely into her dressing-gown pocket. With a dry throat, her heart like a stone inside her chest, she clicked off the lock and opened the flat door.

There were two S.S. men outside. They were in uniform, steel-helmeted, truculent, suspicious. They looked at her grimly and pushed past her into the flat.

"What do you want?" she said. Trembling, trying to summon up indignation, she snapped, "There is no one here except my child and myself."

Without a word they walked from the lounge. They glanced at Alenka, who looked back at them with a child's steady, level gaze. While one examined the bedroom and kitchen, the other walked through into the sitting-room. Mrs. Tereza followed him. He opened the small cupboard door, poked around inside with his rifle, then fumbled round with his hand. His eyes roaming over the settee alighted on the cushions at the end. He took a step towards them, glancing across at Mrs. Tereza as he did so. With a hopeless feeling of terror she darted a glance at the bureau in the other corner. It stopped him in mid-stride. Glancing at her suspiciously he turned back and rummaged through its drawers. He found nothing which interested him. He glanced back at the cushions again, and her heart went cold. He must not touch them! At all costs he must not touch them! As he moved to pass her she attempted, apparently, to pull a chair out of his way. In some odd manner it got into his path. He paused, and at that moment the other soldier came into the room.

"Nothing," he said. "Let's get on and finish the others." The S.S. soldier glanced for the last time at the cushions. "All right," he said.

She followed them out and locked the front door behind them. She stood with her back against it, sweat beading her forehead. She felt sick; she knew by Alenka's face that she must look dreadful.

She tried to smile at her and grimaced as if her facial muscles were stiff with cold.

"It's all right, darling," she whispered softly. "It's all right now."

She waited until she heard the front door slam downstairs, and the lorries start up, before letting Opalka out of the cupboard. He stretched and tossed his revolver on the settee.

He took both her hands in his own. "When it's all over," he said, "and if I'm still alive I shall come back and give you a golden key." They turned out the light and peered through a crack in the black-out shutters. The first greyness was starting in the sky. A bird was chirping somewhere down in a tree.

They walked back into the lounge. Alenka was still in the armchair but she was sobbing quietly to herself.

All that night the searches continued. The people of occupied Europe came to know them well, and to taste the agonizing fear and anxiety which always accompanied them. There was, in the deliberate and systematic use and repetition of the hours before dawn as a time of search and arrest, a threat and an intimidation more potent than the sound of bombers overhead; a terror as acute as the clip-clop-clip of the executioner's feet approaching down the long corridor towards the death cell. That night the stars were cold and hard above the spires of Prague and the air beneath an invisible spider's web of criss-crossing radio waves. That night the voice of Radio Prague was shrill with baffled hate. Someone had to pay for this outrage!

There were special instructions for the people of Prague: no civilian was permitted to leave his house between 21.00 on the 27th May and 06.00 in the morning of the 28th May.

All public bars, cinemas, theatres and places of public entertainment were closed from now on.

All public transport was stopped.

Whoever was found on the streets during these hours of curfew and did not stop when called upon to do so would be shot on sight.

Jan awoke at five-thirty. Uncoiling from the armchair in the Moravecs' flat, his whole body was stiff and sore; he still felt immensely depressed. The wound in his chest was painful and his eye throbbed under the bandage. He yawned out at the cold grey light through the window, and then looked ruefully at himself in the bathroom mirror. He fingered his puffy swollen face. All over Prague, people were waking under a clear June sky to start another day of terror, to switch on the radio and hear what had happened in the night. They learned that the executions had started. The early radio bulletins carried the names of five people

who had nothing whatever to do with the resistance but had
been executed for sheltering unregistered persons.

Jan went into the kitchen. Auntie Marie was already
there in her dressing gown and slippers, making coffee. He
had never noticed how grey her hair was before. She smiled
at him. She spoke in the hushed tones that one adopts when
the rest of the household is not awake, and the day has only
half begun.

She asked him what they would be doing in England at
this time of morning.

He knew then that she was thinking of her son in the
R.A.F. and Jan wondered at which bleak airfield he was
stationed. Would he be perched in one of those little huts
around the perimeter track, watching the black bombers
homing after their nightly raids? Or would he be sleeping
in a draughty Nissen hut with the orderly corporal already
on his rounds, crying "Wakey-wakey".

He tried to tell her of life in England; how, in some towns,
the people would be counting their dead after an air raid
while others stared at their ruined houses and wondered
what would become of them. He also told her that in some
parts of the country they would hardly know there was a war
on. He told her of a place he knew, a village called Ightfield.
Josef and he had stayed there so many times with a family
called Ellison. It was in the country and the house stood at
the edge of a field in a tiny village. There was a long path
through the vegetable garden up to the door. From the room
where Josef and he used to sleep, they could see out over the
fields, and about this time the black and white cows would
wake up and start mooing to be milked. It all seemed very
far away now.

They chatted a little longer, and then Jan told her he
would be leaving after breakfast.

She turned in astonishment, the coffee pot poised in her
hand. But why? He was safe here. With his injured face he
might easily be recognized.

He explained why he had to leave. The Germans would
immediately make exhaustive inquiries about that bicycle;
it was their most promising clue. They might, somehow,

Heydrich's body lies in state in the forecourt of Hradcany Castle

The Orthodox Church of St. Cyril and Method in Resslova Street

S.S. men and Czech firemen thrust smoke-making equipment through the outside ventilation slot into the crypt

connect it with Auntie Marie. If they caught him in her flat it would be hopeless for her. Without him there, she could always say that the bicycle was lost or that it had been stolen. They might not believe her, but at least she would have a chance. His voice was calm and his mind was made up. When the workers started off for the factories he would join them, he said. As a railwayman he could mingle in their ranks and not be noticed. He could take the bandage off his eye and pull the cap well down. He had thought it over and decided it would be much safer for everyone if he kept on the move. She did not try and dissuade him. She knew him better than that.

He also told her that there was to be a meeting at three o'clock. After that he should be all right. And, anyway, she had already accepted far more of her share of danger than was right.

As he left the flat to join the thin streams of workers pouring from their homes and coagulating into small groups at tram stops and road crossings, he heard the radio booming from half a dozen flats. It was not difficult to hear the whole sequence of the announcement.

"In consequence of the attempt on the life of the Deputy Reichsprotector the following is decreed:

"A state of emergency for civilians in the whole Protectorate of Bohemia and Moravia is declared and takes effect at once.

"Whoever hides the criminals, or gives them any help, or has any knowledge of their identity, or description of their appearance, and does not inform the authorities will be shot with his entire family." The radio made a point of repeating that fact at least once an hour.

He kept pace with the other workers. His overalls suggested that the best place to move around unnoticed was the railway station. He joined the streams of pedestrians walking towards it.

Inside the huge hall it was crowded and echoing with distorted noise. He walked backwards and forwards through the halls and booking offices, keeping the wounded side of his face as much as possible towards the walls. He picked a newspaper from a wastepaper basket and found a seat in a busy part of the booking hall where relays of people sat to eat their sandwiches. He sat half-hidden behind the newspaper, occasionally pretending to doze, holding his hand carefully over his wounded eye as if he was supporting his sleepy head. At lunch time he joined a party of railway workers eating their bread and sausage on a pile of logs, staying far enough away to avoid identification yet close enough to appear attached to them.

By the time it got close to three o'clock, he was weary of these subterfuges, and with a sense of relief walked through the streets towards 1837 Bishop Street. He waited until the street was empty and then pressed the bell. A young resistance worker, whom he knew slightly, let him in, and he found only Uncle Hajsky awaiting him. Behind his large horn-rimmed spectacles his eyes looked red and tired, and he greeted Jan wearily. None of the others was coming. Everyone must stay under cover until this blew over.

They did not have much to say to each other. Jan thought they had botched the whole business up pretty thoroughly. Uncle Hajsky stared at him owlishly, and said that he had heard that Heydrich was on the danger list. If his condition were not serious, the Nazis would undoubtedly have been boasting in every news broadcast that the attack had been a failure.

He told him that the S.S. troops and the Wehrmacht had surrounded and cordoned off entire areas in the Liben and Vinohrady districts. They had nearly got Opalka, and two of the newly-arrived parachutists had had to hang outside a skylight for nearly an hour.

There were bound to be more searches tonight. The curfew started at nine o'clock, and everybody on the streets after that hour was liable to be shot. With an edge of bitterness in his voice Jan inquired where he should spend the night.

He should go back to the Ogouns, advised Uncle Hajsky. The group had been offered a secure hiding place right in the heart of Prague. If all went well it would be ready for occupation tomorrow. Then he would get in touch with Jan again.

Uncle Hajsky left first, and after a discreet interval Jan followed. He went back to the railway station. Amongst the crowds there he felt safer than anywhere else, but as the homegoing workers began to thin, he knew that if he stayed much longer it would be dangerous.

He left the station and wandered out into the streets. He turned over and over in his mind the idea of returning to the Ogouns. It did not seem fair to them, but who else could he turn to? Anna would shelter him, but her flat was overlooked. A stranger—and a man at that—would certainly be noticed. He would endanger her needlessly. There was really nowhere else he could go except to the Ogouns. Wherever he went he took the chance of death for all whom he encountered. He could rejoin Josef—almost certainly he'd be at the Fafkas with Liboslava—but it would be far safer if they stayed apart for the time being. The fact that two young men had made the attack was well known. He made up his mind, therefore, that he would approach the Ogoun house and see what was going on. If it looked quiet he might chance it. He waited until dark before he turned into their street. There was no one about; everything looked perfectly normal.

He rang the bell, giving the usual signal: three short rings and one long one. Within a few seconds the door opened, slowly. The Professor stood there. His face told Jan how sick he was with worry. "Come in," he said simply.

Jan walked through into the living-room. Mrs. Ogoun had just risen from the settee, her face stiff with fright. As Jan came in her lips said, "We're expecting another search . . ." and then she stopped, catching sight of her husband, waiting for a lead from him. Jan halted in the middle of the room, looking from one to the other.

"They surrounded our district last night and searched everywhere," said the Professor quietly. "They came here. We have heard they are likely to repeat these searches."

Jan looked from one to the other. They had been very good to him, and he knew now he should not have come back.

"You are my last refuge," said Jan slowly. "I can go no farther. But I understand——"

The silence was almost tangible. Words were unimportant. Jan knew that if for one moment the Nazis suspected this household, all would be killed. The elderly man standing before him with the tired face carried this responsibility. He carried it for the wife he loved so well, and for the two athletic sons of whom he was so proud. Therefore he had to choose for them as well as for himself.

Professor Ogoun looked at the figure in the dark blue creased overalls. He observed the wounded face; he noted the lines of intense weariness; the look of despair, and suddenly he knew that if he turned this young man away from his door he would forever forfeit his own self-respect. He had entered this thing of his own free will; he could not back out at this moment of intense danger.

"My son," he said quietly, "your mission is higher than ours and therefore your life is more valuable. Stay here with us."

Jan sat down suddenly on the settee. Mrs. Ogoun, heartened by the courage of her husband, sat next to him and put her hand on his knee. "You're all right now," she said gently. "You must be hungry. I will get you some food."

"Your friend is safe," said the Professor. "He's staying with the Fafkas. Mrs. Fafka came round this morning. He'd left some ammunition in the pocket of his overcoat."

"But they searched——?" said Jan.

"They were looking for men, not bullets," said the Professor. "They had no reason to suspect us. They looked in all the rooms, the cupboards, under the beds. It was not a systematic search."

"You know what happened?" asked Jan.

"Only what the newspapers and the radio told us."

"What about the cap?" said Jan. "I'm sorry about the cap."

Professor Ogoun nodded. "Yes, we know. We were a little worried at first because everyone knows that our younger son wears it at school. But we found a piece of camel-hair material in the lining of my wife's coat and we have a good friend who is a tailor. He made us a replica. Don't worry. We've dirtied it, and no one could tell the difference."

Mrs. Ogoun brought in a bowl of hot water and a pair of tweezers. "Let your head rest back on the settee and I'll see if I can get out the rest of the bomb splinters."

For two hours with gentle fingers she probed and bathed. During this time they discussed where he could hide should there be another raid. Jan had thought about it before he arrived. The kitchen window was blacked out with a panel of cardboard an inch away from the window pane. If they opened the kitchen window, he could stand outside on the sill in the darkness, and the black-out panel would conceal him. If, moreover, they moved the large cupboard in front of the window and hung their overcoats inside, they might further deceive any searchers by going straight to the cupboard to get their identity cards from the pockets. If Jan slept in the large armchair in the living-room, he should be able to take up such a position within a few seconds.

They agreed on this plan and rehearsed the move many times. After several rehearsals, from the moment the alarm was given to the time Jan was hidden, the operation took only twenty-five seconds. During their final practice Professor Ogoun suddenly stopped and looked sadly at Jan.

"Such a silly game for grown-ups to be playing, isn't it?" he said quietly.

CHAPTER FOURTEEN

THAT Vladimir Petrek, the black-bearded chaplain of the Czechoslovakian Orthodox church of St. Cyril and Method in Resslova St., should choose to involve himself with the parachutists at this hour of critical peril and offer to provide them with a secure place of refuge, is indisputable proof of his personal integrity. But there was more to it than mere courage. He offered sanctuary in its simplest religious sense. The parachutists, he believed, were soldiers fighting against the bleak ungodliness, the merciless inhumanity of the Nazi regime. It was his duty and the duty of his church to do all possible to aid them.

This decision, after consultation with his bishop and the church elders, he communicated to Jindra, who welcomed his intervention. To allow the parachutists to remain scattered about Prague meant that they were a constant danger both to themselves and to the people who sheltered them. The Nazis were still organizing swift surprise searches. Much better therefore to congregate them safely somewhere and eventually smuggle them out of Prague when the time was right.

Chaplain Petrek volunteered to guide each parachutist personally to the church. This was the best way to avoid suspicion. Once there, he was certain they could not be found.

Jan had slept soundly under his blanket at the Ogouns during that second night after the attack, and when he awoke, fit and refreshed, it was at once apparent what an enormous difference Mrs. Ogoun's poulticing and bathing had made. The swelling around his eye and cheek had gone, and except for the dark wound at the side of his eye, his face looked almost normal. His depression too had disappeared; now he felt ready to go and meet Josef. He changed into his best suit, pulled his trilby hat well down over his wounded eye and announced to the Ogouns that he was off to the Fafkas. He would see them again soon.

He strode blithely through the streets with the sunshine on his face, and feeling that somehow the worst was over.

At the Fafkas, Josef greeted him boisterously. He stood back, regarded Jan's face critically and observed, tongue in cheek, that he never was very good-looking anyway, so a few scars on his face would not make much difference. They were very pleased to see each other. It was the first time they had been separated since landing in Czechoslovakia.

They talked solidly for an hour, exchanging experiences, and Josef revealed that Uncle Hajsky had visited him and told him about the church. It was to be kept a strict secret; he must not even tell Anna about. Only Uncle Hajsky, Jindra and Auntie Marie, who would try and cook them occasional hot meals, would know where they were.

That afternoon the man with the black beard called for Jan. On that hot May afternoon few people were about, and Jan followed the chaplain through the centre of Prague, walking about fifty yards in his rear. From the river bank the priest turned up Resslova Street. Three hundred yards up on the left-hand side, unobtrusive in the climbing perspective of the other buildings, stood the Church of St. Cyril and Method. Stone steps led up to its imposing baroque entrance and huge iron-studded door. But the chaplain avoided this. Set back from the main road in the side wall of the church stood a small door. Petrek opened it with a yale key, and when Jan pushed against it he found himself in the small ante-room which the chaplain used as his office.

Petrek preceded him along a short narrow passage which led to the church and the altar. A thin painted wooden screen separated the altar from the main body of the church, and in its high vaulted interior Jan gratefully inhaled the cool air. At the far end of the church above the main doorway and reached by a flight of wooden steps, ran a wooden balcony.

In the shelter of his own church Petrek smiled for the first time, his white teeth glinting against the dark beard. Affably he took Jan's arm and led him around the building,

199

explaining its history, as if they both possessed time and leisure for scholarly appreciation.

Petrek was that sort of man. He was deeply immersed in the aesthetic mysticism of religion. It was to preserve his own values that he was aiding them all, but Jan was still a little puzzled by this attitude. He had had scant time either to think of God or to theorize about religious philosophy. Instinctively, he liked and trusted the chaplain, but to the end regarded him as an enigma.

Petrek explained that the church had been built between 1730 and 1736 on the site of a much older monastery. He pointed to the ceiling, white and gracefully arched, where coloured panels depicted angels lounging negligently upon billowing white clouds, whilst small rosy-bottomed cupids fluttered coyly overhead. He informed Jan that a German artist had painted them a century ago. He also spoke of a rumour which stated that, from some point in the crypt, an ancient underground tunnel ran down to the banks of the River Vltava. Apparently it had been bricked up long ago and no one had ever rediscovered its whereabounts. Wryly he observed that perhaps Jan and his friends would have time to do some further research regarding its existence.

As he spoke, he walked slowly towards the far end of the church and the huge main doors, studded with heavy nails. He told Jan that they were usually open in the morning so that worshippers might come in and pray. He also warned him that during these periods they would obviously have to exercise extreme care.

Three wide strips of coconut matting covered the main floor of the church, and a narrower strip ran between a glass and wooden draught screen to the main doors. The chaplain beckoned Jan to stand aside, then stooping, and with a theatrical gesture, he pulled the strip of matting aside. Beneath was a flagstone, two feet square, with an iron rung set in its centre. The chaplain braced his feet one on either side of the flagstone and took a double-handed grip on the iron rung. Straining upwards he lifted the slab three inches clear of the floor and swung it back between his legs. It needed all his strength; it was a very heavy stone. No light or sound came from the black hole he had uncovered.

He took a small torch out of his pocket and shone it down through the hole, and Jan could now see the top rungs of a thin ladder protruding to within a foot of the level of the church floor.

The chaplain led the way down into the ancient crypt. Gingerly, Jan followed him. It was not completely dark. High up on one wall was a ventilation slot about nine inches wide and eighteen inches long, barred by a jagged iron grill which admitted fresh air and daylight.

From outside the church, the chaplain explained, it was hardly noticeable, set as it was in the wall, ten feet above the pavement. When Jan's eyes became accustomed to the light, he saw that honeycombing either side of the crypt, between the thick stone buttresses which supported the roof, was a series of square holes. These apertures were roughly two feet six square and ran back into the wall for about seven feet. Those which contained the bodies of the old monks were closed with a brick and mortar seal, but many, still awaiting occupants, gaped blank and empty.

The chaplain led the way to the far end of the crypt. It was—as Jan was to discover later—twenty-two paces long and between three and five paces wide. At the far end a short but steep flight of stone steps ran upwards to the level of the church floor. This exit was sealed off by an immense stone slab mortared into the floor overhead.

The only way down into the crypt, therefore, lay through the narrow funnel through which they had both descended. It would be easy to defend; in fact it was well-nigh impregnable, but a colder, more cheerless and depressing place one could not imagine, and the use of a tomb as a refuge was an anticipation not greatly to the liking of either Jan or Josef or any of the others, when they eventually arrived. The chaplain brought them in one by one, and by that evening six were assembled: Jan and Josef and Valchik, of the old-timers, and three of the newly arrived parachutists who so far had seen no action. Their names were Bublik, Hruby and Svarc. Lieutenant Opalka and Ata Moravec were also joining them later. They both knew too much to be left outside.

The chaplain explained that they could use the crypt as a hiding place for at least sixteen or seventeen days if that was necessary. His churchwarden knew that they were there but he had a wife, a talkative wife, and she could certainly not be trusted with such a secret. However, she was on holiday and would not be back for almost three weeks. Well before that time, the search for them should have petered out, and they should be able to return to more comfortable lodgings.

In his summing up the future the chaplain was to be proved quite wrong. The hue and cry would not die down. It would increase in tempo.

The Germans were masters of Europe. Wherever they had fought, they had been victorious. That a defeated subject people should have dared to strike against their military omniscience, enraged them to a point near apoplexy. Executions and more executions were the quick and obvious means of demonstrating that fury. Blindly, indiscriminately, mercilessly, they lined up people before their firing squads. Scores and sometimes hundreds were executed every day, and their names published in the newspapers and gabbled over the radio. The wrath of the Teutonic gods, Hitler and Himmler, must be appeased! Frank, who had taken over Heydrich's post, was empowered and urged to use any means or methods he liked; not only to find the guilty men, but also to punish the whole Czech nation.

Road blocks were set up, whole areas cordoned off. Wholesale arrests were carried out and the mass executions increased.

Radio and newspaper exhortations continued at full blast. Unless the guilty men were found all of Czechoslovakia would suffer, they said.

To Reinhard Heydrich lying in his bed at the Bulov Clinic all this meant very little. Doctors were constantly in attendance; blood transfusion after blood transfusion was given, but his skin grew gradually more sallow, his features more pronounced, his pulse weaker. He died on the morning of the fourth of June, and the autopsy made by the president of the German Pathological Institute declared that death came as a result of damage to the vital parenchymatic organs, by bacteria, possibly from poison which entered with particles of explosive, and which was mainly centred in the chest, the diaphragm and around the spleen.

The Acting Reichsprotector was dead. Now the real fury of the Nazi Empire could be demonstrated.

Orders were at once given that the city should mourn, and black flags and black drapes and black bunting were hung from every building. Even the Germans realized that the Czechs were mourning their own dead and the indignities heaped upon them. The bands played elegiac music in the streets and upon the radio, but between the mournful melodies the Minister of Education was heard threatening that "the terrible murder committed by agents has put the question of our national existence upon a knife edge; it is quite right that seven thousand traitors should perish in order to save seven million people!"

Jindra walked slowly to the church in Resslova Street that afternoon. He walked under the black flags and bunting, along the river bank and up the street where the church stood. In the chaplain's office he chatted with Petrek for a few seconds and then went through into the church itself. Uncle Hajsky was already there and so were Opalka, Valchik, Jan and Josef. The other three were out in the spring sunshine. They had identity cards; there was nothing to connect them with the attack; they would be reasonably safe.

Jindra looked anxiously at Uncle Hajsky. It was quite obvious that he needed a rest; he must go into the country somewhere and get away from this atmosphere for a while. He seemed to have shrunk in his clothes, to have aged ten years in as many days. The cords in his neck stood out when he spoke, and from his collar his bony head protruded like that of an old turtle.

They talked amongst themselves for a while, and Lieutenant Opalka, grave and composed in a grey polo-necked sweater, seated with his legs crossed upon a high-backed chair, acted as spokesman for the parachutists.

By this time, blankets and mattresses, tinned food, utensils and a primus stove had been smuggled in to them. They had also brought in their store of weapons and ammunition. They were as snug as they could be in the crypt, even though it was not possible to be very comfortable. At night three remained on watch upon the wooden balcony, and the other four slept in the crypt. It was warm on the balcony during those June nights, and one could see the bright stars through the great windows. In the crypt it was cold and black, and smelt of ancient death, so there was much competition for guard duty on the balcony, and Opalka had found it necessary to work out a roster.

A woman eye specialist duly visited Jan and attended to his eye. It had not been seriously damaged and he could now venture outside the church without much fear of being recognized as the man with the wounded face so wanted by the Nazis. The curfew and restrictions upon public places of entertainment had also been relaxed, so that now the parachutists could leave the church quite freely, singly or in pairs, without arousing undue suspicion. In the morning, those on guard mixed with the congregation. On two occasions S.S. troops had made a spot check of identity cards, and both times Jan and Josef had presented their faked cards without arousing any suspicion. As long as the parachutists were back inside the church by midnight Opalka had no objection to their going out. He knew, and so did Jindra, that it was better to take some slight chances and preserve morale than to insist that everyone rotted in that dark tomb beneath the church floor. Jindra now had moved from his flat on the outskirts, where so many of their important meetings had taken place, and he had given the keys to Opalka, so that the parachutists, a few at a time, could go there for a couple of hours of comparative comfort and relaxation.

When Opalka had finished, Uncle Hajsky reported the situation from his angle. He had news concerning several other members of their group. Ata Moravec was out in the country in hiding; Auntie Marie had gone to Pardubice to give the group operating "Libuse" some idea of what was happening, and to hear what they were doing; she, however, would not be away long; she had been indefatigable in cooking hot meals for those in the crypt and bringing them to the church, and she wished to continue this service.

Karel Curda, as far as Uncle Hajsky knew, was still in the country hiding at his mother's farm, and Pechal was still lurking in the forest near his home. For the time being, at least, they would have to fend for themselves.

In their investigations the Nazis had learned that a fourteen-year-old girl had wheeled a blood-stained bicycle from outside a Bata shoe shop to some address in Liben. Several people had come forward to testify that they had seen her, and in this district the Nazis had intensified their search. All the schools had been visited and hundreds of little girls interrogated. Mrs. Novotna had decided at once that Jindriska should become "very ill", and even when German agents visited her house, she was able to convince them that her daughter had been sick in bed long before the attack had taken place.

When Uncle Hajsky had done, Jindra delivered his report. He brought good news; undoubtedly their plan had succeeded, and already a variety of government spokesmen were hotly denying that conscription of the Czech nation was ever in the mind of the Protectorate government. That Heydrich had been assassinated to prevent such an occurrence was stupid propaganda, they said.

So great was the anger of the Czech government circles that they even referred to the "lying reports broadcast from London". They quoted at length from these despatches and then went on to reiterate how false they were.

Such denials, said Jindra, revealed plainly how dangerous the Protectorate government considered the broadcasts from London. "Under Heydrich's beneficial guidance," boomed the speaker, "the workers were better off than ever; had he not, only a few weeks before the vile attack which ended his life, enabled over three thousand Czech workers from the armament factories to take a prolonged holiday?" The voice of Prague Radio went on enumerating the splendid things General Heydrich had done for Czechoslovakia. What is more, it announced proudly, the Protectorate government, in honour of his memory, were renaming the Vltava embankment the Reinhard Heydrich embankment; a statue was to be erected in a public square; and a plate was to be let into the roadway at the place where the grenade ended his life. There was a spontaneous jeer from the parachutists at this point. Uncle Hajsky interrupted it by saying sombrely, "But the executions are continuing."

Jindra looked at him sternly. "We expected reprisals," he said shortly. "This is a victory. London considers it a victory and victories must be paid for."

On that note the meeting dispersed. Jan went out into the sunshine to meet Anna, and Josef to see his Liboslava. Neither of them, not even Jindra, could guess what payment for that "victory" the Nazis were about to extort.

In the state rooms of Hradcany Castle, Karl Frank drew up his plans for one implacable gesture which would prove conclusively that no one dare trifle with Nazi pride or power; that no country could connive at murdering a senior member of the Nazi hierarchy and escape without the most fiendish reprisals. This action was meant to establish a precedent. It did more than that; it horrified the entire civilized world.

Upon the 10th of June, at dawn, Nazi troops surrounded a village a few miles outside Prague and began their grim and desolating work. Frank's propaganda was already prepared.

"In the course of the search for the murderers of General Heydrich," it ran, "it was ascertained that the population of this village supported and assisted the perpetrators. Apart from the help given to them, the population also committed other hostile acts, such as the keeping of an illegal dump of munitions and arms, the maintenance of an illegal transmitter, and hoarding an extraordinary large quantity of goods which are controlled."

All this was flagrantly untrue. No one in the village had ever heard of Jan Kubis or Josef Gabchik or assisted the resistance in any way. There were never arms or transmitters or "goods which were controlled", in any house. The men of the village worked in the nearby mines or in the fields, and the women attended to their needs and bore their children. They lived a simple hard-working life, and when the terror began, their attitude was one of complete bewilderment. What had Lidice done to deserve this?

All the men and boys were taken from their houses, lined up against the wall of a barn and shot. All the women and children were piled into lorries and driven off to concentration camps.

It was not that they simply shot the men and deported the women and children. They completed, in its fullest medieval meaning, the operation of razing a place to the ground.

Lidice was a large village of many houses and farms, several shops, a church with an imposing spire, and a schoolroom. The business of reduction was a considerable task. For that was the Nazi intention; to obliterate the village from the earth, and erase its name for evermore from the map.

German photographs reveal that bulldozers and whole lines of wagons and lorries were needed to transport the rubble and level the sites of the houses. Removing the human rubble was an easier task. The one hundred and seventy-three men and boys, after execution, were buried in a pit on Horak's farm. The workers on night shift were quickly arrested as they returned home and immediately shot; only one, sensing disaster, escaped into the forest but he, also, was later betrayed and shot. Another miner was in hospital with a broken leg. By October he had recovered. He was then shot.

The women were transported to the concentration camps of Ravensbruck and Oswiecim where most of them died. Eighty-two of the children were killed; a few, born to their mothers in concentration camps, were adopted into German families, and years afterwards were found by the Red Cross and the International Tracing Service.

On the whole, the dissolution of Lidice was undertaken

very thoroughly and very competently. It had, of course, upon the conscience and emotions of the outside world, an effect diametrically opposite to the one the Nazis intended and envisaged.

Even in those dark war years when the mechanism of civilization had gone completely awry, when death in many hideous forms was commonplace and truth had been replaced by propaganda, the fate of Lidice bewildered and horrified world opinion. It certainly did not cow or intimidate as the Nazis intended it should. The immediate reaction was one of enormous anger. That the regime of even Hitler should boast of this act was received with an incredulity that bordered upon disbelief.

Perhaps more than any other atrocity, in a war full of atrocities, Lidice jolted the conscience of the world. At first it seemed only a small pebble dropped into the ocean of war, but the ripples quickly spread and touched people everywhere. The uncommitted ones now knew that there could be no compromise with an enemy such as this. This behaviour, aboriginal in its inhumanity, was outside all conventions or unwritten charters of decency. Men now knew that the fight must continue to the very end, and that end must be the defeat of Nazi Germany. Without that there could be no safety, no honour and no hope for anyone anywhere. Men took care that the name Lidice, far from being erased for ever, was perpetuated in a variety of ways. An American town and a Mexican village both changed their names to Lidice. Tanks roared into action with "Lidice" painted upon their turrets; block-busting bombs were loaded into aircraft for delivery into the heart of the Reich with the same inscription chalked upon their cases. Even in the hearts of Germans, in or out of uniform, the name and its implications must have bewildered and disgusted them.

To Jan, upon the sunny afternoon of June 10th, the news of the slaughter was crushing in its implications. It was the final bitter and bloody straw. The eventual death of Heydrich had brought him no personal feelings of triumph. The subsequent series of executions had sickened and depressed him. Jindra knew this; Jindra had sensed his mental despair, as the firing parties went about their daily ritual.

Already Jan had approached Jindra, and told him that both he and Josef were ready to give themselves up. They had to do something to end this unending slaughter of innocent people. Jindra recalls how he put his arm around Jan's shoulders and told him that this was a burden he had to bear; it was a price that all Czechoslovakia had to pay, and in the final assessment it would be shown that they paid it willingly.

Jindra was fifteen years older than Jan; his was the mind and the strength behind the whole of the organization. He realized that he could do little to assuage Jan's mental agony. He could only try and bolster his determination to go on. With Josef it was easier. Josef was more of an extrovert, gayer, better equipped and with more mental resilience than his friend; he did not worry so deeply; though he, without question, was also willing to sacrifice his own life to end the slaughter.

When Lidice was annihilated Jan reached the very depths of despair. He had dropped out of the skies above Czechoslovakia with high hopes that he would be of lasting service to his country. He had fallen in love in the execution of that service, and for just a few brief moments he had entertained some small hope that a future might still exist for him. Now he knew that, whatever happened, his conscience had to carry a burden he was not certain it could endure.

Upon the afternoon that the news of Lidice reached them, Vladimir Petrek was sitting in his office when both Jan and Josef appeared in the doorway. He knew from the grim and anxious looks on their faces that they had weighty news to convey to him. Indeed, they had come to ask his advice as to what he thought they should do.

Somehow, they declared, someone had to stop the dreadful and continuous slaughter. They had already suggested to Jindra that they should give themselves up, and he had abruptly and finally vetoed the idea. Lidice had now made it imperative that some action had to be taken. There was every reason to suppose that this was only the first move in a campaign of remorseless terror; other Lidices might follow.

Jindra's decision was made of military necessity. What was the advice of a man of God? How deeply they were troubled, and how they hung upon his words, was pitifully apparent to the chaplain. As he explained to Jindra, when he later reported the incident, he had had to choose his words very carefully.

"First," asked Vladimir Petrek, "what are you thinking of doing?"

They told him they intended finding seats in a public park, and then hanging small cardboard placards around their necks which announced that they were the assassins of Heydrich. They would then swallow their poison pills. Their dead bodies, plus the placards, should supply enough mute evidence to satisfy the Nazi authorities.

Petrek looked at them sadly. The scheme was wildly melodramatic, but then everybody's lives in wartime were wildly melodramatic. There was no doubt about the seriousness of their proposal. The chaplain realized that, if he concurred and said he thought their plan feasible, they would act upon it at once. That was the measure of their utter desperation.

He declared at once, firmly and unequivocally, that the entire plan was futile and meaningless. In the first place the possession of two dead bodies would never appease the Nazis. Secondly, as a minister of God, he could not for one second condone or even contemplate the act of suicide. It was cowardice, abject, pitiful cowardice.

At that word he saw their faces change, and knew his point had gone home. Sacrifice, they could endure, but cowardice was anathema to their pride. He talked and argued with them for a long time and unconsciously repeated the arguments of Jindra. Victories would never be won without agony and suffering; their personal deaths would solve nothing and might indeed provide a material victory for the enemy.

When Jan and Josef left him he knew that, for the time being, he had delayed the action they so seriously contemplated, but he also guessed that he had not completely driven it from their minds. The desire to atone in some way for the dreadful revenge their actions had brought down upon the heads of their countrymen, was still burning in their minds. Only time could decrease their anguish.

In this process Anna Malinova played an important rôle. Jan saw her every day and almost every night now. She was gentle; an oasis in a world full of brutality and hate. She did not even mind the scars. She touched them with such pity that they could have been burnt upon her own smooth skin instead of his. To Jan she appeared at times to be his only link with sanity and reality in a world without either.

He met her on the bridge in their usual place. She also had heard of Lidice, and with one glance at his face she knew the mental agony he was experiencing. She held his arm tightly as they walked along the Vltava embankment before catching a tram out to Jindra's empty flat. In the afternoons, in the warm June sunshine, it seemed to the people of Prague that the all-pervading atmosphere of fear which hung in the air like a heavy pollen dispersed a little. Now, lovers walked in the shade of the chestnut trees at the side of the river, their feet trampling the thin drifts of blossoms fallen on the banks. Women with prams and children sat on benches and watched the swans. People strolled idly backwards and forwards, looked up at the blue sky, or down at the dark Vltava, and tried to forget that madness existed everywhere. It seemed to many people in Prague during those days almost odd that the sun should still rise and set, the river flow and the flowers still bloom as if these bloody and lunatic gyrations of homo sapiens were of not the slightest importance to anyone. Somewhere, in the scheme of things, it seemed that God and Nature were not collaborating; otherwise the grass would surely wither and the sun pause in its daily arabesque across the sky, at the spectacle of a world so torn by hatred and diminished by pain.

In Jindra's flat all Jan's despair poured out, and Anna Malinova let him talk. It could not go on, he said. Not for a single day more. They had to give themselves up. Somehow they had to stop the insensate, useless slaughter. They had completed their job; their own lives were now of small account in the general scheme of things. No longer could he bear the responsibility for so many deaths. Did Anna understand that? Did she really understand that?

It was rhetorical rather than real, but Anna held his hand and tried to soothe him. She brewed hot ersatz coffee and made him drink it. She made him walk around the flat with her, examining the bedroom and the bathroom and the kitchen and criticizing their defects. But even she did not now have enough courage to say, "one day we shall have an apartment like this".

This scene she later reported to Auntie Marie, hoping perhaps that Auntie Marie might possess healing skills that she, Anna, through her inexperience, did not have. She told her how they tried to equate, somehow, the utilitarian order of the flat and its furniture, the simple order of living which should rightly have been theirs, with the holocaust which seemed to tower above them and hang in the very air. Against the enormity of the Nazi vengeance, their lives and actions seemed pitifully unreal. Even grief seemed unreal, perhaps because when grief becomes a national calamity, it belongs to somebody else.

They sat upon the settee and watched the sky darken to indigo and the stars appear. They kissed and clung together in their small room, fashioning momentary forgetfulness, searching desperately in the human oblivion of passion for comfort and some reason which might give shape and meaning to their dilemma.

This perhaps was all they were to have. It was perhaps as good as anything that might come in the future. Why should they put faith in the future? Was not this sunlit afternoon, this evening of completion, sufficient? If the next spring and the next summer came and went without them, did it matter?

But they knew it did matter. The sinews and the mind and the blood cells yearned for fusion and continuity; the flesh shouted to go on. Even though their agony might continue, the will to exist remained, and must remain. It was Anna Malinova who made this plain to Jan.

CHAPTER FIFTEEN

THE news of events in Prague brought a growing fear to Sergeant Major Karel Curda, hiding out upon his mother's farm, many miles out in the country near the village of Nova Hlina.

He was surrounded by terrified people. From the very moment he had arrived in Czechoslovakia, and his mother, sister and two married brothers knew that they were sheltering and associating with a parachutist, they had been frightened. More and more those days he heard the sound of his mother's weeping; more and more he saw her reddened eyes and the reproachful face of his sister.

When he returned after the Skoda episode, they begged him not to continue in such things: but when they heard about Heydrich they knew they were too late. Now he had brought them all to ruin and destruction.

It was in this sort of emotional climate that the courage of Karel Curda slowly began to leak. The newspapers and the continual radio bulletins forced new cracks in his mental façade. Slowly his morale drained away.

Daily he read of the mounting list of executions; morning, noon and evening, he heard the staccato reports threatening death and torture to the guilty men, but promising safety and rewards to those who confessed.

Two names amongst the roll of victims impinged particularly upon his consciousness. They were the names of Frantisek Miks, gendarme of Tabor, and Antonin Miks, clerk of Prague, the brothers of Arnost Miks. They were the brothers of the man who had flown back to Czechoslovakia with him, who had trained with him, lived and laughed and drunk English beer with him, and above all trusted him. These brothers had not even known that Arnost Miks was back in the country. They had no contact whatsoever with the resistance, yet they had been executed!

This would happen to all his own family should suspicion

fall upon them. Even his fiancée and his child would probably die. Alone in that farmhouse, wrestling with his conscience, the idea was growing unbearable.

He heard also the voices of the ministers of the Protectorate government which alternatively pleaded, exhorted or threatened. It was the duty of the entire nation to hunt down these murderers, they said. Immediately they were found all measures of terror and repression would be lifted. People should ignore the traitorous transmissions from the Czechs in London. Their false propaganda, which suggested that anyone who denounced the murderers, or helped the authorities in any way to find them, would be executed, was nonsensical. What could *they* do against the mighty power of the Reich? The government guaranteed that whoever helped to find the assailants would be reprieved, even though he himself was guilty. This applied equally to his family.

All this had its effect upon Karel Curda, but the occurrence which had the greatest effect upon him came at the end of a tortuous chain of circumstances. And it was poor unlucky Pechal miles away who started the chain.

Ever since he had dropped into Czechoslovakia, Oldrich Pechal, the last operational member of the team of Pechal, Gerik and Miks, had been hiding in the forest. The Jindra Group had tried to contact him without success. Stubbornly he eked out an existence in the forest and waited to see what would happen to his family.

The Germans, because of Gerik's betrayal, knew approximately where he was; they certainly knew about his family. In vain Pechal secretly visited his father and mother and told them to flee. But his father said wearily, "Where shall we go, my son? We are too old now, your mother and me, to run away."

When Heydrich died they were at once arrested. It was shortly after this that Pechal made contact with what he believed to be the local resistance organization. He was tricked into a meeting at a lonely spot in the forest, and when he fought desperately to escape, he was beaten into unconsciousness. They strapped him to a stretcher and carried him to one of the local Nazi hostelries, and the brutal interrogation began. But Pechal betrayed nothing. He might be hesitant and emotional and he was certainly much too concerned with his family, but of his personal courage and fortitude there was no shadow of a doubt.

There was, of course, no further point in the Nazis preserving the lives of his father, mother and brother any longer. They were shot, and news of their execution was published in the newspaper; but it is highly unlikely that the Nazis realized that the news would intimidate or influence anybody.

But intimidate it did. It pushed Karel Curda to breaking point. He read that news item over and over again. Miks' brothers and now Pechal's family! What could prevent it happening to his own family? His mother, sister and two married brothers and all their families would die before the firing squad. Somehow he had to prevent it. But how? Even if he betrayed his comrades and all they stood for, what good would that do?

Could he trust the word of the Protectorate government's ministers? Could he trust the Nazis not to destroy his mother and sister and brothers? He reassured himself by recalling that so far he had caused them little harm. Yes, he had landed in Czechoslovakia illegally by parachute; he had lit a candle in a barn which had caused a blaze to guide R.A.F. bombers, but that was all; and the raid had proved abortive.

He went back to his radio and his newspapers and there he read Karl Frank's latest pronouncement and last offer. If information giving the identities of Heydrich's murderers was revealed before the 18th June, not only would the informant and his family be protected even if he was guilty, but he would also be rewarded. And the reward now stood at twenty million crowns!

So Karel Curda took his first step. He wrote a letter to the police chief in his nearby town, but took the precaution of posting it from a point well away from his own village. He did not sign the letter, and in it simply revealed that the names of the men who had killed Heydrich were Jan

Kubis and Josef Gabchik. His journey towards betrayal had started.

Almost certainly the police post which received the letter ignored it completely. They were possibly quite used to receiving vindictive and anonymous letters. For two days after this initial step, Karel Curda waited and wondered. And as he waited he realized he had committed himself. Now they might trace the letter back to him. If that happened all was lost. There was nothing for it but to go to the police or better still to the Gestapo itself and confess everything. Only in this way could his family be saved.

He caught a train to Prague. As if to reassure himself that he was following the right course, he went first of all to a flat where Uncle Hajsky had found him lodgings for a short while. The couple there regarded him with horror. What was he doing in the city? Did he not know that sudden searches were likely to take place at any hour of the day or night? Everyone was lying low. He should return to his country hide-away at once.

So Karel Curda left and walked back down the street. Some peculiar little pocket of integrity in his mind had satisfied itself that the resistance could not help him; therefore he had to turn to others who could. His dragging feet took him towards the Gestapo headquarters in the Petchek Bank.

The rest of his story is documented by official German sources. When the S.S. Corporal snapped to attention before Commissar Jantur in his office, he reported with some excitement that there was a Czech down below who maintained he knew the identity of the assassins of General Heydrich! Commissar Jantur was not over-impressed. In his time he had examined cranks, patriots, religious maniacs, self-styled martyrs, the stupid, the soft-headed and the completely insane. He knew that most probably this new informer could be numbered amongst such people. However, there was no harm in seeing him.

When they brought the man into his office, Jantur looked at him with new interest. The man was plainly not a lunatic, but very frightened. That, Commissar Jantur knew, was an encouraging sign. The Gestapo had much experience of dealing with frightened people.

The man was of medium height and build. He had a small black moustache and black hair brushed straight back from his forehead. He was untidy, a nondescript fellow, and no one would have picked him out in a crowd. Jantur beckoned him to a chair and the man sat down, looking nervously upwards at the two huge S.S. men flanking him on either side.

Jantur began his interrogation quietly enough. The Gestapo had worked out, through long experience, exactly how to extract information from nervous witnesses. Name? Age? Occupation? It was at this point that Curda confessed he was a parachutist.

Jantur said quietly, "I understand you wish to make a statement?" Curda nodded.

"You realize," said Jantur ominously, "that whatever you may wish to tell us, may not have the value you seem to put upon it. We already have one parachutist named Gerik who has told us much."

"I know who the men are who killed Heydrich," repeated Curda. "I can identify the briefcase they carried. . . ."

Jantur's head inclined slightly. The average onlooker would not have noticed the movement, but the two S.S. thugs were practised in such signals. They went into action at once. One hauled Curda to his feet by the scruff of his neck and grabbed both his arms behind his back. The other, almost simultaneously, smashed each fist alternately into his face. Then they flung him to the floor and began to kick him. As he lay there, squirming to avoid the kicks, Jantur rose in his seat and began to bellow. The words were unimportant. The thing was to make a great, threatening noise. By this time the suspect was usually confused enough to admit anything. "You think you can come here and bargain with us?" roared the Commissar. "Who are these men? What are their names? Where are they hiding?"

One of the thugs picked Curda off the floor and the other began to punch him in the face again. Then they slumped him back in his chair.

"Now," said Jantur, "you'll tell us what we want to know."

Before Curda had time to speak, another fist smashed into his face. He crashed back against the wall. His lips were bleeding, swollen and puffy, and one eye was almost closed. The boots thudded into his ribs again.

They saw him reach down to his coat pocket. Fumblingly he tugged out his handkerchief. In one corner he had folded his small brown capsule of poison. He moved his hand containing the handkerchief towards his mouth, but there was no determination behind his gesture. Karel Curda did not want to die. That same little pocket of integrity was still trying to convince itself that his behaviour was that of a man. Curda allowed them to snatch the handkerchief from him; he saw the little brown pill drop and run for a couple of yards on the carpet, a tiny brown marble, glossy and shining and very pretty. It was pounced upon by one of the S.S. guards. He handed it to Jantur, whose yelling had been almost non-stop. Now the guards began to kick Curda again. He was half unconscious by the time they hauled him to his feet and jammed him back into the chair.

Jantur carefully propelled the little poison pill along the blotting pad with a stubby finger. Miraculously he had stopped bellowing. With an almost kindly intonation he said:

"Now tell me, who did you say committed the crime?"

Through bleeding swollen lips Curda began his betrayal. "Jan Kubis and Josef Gabchik," he said. "They are both parachutists dropped here from England. They have been operating in Prague for the last five months."

"And you yourself? Your part in this?"

"I was a parachutist too, but I only took part in one operation at Pilsen which was a complete fiasco."

"Why should we believe your story?" demanded Jantur. "Doubtless you have heard we are offering a large reward for the capture of the assassins." Curda hesitated.

"Well?" said Jantur. "Why are you betraying them? Judas only received forty pieces of silver. I see you are after twenty million."

218

Still Curda hesitated. Perhaps some faint realization of how, from this time forward, he would have to live, was beginning to filter into his consciousness.

"I want to protect my mother," he said in a low voice. "I read that the family of Lieutenant Pechal who dropped with me had been shot. I do not want my mother to be shot."

Jantur looked at him and grinned. "We will see about that later."

A few moments afterwards they brought in a bundle of briefcases and tossed them down in front of Curda.

"Now," said Jantur, "we'll soon see if you're telling the truth. Tell us which briefcase was found at the scene of the assassination."

It took Curda only a few seconds. He remembered Josef's briefcase during their stay in Pilsen very well, because he had noticed one peculiar thing about it. He pointed to a black stain under the lock.

"This is the one," he said. "It belongs to Josef Gabchik."

Jantur's face changed at once. Before that moment he had been inclined—if not to disbelieve—then certainly to underrate the evidence of this craven betrayer who had surrendered so weakly. After all, they had had Gerik for some time now. He had not been of much use to them, and no use at all in the Heydrich affair.

"He carried his Sten gun in this case," continued Curda. "It broke into two pieces."

"Where are these two men?" snapped Jantur.

"I don't know. Hiding in Prague somewhere."

"Well, describe them! We want an accurate description."

Curda put a hand to his aching head. "Kubis is about five feet ten," he began, trying to recall every detail he could remember. "He has fair hair, blue eyes . . . ." The shorthand writer copied down the details.

"Have you any idea where they might be hiding?"

"No," said Curda, "but I know the flat where they used to have meetings. The son, Ata Moravec, took me there once."

The other Gestapo chiefs, Panwitz and Fleischer, were crowding into Jantur's office now, both summoned to hear this eventful news. The three of them cross-questioned him, and the minutes grew to hours as the merciless interrogation continued. Curda betrayed all he knew. He told them about the organizations in Pilsen and Brno, Pardubice and Prague.

He gave names and addresses of all the men and women he had met. He held nothing back. It was not necessary to beat or bully him any more. His duty, he had decided, was to save his mother's life. If in so doing, he destroyed a hundred other mothers, that was outside his responsibility and beyond the demarcation lines of his conscience.

The Gestapo could hardly wait to act upon the information they had extracted, but they knew if they acted too hastily that the birds might escape the net. They did not begin operations, therefore, until their favourite time for arrests: the early hours of the morning.

The ringing of the bell at the front door woke up Auntie Marie at once. Her husband stirred but did not wake. Instinctively she knew something was wrong. With a dull sickness in her stomach she got slowly out of bed and pulled on her dressing gown. As she walked into the hall she saw Ata's worried face appear from behind his bedroom door. He had only come back that afternoon from his hiding place in the country.

She motioned him to go back and called out, "Who is it?" There was a pause, then the caretaker's voice answered her, "It's only me, Mrs. Moravec." The woman caretaker was old and infirm and could be trusted.

With a great, upward welling of relief, Auntie Marie lifted the yale latch and began to open the door. When it was a quarter open, a shoulder was suddenly thrown against it and the door was smashed open.

The landing outside was full of men in plain clothes! Gestapo! She knew at once that they must have forced the caretaker to bring them up at revolver point. The horror of it stunned her into silence as their orders rapped out.

"Back! Raise your hands! Turn and face the wall!"

This short fat one she had heard about. It was Fleischer, one of the most important Gestapo chiefs in Prague. The men rushed past her into the flat, revolvers in their hands. They crashed into all the rooms; they hauled out her husband and Ata; they flung open wardrobes and cupboards. As she stood immobile, her eyes roaming despairingly over the small floral decoration of the wallpaper in her hall, she knew that all was lost. Fleischer would not personally make an arrest unless matters of vital importance were concerned. They had been betrayed. Someone had broken.

She heard them forcing her husband and Ata into the hall.

"Turn round and keep your hands up," rapped Fleischer. He was now very angry. Alas for his dreams of fame. The two assassins were obviously not hiding in the flat.

Seven men in trilby hats with flat faces and hard eyes faced them across the hall. Two were sent off to continue searching the apartment.

"Where are they?" barked Fleischer. "Where are they?"

It was Mr. Moravec who spoke. He was dazed with sleep and shock but he said, "I do not know what you are talking about."

Fleischer raised his revolver to strike him, then lowered it again.

"You're finished now. Either you tell us or you know what will happen."

Mr. Moravec slowly and painfully repeated his answer. "I do not know what you are talking about. There is no one here."

And Mrs. Moravec could think sadly, "How true that is. How little he knows. He has observed—even mildly disapproved—but he knows nothing, and he will say nothing."

Ata? She glanced sideways at her son. Ata knew everything but he was safe. He would not speak. He was her son.

But she hereslf? The Nazis were aware now that she possessed information. They would try and make her talk. They would try and drag the secrets from her body. On several occasions previously, she had privately considered what her reactions might be under torture; she had even discussed just such a hypothetical situation calmly with other people. She had admitted she did not know how she would react in such a situation, if such a thing ever happened. But she dreaded it and she had taken precautions.

The bicycle had worried her very much. On one visit to Pardubice she had confessed as much to the Lieutenant operating the "Libuse" transmitter, and asked him for one of the poison pills which she knew all the parachutists carried. He had obliged her. Now she must decide what action to take, and act upon that decision. In her heart she knew what she had to do. She had to die, quickly, and at once.

She glanced at her husband who intercepted her glance. Intuitively, he knew what she was considering. He shook his head quickly, almost as one shakes it to clear a slight pain. He did not speak.

The means of death she carried inside a medallion hanging from a chain around her neck. Within lay the small brown pill she had obtained from Pardubice. It *must* act as quickly as they prophesied. But with her hands held high above her head, how could she use it?

There was a shout from the drawing-room. One of the searching men had found some papers. They looked incriminating. Motioning to the interpreter to accompany him, Fleischer walked swiftly from the hall.

Only three men guarded them now. Mrs. Moravec knew then that God had intervened on her behalf.

The door of the lavatory stood almost opposite. She said to the guards, "Please? I must go to the lavatory."

The three men stared at her suspiciously. "It is forbidden," said the shortest. Ignoring the pointed revolver, she dropped one hand to her stomach and groaned, "Please! I must go!"

The three Gestapo men exchanged glances. The tallest said, "Let her go. She can't escape now."

The shortest man gestured with the muzzle of his revolver. "Hurry, a minute only."

She turned to glance at Ata, then at her husband. Her eyes met his, and he understood. How could she tell him of the love she still felt for him? How could she say in one glance, "Goodbye, my dear husband. God protect you."

She took three swift steps into the lavatory and closed the door. She flooded the toilet to cover the sound of the snap of the locket. The small brown pill lay in the palm of her hand. Oh God, was death this easy? She threw it into her mouth, gulped and swallowed.

She fumbled for the door handle and stepped through. She heard the bull-like roar of anger as Fleischer, hearing the toilet flush, came racing back. Then the floor began to move upwards and she saw the agonized look upon her husband's face. If the look in her eyes was meant to comfort him, only God will know, for she crashed forward on to her face and lay very still.

Ata, his face a blank mask of misery, watching his mother die on the floor, and wishing that her last few moments might be peaceful, said brokenly, "It's her heart. She often has these turns."

And Fleischer, an expert in these things, turned and stared at Ata with the saurian eyes of an expert torturer, and said softly, "Take him away, he's got things to tell us."

They gave Ata no time to forget what he had seen. They took him to the Gestapo Headquarters at the Bank and began their fiendish operations.

Ata was just twenty-one. At twenty-one a man will take incredible risks coolly and competently. He will fly an aeroplane at fantastic speed in combat; he will take his tank through heavy shellfire; he will suffer bombardment from depth charges, locked in a tin cigar hundreds of feet under the sea. But this is in hot blood, in the heat of combat. Torture, cold, competent and clinical, is different.

In the vaults of the Petschek Bank, the first attack was on the mind. The interrogator in the blood-stained room, the still wet traces of human agony; the devilish instruments hanging within eye level; the brutish torturers grinning sadistically in anticipation.

They had dragged him from his bed, and his mother had died before his eyes. To sit there waiting for pain when the only person he had ever loved was dead was more than he could stand. Perhaps also, from the time the Germans captured the bicycle, he had harboured resentment somewhere. Perhaps when his mother died his own courage died, although it took a little time for him to become aware of this. He held out as long as he could. Doubtlessly he did not realize it, but *everything* depended upon his holding out.

They beat his father brutally, but he was numb with shock at the death of his wife. Life for him was finished. He was not confusing the end of it with blabber-mouth talk to hired bullies. Pain was merely another step on the quick road to the grave. He looked up at them from numb and lifeless eyes, and soon they left him alone. They had had much experience in selecting who would talk and who would not.

Ata, they decided, would talk. He was beaten, punched and kicked. He was threatened and screamed at. And when they had softened him up sufficiently they brought him face to face with the thoroughly cowed and beaten Curda.

"There you are," said Fleischer. "Now you know that we've got everybody. All we need from you is corroboration." And eventually after hours of interrogation, to spare himself more pain, to give himself some small respite, Ata gave away his first name.

Uncle Hajsky had finished shaving, and his wife was in the kitchen preparing breakfast when the loud knock came at the front door of their apartment. He looked through the peephole in his front door before opening it, and knew at once that all was lost. Like Auntie Marie he had rehearsed in his mind what his move would be. As heavy boots began to kick the door open, he dashed for the bathroom. Like Auntie Marie he knew there was no time for farewells. In the bathroom he swung open the cabinet door. He knew exactly where he kept the pill.

He heard the front door crash open and one of the invaders begin to fire his revolver, although at what he could be firing he had no idea. Then they were outside the bathroom door firing into the lock and through the woodwork of the door. He felt the sharp pain in his hand and he jumped back. As he gulped down the small brown pill he watched the blood spatter to the ground from his shattered fingers.

When they paused for a second he called:

"If you stop shooting, gentlemen, I will come out."

There were no more revolver shots. Uncle Hajsky managed

The church balcony photographed just after the attack

In the crypt Alan Burgess looks up at the shaft and stone slab which leads to the church overhead. This was the single entrance so desperately defended

The memorial on the church wall above the outside ventilation slot.
Bullet holes are still clearly visible

to open the door. He took one step forward, toppled to the ground, and lay there face downwards.

They cursed and kicked him, but Uncle Hajsky did not move. The shy quiet teacher who—if fate had been kinder —would have wished only to instruct his pupils in the intricacies and formalities of a civilization he was willing to die to preserve, had also escaped them.

Auntie Marie and now Uncle Hajsky. Auntie Marie had not spoken, and neither had Uncle Hajsky. Uncle Hajsky's wife knew nothing whatsoever. Her husband had protected her from that. They rushed his body back to headquarters, but even the Gestapo could not bring him back from the dead.

Now Fleischer, Panwitz and Jantur knew they were in difficulties. Telephone calls had alerted the Gestapo in Pardubice, and they had rushed to make arrests. But so far they had only succeeded in catching the young and pretty Mrs. Krupka—who had acted so often as a courier between Pardubice and Prague—and her husband. A fast car was bringing them to the capital.

The Gestapo commissars knew very well how quickly news of arrests got around. They had drained Karel Curda of information, so now Ata Moravec was their only hope. News of the deaths of Auntie Marie and Uncle Hajsky would soon filter out to the underground; the men they wanted above all others would find new hideouts.

They had to make Ata Moravec talk, and they had to do it quickly. Time was not on their side.

CHAPTER SIXTEEN

On that evening of the 17th of June, Jan met Anna at their usual place on the Charles Bridge, and they walked arm in arm back towards the old town. Even to breathe the warm summer air, a little cooler now after the heat of the afternoon, was a relief to Jan, for only ten minutes previously he had literally emerged from the tomb.

At the foot of the bridge they stood together, looking at the tram tracks embedded in pale grey cobblestones and glinting in the sun. The electric cables high overhead shone like golden wires. There was a film of dust on the pavements, a dry powder of dust in the gutters; a softness in the air. It was June. High summer. All over Europe the grapes were forming on the vines, and generals to whom the summer was simply a period when tanks could operate at maximum velocity, with not a patch of mud to delay their progress, drew concentric lines on their operational maps and rehearsed the heartening speeches they would make to their troops.

At the foot of the bridge the tram tracks meshed in a fantastic confusion interpreted only by drivers: some lines swept across the bridge; others lipped the river and ran onwards to some unknown haven of trams far away.

Jan talked eagerly. The news was good. Tomorrow they were leaving the crypt—Anna knew by this time that they were hiding in a church, though she did not know which one—because the churchwarden's wife was expected to return from holiday within the next thirty-six hours. Arrangements had been made to billet them in Kladno, a small town some fifty miles to the north-west of Prague.

News—and this was wonderful news—had also come through, via "Libuse", that very soon it was hoped to fly an aircraft to some landing strip in the forests near Kladno, and ferry Jan and Josef and Jindra back to England. Jindra, as head of the resistance, could instruct Czech Intelligence regarding the precise conditions and requirements of the home resistance; Jan and Josef would presumably return to the army. It was the best and most heartening news they had received for months.

So it was with a lightness of heart that Jan and Anna walked through the narrow streets of the old town and into Wenceslas Square where they caught their tram. Their destination for the last evening together was Jindra's empty flat. As the metal wheels clattered over the steel rails, they felt at peace for the first time since that morning when Jan had thrown the grenade. Now they had a future again. For them love had had to bloom quickly to speed its courtship; the spring, the summer and autumn had to be compressed; the growing up and growing old telescoped into each other. Time had not been expendable; it had ticked past with ruthless speed. Yes, they could imagine as they walked along the Vltava embankment in the summer evenings that the war was far off. They could imagine, as they dropped a pebble from one of the seven graceful bridges, that their love was indestructible. But all the time they knew they were avoiding reality, shutting out the certainty that, without a lucky turn of chance, their days together were inevitably numbered. Now that turn of chance had come. Now they were lifted in spirit to a height they had not dreamt possible. Now they were young, and in love, and only the immediate present was of concern to them.

That evening all over Europe, young men and young women looked up at the darkening sky and felt the urgency of that passing summer. Young men at war, in the coarse, ill-fitting uniforms of half a dozen nations, nursed heavy rifles, looked up at the sky and yawned; sailed over empty seas and yawned; thin men in prison camps looked at the barbed wire and yawned. Yawned and yearned for intoxication and love, for women and the growing earth and freedom.

Jan and Anna Malinova did not yawn, for they had no time to waste. They possessed a few hours of precious time, a flat, and each other. In this war it was all one could expect.

Their tram clanked to a halt at the turning which led to

the Petschek Bank, and after a pause rattled its way onwards again. They felt no presentiment of evil. They sensed no voice trying to reach them from that ominous building. They had no premonition of danger. They had not the slightest knowledge that only a few hundred yards away Ata Moravec was fighting to preserve his courage and trying desperately to buy time with agony.

On that night of the 17th of June they dragged young Ata from his cell again, sneered at the terror growing in his eyes, and instead of smashing a fist into his face, pushed a cigarette between his lips and lit it for him. Since he had been pulled from his bed fourteen hours previously, he had not slept, rested or eaten. Interminably the interrogations had gone on, the beatings, the tortures, but they had had to be careful. They had to preserve him. He must not be destroyed or allowed to sink into unconsciousness. He *had* to talk.

Now they had something new to try. They led him into a bare, brightly-lit room furnished only with a table and two chairs, one on either side. Upon one chair was already seated pretty Mrs. Krupka who had just been driven in from Pardubice.

They shoved Ata across to the table opposite her and said, "Do you know this man?"

Mrs. Krupka, her pupils dilating in terror as she saw Ata's bruised and bleeding face, hesitated, then said "No!" Her voice was steady.

They said to Ata Moravec, "Do you know this woman?" He looked at her for perhaps half a second, then his eyes dropped. To her utter amazement Ata answered, "Yes."

They pushed him down into the chair and crossed to the far side of the room. Strangely, they seemed for the moment to have lost interest in them both.

Mrs. Krupka stared at Ata with wondering eyes, and he, intercepting her glance, mumbled, "It's no use, they know everything."

This was, of course, quite untrue. So far Ata had surrendered only the name of Uncle Hajsky, but in giving one name, he had yielded all self-respect. His spirit had broken

228

and it was only a matter of time before he gave away all their secrets. Dazed and semi-conscious, this was the breach of faith he tried to communicate to Mrs. Krupka.

"But your mother?" she whispered. "What about your mother?"

"She's dead," he replied, slurring his words through broken lips. "I couldn't hide anything."

The S.S. men who had allowed Ata just enough time to implant the doubt they anticipated in Mrs. Krupka's mind, dragged him away. To impress her with their brutal efficiency they kicked him out of the room. Then they returned. The bigger of the two sat in the chair opposite her and said, "There are many things we can do with women who refuse to talk."

She stared at him. She was very frightened and her lips trembled, but more frightening than anything else was the dreadful knowledge of Ata's defection. It dazed her mind and weakened her resolve. If she bore stoically the dreadful things she knew they could do to her, of what use would it be? How much had Ata betrayed? Did they already know all she could tell them?

She did her best. She protested she knew nothing about the resistance movement; she knew nothing about parachutists. But as she lied, turning and twisting under their cross-examination, their real objective began to emerge.

"Where are the parachutists hiding?" they demanded. "Where? Where?"

She said she did not know. They repeated the question, and still she protested she did not know.

Then suddenly the big one leaned forward and struck her across the face. Suddenly with the back of his hand he slapped her hard, jolting her head back. The tears welled in her eyes. She was so tired, and she felt sick.

"I don't know," she wept. "I don't know. They never told me."

"You must have heard something. Speak!"

"I don't know. I don't know."

"You will co-operate of your own free will or we shall use other methods."

They hit her again. She was very young and pretty and near hysteria.

"What have you heard? What?"

They jerked her to her feet and punched her again. She should not have known where the parachutists were hidden; it was not her province to know, but somehow in some unguarded conversation she had overheard a remark. Surely it would do no harm if she told them? There were hundreds of churches in Prague. The boys would be gone long before they found the right one. And she did not know the right one, so she could never tell them that.

"Something about a church," she sobbed. "That's all I know. Something about a church."

They soon confirmed that was all she knew. They left her and went to find Ata again. This time as the cell door was opened there was no cigarette for him; they smashed a fist into his face, and as he reeled back, crashing against the wall and slumping to the floor, they were after him, booting him in the ribs.

Beneath his scrabbling fingers he felt the cold, unfriendly concrete. His whole body was a mass of pain; he could not breathe. He knew then that he would have to tell them more.

They hauled him to his feet. "Now," they said, "where is this church where the parachutists are hiding?"

Ata should not have known either, but yesterday afternoon, because he was soon to join the others in the crypt, his mother had told him about the church in Resslova Street. It was fatal knowledge.

And so the luck turned. As a rule hardly a day passed without Jan or Anna visiting Auntie Marie. But now, because it was thought safer not to mix too much, they had not seen her for forty-eight hours, and in Jindra's flat they were quite oblivious of the outside world.

Why, demanded Anna, should they leave the flat at all? Why should he return to that horrible crypt, and why should she go back to her lonely room?

This was to be their last night together, perhaps for weeks

or months or even years. Let them spread each minute into an hour and each hour into a day. Desperately she wanted him to stay; she was not really appealing with her body; some inchoate instinct buried deep in the marrow of her bones forced her to hold him there.

But Jan only smiled and kissed her, and said she was being too serious. This was not their last night together; there would be plenty of other nights in Kladno. It was only fifty miles away, and even if he went to England, the war would soon be over; it couldn't last for ever. She should see the great international army forming there.

She said that she did not mind him going to England. In many ways it would be a great relief. She would know finally that he was safe, and once the Nazis knew for certain that Heydrich's assassins had escaped them, they would have to end their persecutions, or continue to advertise and dramatize their abject failure.

But why not stay in the flat that night, she begged him. She was so persistent with her appeal that Jan explained that he was taking the last watch on the balcony that night. Lieutenant Opalka, Svarc and he had had the good fortune to win the toss for balcony guard. He could not, therefore, desert his post or his comrades. Tomorrow they would be in Kladno, and all this watchfulness, this mounting of sentries would be over. Didn't she understand that? Didn't she understand what wonderful news it was?

So they lingered a little longer in the flat and then made the journey by tram back into the centre of the city. Upon the middle span of the Charles Bridge, near the statue of Christ upon His Cross, they kissed and clung for a moment and then parted.

Jan walked back across the bridge to go in search of Josef, and Anna, looking back over her shoulder, walked slowly to the arch on her side of the bridge.

So the minutes of that night ticked past. Jan and Josef walked back to the church, and Anna climbed the stairs to her lonely room. Josef descended to join Valchik, Bublik and Hruby in the tomb. The stone slab was swung back into place, and the coconut matting stretched across it. Jan and Opalka and Svarc stretched out on the balcony. Opalka was taking the first watch, Svarc the second and Jan the dawn watch. Only the man on watch remained awake, whilst the other two slept.

The hours of the night slid past. Outside it was dark and warm and quiet, and the sky was bright with stars above the spires of Hradcany Castle. The river rustled softly under the seven bridges, sighing away into the darkness.

Only in the deep vaults of the Petschek Bank was there activity, as Gestapo Chief Panwitz gathered his senior officers about him and outlined the plans for capturing the assassins of General Heydrich.

They had now discovered their hiding place. It was a church located near the river in Resslova Street. S.S. men, reported Panwitz, were at that very moment on their way to arrest both the chaplain and churchwarden. The Bishop and other elders would be arrested at an opportune time.

S.S. troops were also, at that very moment, leaving their barracks in various quarters of the city, and by five-thirty a.m. they would be in position to form a solid cordon around the church in Resslova Street and the neighbouring buildings. There would be absolutely no chance for the assassins to escape. Panwitz briefed his officers by means of a large map on the wall. He pointed out that the windows of a commercial academy on the other side of the street overlooked the church, as did the windows of various flats and houses on other sides. Picked marksmen were to be placed in these vantage points, and they would open fire after the first wave of troops had made the assault.

A guide who knew intimately all parts of the church had also been secured. This was Herr Streiber of the Prague police, who would lead the first special detachment through the back door; the chaplain would undoubtedly possess the key to all the locks. With a little luck they would take the parachutists completely by surprise.

Panwitz also pointed out that a cordon of troops stretched as far as the bridge which crossed the Vltava at the bottom of Resslova Street. The reason for this precaution was that

Herr Streiber had heard rumours of a secret passage which was reported to run from the church to the river. The parachutists might be aware of this passage and attempt to make their escape through it. It was necessary, therefore, to press home the first attack with all possible force and speed.

He ended his lecture with a short reminder of the importance Reichsfuhrer Himmler, and indeed the Fuhrer himself, attached to the capture or deaths of these assassins. If this job were bungled, the repercussions were likely to be very severe indeed.

So the night moved on towards the dawn. Upon the balcony of the church in Resslova Street Jan was awakened for the last watch, and Jaroslav Svarc lay down on the wooden balcony floor beside Opalka to snatch a few hours' sleep.

It was warm on the balcony; all three of them were dressed very lightly. Jan wore thin grey trousers, a T-shirt and a navy-blue windbreak with a zip up the front. No one will ever know what his thoughts concerned during those dawn hours. Possibly he thought about Anna Malinova, from whom he had so recently parted. Possibly about tomorrow's journey to Kladno, and the aircraft trip back to England. What a surprise it would be for Mrs. Ellison and her daughters, when he appeared upon the doorstep! And what a story he would have to tell them!

And then suddenly he must have become aware of danger. From the huge glass window almost completely filling one side of the balcony, he could have seen the movements of troops in the streets; possibly he saw the first platoon move towards the back door. Certainly he awoke Lieutenant Opalka and Svarc. Certainly they moved to positions which had been well rehearsed, and with Sten guns, revolvers and grenades prepared to fight to the very end.

There would be no time to run down the balcony stairs, pull back the coconut matting, lift the stone and warn the others. They knew that the sound of gunfire soon to fill the church would warn them anyway.

They must have heard the S.S. boots moving quietly along

the narrow corridor which connected the chaplain's office with the church. Vaguely in the darkness they would have seen the figures moving across the wooden screen.

They must have been aware of all this, and in position— Jan and Svarc upon the balcony, Opalka down below—when simultaneously they opened fire from three different points. Under the high roof of the church the sudden crash of gunfire echoed and re-echoed in deafening diapason.

The S.S. troops, fumbling around in the darkness, were caught completely by surprise. The white walls were hit by the three Sten guns spouting flame. Bullets screeched from jerking barrels, ricocheted from stone walls and floor, and smashed life from nerve, brain and bone. The S.S. men were massacred; they dropped where they stood before they had time even to return a shot; the few survivors scrambling frantically back into the protection of the corridor. A grenade, thrown probably by Jan, exploded behind the altar screen to hasten their terrified exit. There was no more silence. Now the night was broken with the groans and cries of the wounded, boots clattering and shouted orders in the darkness.

Jan, Opalka and Svarc, reloading their guns, must have watched the first grey streaks of daybreak lighting the windows of the church, picked out the silent shape of the soldiers lying dead on the floor, and known that this was only a temporary respite.

At a signal from somewhere out in the street, machine guns, rifles and other light weapons, mounted in every vantage point overlooking the church, suddenly opened up. A tremendous fusillade of bullets hit the windows, and with a great crash of glass every pane disintegrated. The firing continued.

To the troops outside, it did not seem possible that anyone could have survived such a barrage. The precise effect it had upon the three defenders, however, was soon made clear. Military training had taught them the fundamental art of finding cover. They saw it out, nursing their guns; all three had seen action in France and bullets did not concern them overmuch. They kept their heads down and waited for the next attack which they knew would follow the cessation of this withering fire.

As abruptly as the fusillade started, it ceased. Down the corridor again, and into the church rushed the special S.S. men. This time several dashed directly across the church, under cover of the thin wooden screen. But the defenders were in a perfect position to dictate events. Their field of fire could cover every foot of the church, up to and behind the altar. Their eyes were accustomed to the light; in the growing greyness of dawn, with an intense and concentrated fire, they drove the Nazis back down their corridor.

Again the church was empty, and more dead lay about the church floor.

Outside, in the shelter of a neighbouring building, Panwitz could be heard yelling furiously. Secretary of State Karl Frank had been warned and was expected upon the scene at any moment. Panwitz had been confident he would have the situation completely under his command by the time he arrived. The surviving S.S. men had reported fire from three separate points; that meant only three defenders. It was ridiculous that three men could hold out against a whole regiment of picked troops. He said as much, loudly.

His temper was not improved when at least two of the defenders made quick sorties to the balcony window, hurled out a couple of grenades and sprayed the street with a hail of bullets which sent everyone scurrying for cover. And so the skirmish continued with sporadic fire from both sides.

But now the sun was climbing remorselessly up beneath the horizon, and the sky was already pink and gold and green with dawn colours. The sun gave its advantage to the Nazis. If more soldiers forced their way into the building the defenders would now be visible and therefore vulnerable. If successive waves came in, firing as they ran and throwing grenades, sooner or later the odds would be too great. Grenade shrapnel could reach corners and niches barred to the direct bullet.

So Panwitz gave his orders. Two hours had been consumed by these unsuccessful attacks. This time there was to be no retreat. Wave after wave of troops were to rush the church. Covering fire would be directed through the balcony windows. These attacks would go on irrespective of casualties until the three men were silenced.

Jan, Svarc and Opalka must have heard them coming all right, for as the first S.S. men stormed through the corridor, defensive fire toppled them in heaps. But other men pushed in behind them, leaping over their bodies, sheltered by their bodies, firing desperately with automatic weapons and finally deciding the encounter by hurling a succession of stick grenades up the church and on to the balcony.

Jan may have seen the thin, bottle-shaped grenades curving through the air towards him. Possibly he heard them thud down on to the wooden platform behind him. Then consuming him, and killing him, came the great splash of orange light, flashing up to colour and distort the pastel painted angels and cherubs on the ceiling. There was the great roar of noise, a hiss and whine of flying shrapnel. And for Jan, darkness.

Svarc on the opposite side of the balcony had both legs shattered by the same stick of grenades. The church was now full of S.S. troops directing fire towards them. Svarc could not raise himself up; he could fight no more. He lifted the revolver lying next to him, cocked it with his thumb, placed it to his forehead and pulled the trigger.

On the church floor Lieutenant Opalka, hit in a dozen places by pieces of shrapnel, also knew it was the end. He had been hit in the chest, legs, abdomen and face. Left like this, he knew he might take half an hour to die, and he did not have half an hour to spare. He must have heard the single shot above on the balcony and known that either Svarc or Jan had ended his own life. They had all sworn to do that. No one was going to be taken alive. More than that they could not do.

Opalka made certain he did not bungle his task. He held his glistening brown poison pill between his thumb and forefinger for a second before swallowing it; then he fired five shots from his revolver at the figures advancing towards him, placed the revolver muzzle against his own temple, and let his last bullet take him upon his short journey to eternity.

The firing died away very slowly. There was silence in the church. The sun was rising now, coming up over the low hills around Prague, glinting off the river, penetrating the vague mists under the chestnut trees, poking thin wands of gold down into the streets. Down through the broken church windows the rays fell, and there they touched the broken bodies of the three parachutists.

They dragged Jan down from the balcony; they hauled him outside on to the pavement, dropping him down on the pavement so that a Nazi official photographer could run up and click his shutter and send a sudden radiance into Jan's eyes with the brightness of its flash.

But Jan did not see the flash or feel the bruises as they dragged him through the church. He was still alive—just. So was Svarc—just. Lieutenant Opalka was dead. A convoy of ambulances was already moving the Nazi dead and wounded away and into one of them Jan and Svarc were quickly placed. With a siren screaming it raced through the dawn towards the hospital in Charles Square. They might still be saved so that General Heydrich's death could be doubly avenged. Modern drugs, it was said, could bring a man back from the grave.

When they lifted Jaroslav Svarc out of the ambulance he was already dead. Jan they rushed to the operating theatre, and there the doctors examined him. But even while they were preparing the blood transfusion he escaped them. His heart, which had been beating very faintly, stopped.

Jan Kubis who had planned to do so much "when the war was over" had fought his final battle. For him, at last, the war was really over.

CHAPTER SEVENTEEN

HANDCUFFED to each other Karel Curda and Ata Moravec were taken from the Petschek Bank and driven to the church in Resslova Street. Someone had thrown a piece of carpet over Opalka. It was pulled aside. Curda looked down again at the man who had been his commanding officer, and whom he had betrayed, and Ata stood with head bowed. He had broken completely. He had little more to reveal.

"Who is this man?" Panwitz demanded of Curda.

"Lieutenant Opalka."

"Is he one of the assassins?"

"No," said Curda. "He is not one.'

"Then it must be the two in hospital. You will go there and identify them, but first you have another duty. Other parachutists are hidden in the crypt of the church. You will go in now and order them to surrender.

The two men were pushed at rifle point into the building. Its disorder was chaotic, but the Nazis had rigged up arc lamps and the interior was floodlit.

Already standing there, with his arms bound behind his back, was the chaplain, Vladimir Petrek. They had struck him brutally with rifle butts, and Panwitz had roared questions at him. They knew from Ata's confession that there should be more than three men hiding in the church. Where were they?

Calmly and with dignity the chaplain stared back at Panwitz. This was his church, his place of worship, and although they might desecrate it, they could not intimidate him. He did not answer any questions, and they would never succeed in making him answer.

But the hiding place was not hard to find. Everyone knew that a church as old as this would have a cellar or a crypt. Where was it? They tore aside the matting; within a few minutes they had discovered the stone and hauled it aside. A blast of Sten and revolver fire sent them ducking for cover.

But the last refuge had been discovered. Now it could only be a matter of time.

Ata and Karel Curda were hauled to within a few feet of the hole.

"Call down and order them to surrender," ordered Panwitz angrily.

Ata looked at him with dazed eyes. Up to this point he had been cowed and defeated, but suddenly a vestige of his manhood returned.

"No, I will not," he said.

It was strange that, having degraded himself so far, he would not degrade himself completely.

They kicked him and punched him but Ata would not speak. He had courage enough to keep his deep shame from the men he had known so well.

For Curda it was a different matter altogether.

"Friends," he shouted. "It is no use fighting any more. All is lost. It is better to surrender."

He was answered by a quick burst of fire. Those in the crypt had obviously decided there was no point in wasting words. The two handcuffed men were booted out of the church. They were pushed into a lorry and driven to the hospital. They were led to the morgue in which lay two bodies. Both they identified. It was Ata who looked down at Jan Kubis, the man he had known so well, laughing and gay, and joking with his mother. He said: "Yes, that is the man who killed Heydrich!"

In the crypt, Valchik, Josef, Bublik and Hruby were obviously woken by the noise of the first attack of the troops overhead. They would have tumbled off their mattresses, grabbed their weapons and waited.

For the time being there was nothing they could do, but then, after consultation, they would have remembered. There was perhaps one slight chance left. The secret passage. Chaplain Petrek had often pointed out the stonework behind which the passage was supposed to lie.

They had laughed about the idea, never dreaming that a contingency such as this might arise. In fact in their long hours of vigil they had often discussed how it would be possible to break through into such a passage. The level of the crypt floor was far below the level of the road, therefore even if there was no secret passage, it seemed quite probable that they might well strike a sewer. And a sewer pipe might provide an escape route.

At once, using an old iron bar probably left by stonemasons of long ago, they began to attack the wall. The stonework was old and solid, but they worked with frenzied desperation, spurred on by the muffled noise of the battle above their heads. They needed time. They knew that Jan, Opalka and Svarc would give them all the time they could, but would it be enough? Soon they had removed four of the facing stones and were burrowing into the rock filling behind it.

They pulled the ladder away from the funnel entrance. It was unlikely they would be using it to climb through the hatch and out into the church now. There was perhaps a bare chance that the Germans might be satisfied with the elimination of the three in the church, and not search any further. But it was a slender hope.

The knowledge that their three comrades were dead came later. They heard the battle going on overhead, and then the final assault. They heard the sudden thunder of the grenades exploding, and the slow dwindling of gun fire.

Then, later, they heard the noise of the stone slab being swung away from its place. From above the Nazis looked down into pitch blackness. From below the defenders could see figures and hear excited guttural voices.

Almost simultaneously the four of them opened up with Sten guns. A fan of bullets churned up through the funnel opening, whining and ricocheting throughout the church. It was such relief to see the enemy, and fire at him in anger.

From above it was practically impossible for the Germans to return the fire. It was like firing down a chimney. The bullets smashed harmlessly into the stone floor.

The small aperture which acted as a ventilator outside above the pavement was equally difficult to use. It was at least eight feet from the ground; it was no more than two feet wide by one foot high, and the field of fire it supplied to anyone rash enough to climb up and attempt to poke a gun through it was small indeed. From the windows opposite, the S.S. could direct shots at this ventilation hole, but any that penetrated were as well channelled as the beam of a torch; they expended themselves harmlessly against the walls.

From behind the buttresses which lined the crypt it was easy to take cover, easy to watch the funnel opening for any sign of an invader, easy to watch the window grating for any other attacks which might be launched. They had ammunition, food and drink. Even though it seemed highly doubtful that they would survive, they knew they could give a good account of themselves.

And so, taking it in turn either to stand guard or pry at the stonework with the iron bar, they occupied the long slow hours of waiting.

From time to time now the Germans up above, standing well away from the aperture, called on them to surrender.

"It is useless to continue to resist!"

"If you surrender you will be unharmed."

"Give up or we shall blow the church down on top of you."

The defenders replied by firing occasional bursts up through the hole. It was light now, and the S.S. had decided that a little attention to the ventilator grill opening on to the road outside might pay dividends. But there were difficulties attached to this plan. It was barred by a jagged piece of iron and much too small for any human to climb through. It was also quite impossible to approach because, as soon as a face or helmet showed near the aperture, a chatter of bullets came hissing towards it.

They stopped firing when a well-known voice suddenly shouted down to them. It was Chaplain Petrek, and it was his only concession to the enemy.

"The German police," he shouted, "have ordered me to call on you to surrender."

One of them shouted back. "We know no priest. Go away!"

241

Probably they did not believe it would help Petrek, but it was the best they could do.

Petrek had been dragged from his bed, kicked and punched in the face, and with his hands handcuffed behind his back, dragged to the church. He was the only Czech to witness the events in the church that morning and, during his long imprisonment, he told his story to his fellow prisoners. The German records are not so explicit.

The S.S. had, by now, also discovered that the main entrance to the crypt lay not through the small funnel hole, but beneath the great stone slab cemented down in the centre of the church floor. Without stonemasons and proper lifting equipment it was impossible to move it. As it was hardly likely that the parachutists would give them time for such orderly methods they decided the only way open to them was to blow it up, in the hope that a quick overwhelming rush would overpower the defenders. Acting upon this idea, orders were despatched back to S.S. Headquarters for explosives experts to come at once to the church with their apparatus.

In Resslova Street outside the church and at a safe distance, Gestapo chief Panwitz was once more annoyed. For three hours the troops had been attacking the church. Their bag during this period had been three killed. Their own casualties were much higher.

Secretary of State Karl Frank, who was soon to become Governor-General, was expected at any moment. And Panwitz had decided that the fact that the few remaining parachutists should still be defending their positions, in the face of such superior odds, was a grave reflection upon the courage and skill of his men. The rattle of machine-gun fire directed at the small aperture opening into the crypt was a continuous noise in his ears, but it accomplished virtually nothing.

"Tear gas," ordered Panwitz furiously.

One of his senior S.S. officers ordered his men to knock out the grill in the aperture and drop tear gas bombs through. They were then to stuff the aperture with blankets and a mattress. This action, they decided, would speedily rout out the defenders.

The fire brigade had now also been summoned to the scene. They stood by with pumps and engines, not enjoying the situation, but there was no protest any one of them could make without losing his life. Indeed they could not even protest when orders were sent back to their headquarters asking for the dispatch of smoke-making equipment. It was a peculiar piece of apparatus used for filling a room with thick black smoke; a valuable aid in the training of firemen.

Meanwhile the troops were busy knocking out the iron bar which barred the ventilation hole. Bullets ricocheting off its jagged edges had already loosened its hold, and without much effort it fell through into the crypt below.

Inside they watched it fall and prepared for action. They knew the Germans were trying something new. Already they had tried tossing hand grenades through the ventilator. This was quite useless. The defenders simply stepped back behind the large buttresses and allowed them to explode harmlessly. At least two grenades had failed to drop through and, falling back on to the pavement outside, had rolled towards their dispatchers. This bred panic and dismay everywhere, and this sort of attack was quickly abandoned.

To be ready for an emergency the parachutists placed the light ladder against the wall near the ventilation hole.

Suddenly a hand appeared at the ventilator, and a string of tear gas bombs fell through on to the floor. A mattress was quickly stuffed into the aperture. With three of the defenders pouring shots into the mattress to keep the S.S. outside disconcerted, the fourth ran forward, picked up the bombs and raced up the ladder. The three others giving him covering fire paused, and he gave a hearty push with the muzzle of his sub-machine gun. A quick burst to clear the pavement, and both mattresses and the string of tear gas bombs landed outside on the pavement.

Outside, the infuriated Nazis heard Valchik, Josef, Hruby and Bublik laughing. There they were, trapped, and with no future except that of a quick death before them. They were laughing, and undoubtedly Josef was leading that laughter.

One of the main disadvantages from which the Nazis suffered was the fact that they had to operate in the light of the bright morning sun; whilst in the crypt, the defenders' eyes were protected against the strong light. An officer reported this to Panwitz, who instructed that the floodlights from inside the church be set up outside. Doubtfully the officer obeyed his orders.

The bank of floodlights was set up near the ventilator and then carefully wedged into position. An order was shouted for the current to be switched on. And at precisely the same moment a skilfully aimed blast from a Sten gun blew the bulbs to smithereens and sent the stand over backwards. Its shattered remains were removed.

The smoke-making machine had now arrived. The Germans left its handling to the firemen. Cautiously they man-handled the foot-thick rubber pipe towards the entrance to the crypt, forced the nozzle through and stuffed the mattress against it.

It was a good idea in theory but quite useless in practice. With little to support them from outside, it was simple for the defenders to prod both mattress and the smoke pipe back on to the pavement again where it sullenly belched smoke.

S.S. Gruppenfuhrer Karl Frank had now arrived and taken over the executive command from Panwitz. The time for sterner measures was due. Frank stood a discreet distance away, completely out of the line of fire, and gave his first order. Water. Why had the firemen not tried water? The river was no more than two hundred yards away; the firemen had enough hose pipes; the crypt was undoubtedly below ground level. If pipes were pushed in through that hole they could flood them out. They could drown them in their hole under the earth like the rats they were.

Panwitz saluted respectfully and relayed the order. The firemen ran out their hoses. Two moved forward and pushed the hose nozzle in through the ventilator hole. The cocks of the pumps were turned on. With all hoses working the firemen could deliver over six hundred gallons a minute at any given target. As it was, they delivered not even six hundred pints! Standing on the ladder, it was not difficult for the defenders to cut the canvas pipes with their razor-sharp knives, so that the weight of the water in the straining hoses outside, lashed them back towards the firemen. Water joined the black smoke in the general confusion. It appeared that "the rats" were not prepared to be drowned in their own trap.

Frank's anger showed upon his thin face and tight lips. It was preposterous that a few men could continue to defy a whole battalion of well-armed soldiers. He ordered the senior officer to act. Volunteers must enter the crypt through the one available entrance and wipe out all resistance.

A rather reluctant troop of S.S. paraded before the Secretary of State.

"Volunteers are needed," snapped the officer. "They will step forward at once." If he had added "into the grave" he might have expected a similar response. Two rows of pale faces, set and determined under steel helmets stared to the front. Not an eyelash flickered. Not a foot stepped forward.

The officer was plainly disconcerted. They were certainly not behaving in the tradition demanded by Reichsfuhrer Himmler.

"Did you hear me?" he barked. "I said 'Step forward, volunteers!'"

There was still no movement and the officer paced up and down the ranks staring at them angrily. "Volunteers!" he bellowed.

In the rear rank a soldier took one pace forward; another moment's hesitation, and a second followed suit, and finally a third. The rest remained statuesque.

It was not enough. Abruptly the officer selected another half-dozen, snapping out the names contemptuously. An n.c.o. ordered them to double into the church. By the side of the hole a rope was coiled. One by one they were to be lowered through and carry the fight to the parachutists.

In the crypt, work still continued upon the hole in the

wall, but any hope that they would find the way into a secret tunnel or a sewer must have been dwindling. They had chipped and scratched nearly three feet into the wall and had found that the earth and rock became only more solid.

They probably still observed the same ritual, with two digging and two on guard. The parachutists covered the only two possible places of attack; through the ventilator, and down the funnel from the church floor. An attack down the latter seemed suicidal. Their surprise must have been intense, therefore, when suddenly down through the hole appeared a pair of dangling jackbooted legs. Two barrels jerked up and a quick spatter of bullets skinned lumps of stone from the walls and smashed the soldier's legs. The man screamed in agony and he was swiftly drawn back up through the hole.

A stretcher was already waiting on the floor of the church. Moaning loudly the man was hurried away to an ambulance.

The next volunteer, grey-faced, tied the rope around his waist. The interior of the hole was pitch black. He decided to jump through, firing with his sub-machine gun as he dropped. The rope would break his fall, and his comrades would then swiftly lower him to the floor. As a piece of military strategy it was completely idiotic. As he dropped through the hole a blast of sub-machine gun bullets hit him full in the chest. Bullets severed the rope and he dropped in a heap on the floor of the crypt. He would make no more mistakes of that sort.

They pulled up the severed rope, eyed it with rather more anxiety than an angler eyes a broken line, and tied on the third volunteer. They had heard the last volunteer loose off a few shots on his way down, but whether this was an involuntary action on his way to eternity or a deliberate action against the defenders, they had no way of telling.

The third volunteer leapt through with such force that he jerked the ropes from their hands, or perhaps the remaining volunteers had no wish to use it. Again there was the shattering blast of bullets echoing and re-echoing in the crypt. Shot to death, his body folded itself quietly upon the inert form of his comrade, and the rope coiled itself neatly about him.

The three real volunteers were now expended. The rope had gone and the remaining men looked at each other with empty eyes. Was it possible to get more rope? No one seemed to think it necessary. The n.c.o., anxious not to have to shoot one of his own men for dereliction of a duty which was plainly suicidal, hurried off to report to his officer that two men were dead, and one seriously wounded, and that to pass any more men through the aperture was tantamount to placing them before a firing squad.

For the moment all action ceased. The crypt was impregnable.

The next point of attack Frank decided must be the wall of the crypt itself. The outlines of a walled-up door outside in the street were plainly visible. A huge lorry, with a timber baulk jammed into the back, was improvised to act as a battering ram. It reversed at speed into the wall. There was a loud crash, and pieces of wood splintered from the interior of the lorry. It ran forward and reversed hard a second time. There was a second tremendous bang and the cab of the lorry visibly moved forward. The engine coughed and subsided, while from the axle came a cracking noise. It was quite obvious that the next ramming attempt would force the driving cabin completely off the lorry. The walled-up doorway was completely undamaged, the stonework hardly chipped. The attempt was discontinued. The lorry low-geared its way up the hill towards a garage and retirement.

The explosives team now arrived and went to work. They drilled holes in the great slab of stone in the church floor which barred the entrance to the crypt. At almost the same time the firemen were ordered to try and fish out the ladder from the crypt by using a huge hook on a piece of rope.

Up to this moment, although an occasional fireman's uniform had appeared within range, the four parachutists had not fired at them. They did not wish to kill Czechs obviously acting under duress, but now their own safety was imperilled. Bullets again splattered on the stone around the window. The firemen and their hook retreated.

The ladder still stood against the wall near the ventilator hole to be used in case of emergency. To risk leaving it in such a position was the first mistake the defenders made, and they could not afford any mistakes. But they had their hands very full. One of the firemen, squinting in from an angle, glimpsed it. On impulse rather than by deliberate design he stuck in his hand, grabbed the top rung, pulled it up through the grating, and threw his weight down upon it. Its end reared up out of the parachutists' reach in a fraction of a second. The S.S. rushed forward to help haul it through the hole.

The parachutists could now no longer parry attacks by smoke or water through the hole twelve feet above their heads. They were unable to cut hoses or push them back through the ventilator.

This was also obvious to Karl Frank. He gave the order for the hoses to be pushed back in and the faucets turned on. The six hundred gallons a minute could now be delivered. Inevitably the crypt must fill with water.

In the crypt, ammunition was almost certainly getting low. They still had revolver ammunition and some magazines of Sten gun bullets, but they had expended it in prodigious quantities to keep the enemy at a respectful distance.

Even at the speed the hoses delivered it, they knew it would take some time for the water to fill the crypt. And it is doubtful if either Josef or Valchik, Hruby or Bublik wasted any time working out the hypothetical problem that if a cellar is twenty-five yards long, five yards wide, and five yards high, and the water is entering at six hundred gallons a minute, how long do you stay alive?

Very soon there was a foot of water, oily and black, sucked up from the River Vltava, swirling around the floor of the crypt. Josef Gabchik climbed into one of the places reserved for dead monks, with his Sten gun and his Colt revolver, and made himself as secure as possible. He could now look down on the thick snakes of water hissing through the distended hoses.

As it struck the surface of the water many feet below it

would churn and froth and the bubbles would dance away to fragment against the cold stone walls. All of them must have known now that they had not long to live.

But the Nazis were not content with this slow method of extermination. Secretary of State Karl Frank wanted quicker results.

The explosives team, working upon the slab below the altar, announced they were ready to fire their charge; orders were given for them to proceed at once.

Above the sound of rushing water the noise of the blasting charges was ear-splitting.

The great slab cracked in two and tilted upwards. A smother of dust rose high into the air. The explosives team rushed forward with ropes and pulleys and hooks to clear the stone and open the wide entrance which led to the short flight of steps.

It is possible that the defenders welcomed this intervention. Now at least they were given the opportunity of fighting to the death, and not drowning slowly in the cellar.

Deafened by the great noise, they hurried to new positions. Josef crouched in his pigeon-hole of stone—an empty monk tomb six feet above the level of the water—his Sten gun and ammunition magazines by his side and his Colt revolver ready for use.

Valchik, similarly equipped, stood opposite behind a stone buttress. The other two, armed and ready and sheltered by buttresses, stood farther back. They waited for the first rush of S.S. troops down the stone steps. But this time the Nazis were not so impatient. In the church itself Chaplain Petrek watched them setting up a new battery of arc lamps so that the light poured down through the newly revealed entrance.

Nevertheless, there was not room for more than two soldiers abreast upon those steeply sloping stairs. It was still a suicidal place to assault. It was still the entrance to a tomb, from which a return was unlikely.

The first six men lined up. At a command, with submachine guns ready, they dashed for the stairs. Undoubtedly the defenders heard the clatter of their boots upon the steps.

The S.S. men were met by concerted fire from four Sten guns. They screamed, toppled and splashed face downwards into the water.

Using the methods by which they had overcome Jan, Opalka and Svarc, a second wave of troops surged immediately down to the attack, but the bodies littering the stones hampered their movements. They also were shot down as they came.

Grimy, wet and close to exhaustion, with their Sten ammunition almost gone, the four defenders waited for the next attack.

They had been defending their position now for some six hours against all that a whole regiment of picked S.S. troops could do. They had inflicted considerable casualties upon them. The stairs were choked with bodies of the dead; the steps were slippery with their blood, and the gently surging black water lapped the steps and was stained scarlet.

The next move of the troops was to mount a light machine gun in the church so that it could fire down the stone stairs of the crypt. It did no damage. No longer could the bullets ricochet dangerously off the stone flags; they simply churned the water up harmlessly.

They fired a long burst with machine guns, then cut it abruptly, as two black objects came hurtling down the stairs. But Valchik and Josef must have been prepared for such an eventuality. The grenades went off with a great bang, and water and hissing pieces of metal bounced off walls and roof. The defenders were unhurt. They raised their heads to meet the next attack. Firing as they ran, the troops poured down the stairs again. They did not lack courage; only intelligence. Many died from the combined fire of the four guns at the top of the stairs; several dived almost vertically over their heads; they landed on hands and knees in the flood, scrambled upwards, their faces distorted, mouths opening and closing like strange fish emerging from the water, and fell forwards face downwards, as the defenders carefully picked them off.

But it was revolvers they were using now. Even from his

position in the church Chaplain Petrek could hear that. It could only mean that the defenders were out of Sten ammunition. On the other hand it might mean that they were setting a trap to lure more Nazi soldiers to their deaths.

Down in the crypt the four of them must have known that the fight was nearly over. Sten ammunition had gone. With only a few revolver bullets left between them, the end could not be far off.

They had fought to the best of their ability. To fight to the last bullet meant inevitable capture. That was unthinkable. To be displayed as live trophies of German conquest after all they had experienced was a degradation they could not conceive, and would not endure. And so they made their final sacrifice.

The Germans crouched in the church heard the four single shots ringing out one after the other, echoing loudly in the sounding chamber of the crypt.

So Hruby fell, and Bublik. So Valchik slumped forward. against his buttress and died. Each shot himself neatly through the temple with his own revolver. Josef lay face downwards in his self-chosen tomb, his head and shoulders protruding from the shelf, his blood splashing slowly downwards into the black waters pumped from the old river which flowed so smoothly through his city. It mingled with the blood of Valchik, floating face downwards in the water, and the blood of the German dead crowded at the foot of the stairs.

Not even in their remotest dreams could the old monks have envisaged such a scene as was now unfolded in the silent crypt. Only the water rushing through the ventilator hole made any sound. The monks had built the burial place so that the bodies of their fellows could crumble slowly into decay in dignity and peace.

Perhaps there was both dignity and peace in the tomb at that moment. There was certainly no lack of macabre horror. Many brave men had died there for reasons which they believed to be just and adequate. So perhaps the old monks might have discerned in this grim, frozen pageant of death in battle, a certain nobility of purpose. Men throughout the ages have often chosen a similar quick step into eternity as their final pledge to the living.

The firing died away. Somehow, in the church, everyone knew that the battle was over. Features sagged in relief. No one grinned or shouted aloud. The cowardly business of butchery and torture and dishonour of the dead is enjoyed by a comparatively small proportion of the people of any nation.

The pumps were turned off and the water settled in a smooth black sheen upon the floor of the crypt. It was no more than two feet deep. The firemen rolled up their hoses, packed them back into their engines and, sick at heart, drove silently back to their stations.

Secretary of State Karl Frank moved cautiously forward to inspect the church. A German officer, Luger revolver in his hand, walked slowly down the stairs into the crypt and paused upon the last step. He stared round at the bloody scene. He waded slowly through the blood-stained water to the far end of the crypt, and back again. He stepped over the bodies and remounted the stairs. His face was grim. He said it was now safe for Secretary of State Frank to inspect the crypt. All resistance was at an end. The butchers could take over.

They dragged out the four bodies and laid them on the pavement next to Opalka. They brought back Svarc and Jan Kubis from the hospital and laid them down next to them. The seven men who had fought so gallantly since daybreak were exhibited for all to see.

Then they brought back Karel Curda and Ata Moravec to identify them. It was Curda who said, "Yes, these are all the parachutists; there are no more!"

They placed Jan Kubis next to Josef Gabchik so that their arms almost touched. The pavement was warm beneath their bodies, and the sun hot upon their cold faces. The river ran smoothly past, no more than a shout away from the place where they lay, and the old city which had known so many valiant sons dozed in the sunshine. A new June day had begun.

EPILOGUE

ANNA MALINOVA was one of the first to be arrested in the damburst of vengeance which followed the deaths of the parachutists. Witnesses declare that she bore her fate stoically and bravely. It was as if her heart died when the ranting voice of Prague Radia jubilantly declared that all the assassins of General Heydrich had been discovered in a church and ruthlessly exterminated.

Her heart and mind were numb long before they arrested her. She wept at their brutalities; she wept because she was a woman, but when in the vaults of the Petschek Bank they confronted her with the head of Jan Kubis preserved in surgical spirit in a glass jar, even this grisly relic of the man she had loved so well could not destroy her because she was already beyond destruction. She had lived through a short springtime of joy, and this savage winter of Nazi vengeance could not dispossess her of its memory.

They dressed her in prison clothes and killed her in a gas chamber at the concentration camp at Mauthausen, along with all the others, as they destroyed hundreds and thousands and millions of people in those bloody and bitter wartime years.

It was a fundamental mistake which the Nazis repeated over and over again, until finally their pomp, their evil, and their stupidity, along with their leader, perished in the Wagnerian hell of Berlin.

It was a fundamental misconception common to most tyrants and their satraps. They believed that oppression and brutality would inevitably crush and annihilate all resistance, both physical and spiritual. They did not comprehend that when they ground Czech, French, Polish, Yugoslav, Greek, Belgian, Italian or Russian resistance into the dust, they ground in also the very seeds of the resistance they sought to destroy. And those seeds waited only for the warm spring rain of opportunity to germinate and leap upwards in greater strength and greater fury.

Mrs. Novotna the Nazis also destroyed, and her small daughter who had wheeled the bicycle; the doctor disguised in his tram conductor's uniform who first attended Jan; and the young woman eye specialist who visited him in the crypt. Ata Moravec, Liboslava and her mother, father and sister; Chaplain Vladimir Petrek, his sexton, bishop, and the church elders; more than fifteen hundred people within a space of five weeks.

But they could not kill everybody; hundreds who had worked valiantly for the resistance movement survived. Professor Ogoun escaped by getting himself certified insane by a friendly doctor; he spent many months in a lunatic asylum safe from all questioning.

Jindra also survived. He was the only one intimately connected with the assassination of Heydrich who did survive the war, and this was due to a number of fortuitous circumstances. He was arrested some weeks after the deaths of Jan and Josef. While he was being taken by car to the Petchek Bank he swallowed a dose of heroin. But his action was detected and he was rushed to hospital. Heroin, unlike the merciful poison pills used by Auntie Marie and Uncle Hajsky, took several hours to bring death. In the hospital they were able to take the necessary counter measures to save him for Nazi interrogation.

He did not talk, and in the confusion which resulted from the hundreds of arrests the Nazis had made, and were continually making, they did not understand his real importance. Nevertheless he was sentenced to death. But as Nazi victories turned to defeats, and as their administrative processes grew clumsier and more inflexible, his sentence was constantly delayed. When the final liberation came he was still alive to testify against the traitors, Karel Curda and Gerik.

The Nazis had rewarded them both with millions of crowns and publicized their generosity widely within the Protectorate, to show how well they repaid collaborators. Not that it did either Curda or Gerik much good, and not that they ever rested easily again. They might change their names and their ways of living; their Judas crowns could buy them material comfort and luxury; but it could not purchase one minute's respite from the fear that eventually their own countrymen would take them. No men in Czechoslovakia were ever as closely watched and carefully marked as Curda or Gerik. In 1946 they were accused before a Prague court, convicted and hanged. Karl Frank was also executed.

So now it is all finished. Over the soft green rise and fall of earth, where Lidice once stood, the wind moves among the tassel-headed dandelions and the curving feathery grasses. The red roofs of the new town stand up on the escarpment to the left, strangely remote and aloof, and in the hollow below the gaunt cross with its circle of thorns, stands the strangely pitiful remains of Horak's farm, where, long ago, they shot the men and the boys. On the slight rise beyond the cross stands the rows of little crosses which mark their graves. The wind blows over the great empty space, and nothing is left except the small museum, the green grass and the larks crying in an empty sky.

Anna Malinova is only a name ruled through with a red line in a concentration camp record book. No remains, or bones, no grave of either Jan Kubis or Josef Gabchik has ever been discovered.

But they are not forgotten. Around the village of Dolnich Vilemovicich where Jan was born, the countryside is very lovely: rolling and green, lonely and unspoilt with its fields of yellow wheat and strips of bright mustard seed burning against the more sober greens. Towards the distant swathes of dark pines crowning the hillsides, the narrow twisting white roads are lined with shady fruit trees.

The villagers smile and nod when you mention the name of Kubis, and point with their fingers. The schoolchildren swarm excitedly behind you, as you pass the open green with the tiny white-painted wooden church and walk to a house at the far end of the village. A man and woman come out when you knock, and you discover that long ago they hid from the Germans during the terror, because they are members of the family whose name is Kubis.

There is also a stone memorial upon the outside wall of the church in Resslova Street, above the ventilation slot which is still pocked and chipped with bullet marks. Down in the crypt there are wreaths and flowers marking the places where the parachutists fought to the death, and each year they are renewed.

There is a small showcase beneath the memorial containing the photographs of those who took part in this legendary action, and small boys, satchels on their backs, pause curiously on their way home from school to examine the pictures.

When they have looked and read they go off up the street, whistling and chattering excitedly, and it is doubtful if Jan Kubis and Josef Gabchik would have preferred any other sort of requiem.

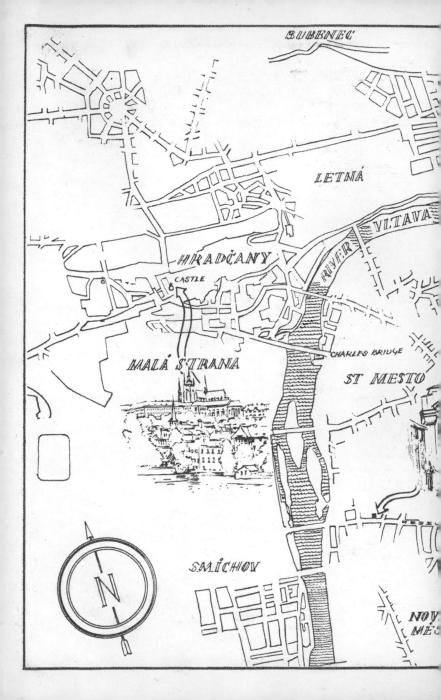